Adobe® Acrobat® 5 PDF For Dummies®

Acrobat 5 Toolbars
(expanded to show all tools)

File toolbar

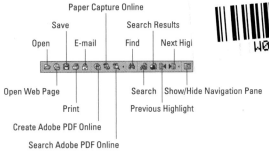

- Paper Capture Online
- Save
- Search Results
- Open
- E-mail
- Find
- Next High[light]
- Open Web Page
- Search
- Show/Hide Navigation Pane
- Print
- Previous Highlight
- Create Adobe PDF Online
- Search Adobe PDF Online

...on toolbar

- [Nex]t Page
- Previous Page
- Last Page

View History toolbar

- Go to Previous View

- Go to Next View

Commenting toolbar

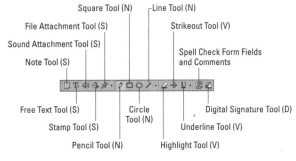

- Square Tool (N)
- Line Tool (N)
- File Attachment Tool (S)
- Strikeout Tool (V)
- Sound Attachment Tool (S)
- Spell Check Form Fields and Comments
- Note Tool (S)
- Free Text Tool (S)
- Circle Tool (N)
- Digital Signature Tool (D)
- Stamp Tool (S)
- Underline Tool (V)
- Pencil Tool (N)
- Highlight Tool (V)

Basic Tools toolbar

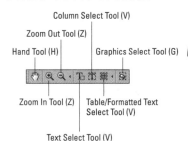

- Column Select Tool (V)
- Zoom Out Tool (Z)
- Hand Tool (H)
- Graphics Select Tool (G)
- Zoom In Tool (Z)
- Table/Formatted Text Select Tool (V)
- Text Select Tool (V)

Viewing toolbar

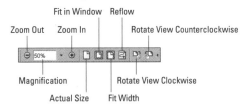

- Fit in Window
- Reflow
- Zoom Out
- Zoom In
- Rotate View Counterclockwise
- Magnification
- Rotate View Clockwise
- Actual Size
- Fit Width

Editing toolbar

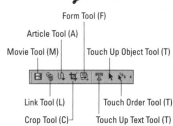

- Form Tool (F)
- Article Tool (A)
- Movie Tool (M)
- Touch Up Object Tool (T)
- Link Tool (L)
- Touch Order Tool (T)
- Crop Tool (C)
- Touch Up Text Tool (T)

Adobe Online toolbar

Visit Adobe on the World Wide Web

For Dummies: Bestselling Book Series for Beginners

Adobe® Acrobat® 5 PDF For Dummies®

Cheat Sheet

Window and View Menu Keystroke Shortcuts

Windowing shortcuts

Windows	Macintosh	Menu Equivalent
Ctrl+Shift+J	⌘+Shift+J	Window⇨Cascade
Ctrl+Shift+K	⌘+Shift+K	Window⇨Tile⇨Horizontally
Ctrl+Shift+L	⌘+Shift+L	Window⇨Tile⇨Vertically
Ctrl+Atl+W	⌘+Option+W	Window⇨Close All

Viewing shortcuts

Windows	Macintosh	Menu Equivalent
Ctrl+L	⌘+L	View⇨Full Screen
Ctrl+plus sign (+)	⌘+plus sign (+)	View⇨Zoom In
Ctrl+minus sign (-)	⌘+minus sign (-)	View⇨Zoom Out
Ctrl+M	⌘+M	View⇨Zoom To
Ctrl 0	⌘ 0	View⇨Fit in Window
Ctrl+1	⌘+1	View⇨Actual Size
Ctrl+2	⌘+2	View⇨Fit Width
Ctrl+3	⌘+3	View⇨Fit Visible
Ctrl+4	⌘+4	View⇨Reflow
Ctrl+Shift+plus sign(+)	⌘+Shift+plus sign(+)	View⇨Rotate Clockwise
Ctrl+Shift+minus sign(-)	⌘+Shift+minus sign(-)	View⇨Rotate Counterclockwise
Ctrl+Y	⌘+Y	View⇨Proof Colors
Ctrl+Alt+Shift+Y	⌘+Alt+Shift+Y	View⇨Overprint Preview
Ctrl+Shift+Y	⌘+Shift+Y	View⇨Use Local Fonts
Ctrl+U	⌘+U	View⇨Grid
Ctrl+Shift+U	⌘+Shift+U	View⇨Snap to Grid

For Dummies: Bestselling Book Series for Beginners

Adobe® Acrobat® 5 PDF FOR DUMMIES®

by Greg Harvey

Wiley Publishing, Inc.

Adobe® Acrobat® 5 PDF For Dummies®

Published by
Wiley Publishing, Inc.
909 Third Avenue
New York, NY 10022

www.wiley.com

Copyright © 2002 by Wiley Publishing, Inc., Indianapolis, Indiana

Library of Congress Cataloging-in-Publication Data:

Library of Congress Control No.: 2002100243

ISBN: 0-7645-1652-3

1B/QW/QW/QS/IN

Manufactured in the United States of America

10 9 8 7 6 5 4 3 2 1

About the Author

Greg Harvey, the author of more than 50 computer books, has had a long career of teaching business people in the use of IBM PC, Windows, and Macintosh software application programs. From 1983 to 1988, he conducted hands-on computer software training for corporate business users with a variety of training companies (including his own, PC Teach). From 1988 to 1992, he taught university classes in Lotus 1-2-3 and Introduction to Database Management Technology (using dBASE) in the Department of Information Systems at Golden State University in San Francisco.

In mid-1993, Greg started a new multimedia publishing venture called mind over media. As a multimedia developer, he hopes to enliven his future computer books by making them into true interactive learning experiences that will vastly enrich and improve the training of users of all skill levels. You can send him e-mail at gharvey@mindovermedia.com and visit his Web site at www.mindovermedia.com.

In 1999, Greg began graduate school at the California Institute of Integral Studies (CIIS) in San Francisco. In the summer of 2000, he received his master's degree in philosophy and religion in the area of Asian and Comparative Studies. Currently, he has finished all his coursework in the Ph. D. program at CIIS and is getting ready to begin work on his dissertation in the area of Chinese and Tibetan end-of-life religious beliefs.

Dedication

To Chris for his unflagging support and encouragement..

Author's Acknowledgments

Let me take this opportunity to thank all the people, both at Wiley Publishing, Inc., and at Mind over Media, Inc., whose dedication and talent combined to get this book out and into your hands in such great shape.

At Wiley, I want to thank Steve Hayes and Tiffany Franklin for help in getting this project underway, Christine Berman as Project Editor, and Kim Darosett as Copy Editor for making sure that the project stayed on course and made it into production so that all the talented folks on the Production team could create this great final product.

At Mind over Media, I want to give special thanks to the following two people: Michael Bryant for his original contribution of the text for Part IV (excellent work, Michael) and Christopher Aiken for his review of the original manuscript and invaluable input and suggestions on how to present the information.

Publisher's Acknowledgments

We're proud of this book; please send us your comments through our online registration form located at www.dummies.com/register/.

Some of the people who helped bring this book to market include the following:

Acquisitions, Editorial, and Media Development

Associate Project Editor: Christine Berman

Acquisitions Editor: Steve Hayes

Copy Editor: Kimberly Darosett

Technical Editor: Bryan Guignard

Editorial Manager: Leah Cameron

Media Development Manager: Laura VanWinkle

Media Development Supervisor: Richard Graves

Editorial Assistant: Amanda Foxworth

Production

Project Coordinator: Ryan Steffen

Layout and Graphics: Stephanie D. Jumper, Brent Savage, Jacque Schneider, Erin Zeltner

Proofreaders: Andy Hollandbeck, Susan Moritz

Indexer: TECHBOOKS Production Services

General and Administrative

Wiley Technology Publishing Group: Richard Swadley, Vice President and Executive Group Publisher; Bob Ipsen, Vice President and Group Publisher; Joseph Wikert, Vice President and Publisher; Barry Pruett, Vice President and Publisher; Mary Bednarek, Editorial Director; Mary C. Corder, Editorial Director; Andy Cummings, Editorial Director

Wiley Manufacturing: Ivor Parker, Vice President, Manufacturing

Wiley Marketing: John Helmus, Assistant Vice President, Director of Marketing

Wiley Composition Services for Branded Press: Debbie Stailey, Composition Services Director

Wiley Sales: Michael Violano, Vice President, International Sales and Sub Rights

Contents at a Glance

Cartoons at a Glance

By Rich Tennant

page 149

page 75

page 7

page 267

page 341

Cartoon Information:
Fax: 978-546-7747
E-Mail: richtennant@the5thwave.com
World Wide Web: www.the5thwave.com

Table of Contents

Introduction

● ●

Adobe PDF (Portable Document Format) is just now starting to fulfill its promise as a truly transportable file format that enables people to share sophisticated electronic documents across a wide array of otherwise incompatible computer platforms without requiring access to either the software that generated the documents or the fonts that they used. Part of the proof of this statement is evidenced in the ever-growing presence of PDF documents, especially on the World Wide Web.

Nowadays, you can hardly browse the Web without encountering sites that present some of their online information as PDF files. In fact, so many sites offer their standard reports, registration and feedback forms, and industry white papers as downloadable PDF files that few seasoned business users remain unfamiliar with the PDF format (even if they're not exactly sure what it is) or the free Acrobat Reader software used to open, read, and print documents saved in it.

Beyond the popularity of PDF for information-sharing on the Internet, PDF is also becoming increasingly popular as the format to use for prepress documents, eBook publishing, document review, and document archiving. To ready PDF files for these additional roles, you naturally graduate from the world of the free Acrobat Reader and Acrobat eBook Reader to that of Acrobat 5, Adobe's latest version of its all-in-one utility for editing, annotating, and managing documents saved in PDF that you must purchase.

As the name *Acrobat* implies, this utility enables you to juggle the many roles it can assign PDF files with relative ease. All that's required of you is a keen sense of the role or roles you want your PDF document to fulfill along with a careful reading of the pertinent sections of this book.

About This Book

This book is your complete introductory reference to the reading, writing, and managing of PDF files for any and all of their many purposes, from preparing prepress documents for printing on sophisticated imagesetters to publishing your life story as an eBook for sale on the bevy of online bookstores. Because the way you make, prepare, and sometimes even read a PDF file varies according to the purpose you have in mind for it, you will find that this book's information emphasizes more the purpose you ultimately have in mind for the PDF file than the features used to accomplish this purpose in the various programs such as Acrobat, Acrobat Reader, and the Acrobat eBook Reader.

As a result, this book is not meant to be read from cover to cover. Each discussion of a topic briefly addresses the question of how a particular feature enables you to accomplish your purpose before launching into how to use it. In Acrobat, as with most other sophisticated programs, there is usually more than one way to do a task. For the sake of your sanity, I have purposely limited the choices, usually by giving you only the most efficient ways to do a particular task. Later on, if you're so tempted, you can experiment with alternative ways of doing a task. For now, just concentrate on performing the task as described.

As much as possible, I've tried to make it unnecessary for you to remember anything covered in another section of the book. From time to time, however, you come across a cross-reference to another section or chapter in the book. For the most part, such cross-references are meant to help you get more complete information on a subject, should you have the time and interest. If you have neither, no problem; just ignore the cross-references as if they never existed.

How to Use This Book

As a reference to all things PDF, you should start out by looking up the topic you need information on (either in the Table of Contents or the Index) and then refer directly to the section of interest. Most topics are explained conversationally. Many times, however, my regiment-commander mentality takes over, and I list the steps you need to take to accomplish a particular task in a particular section.

What You Can Safely Ignore

When you come across a section that contains the steps you take to get something done, you can safely ignore all text accompanying the steps (the text that isn't in bold) if you have neither the time nor the inclination to wade through more material.

Whenever possible, I have also tried to separate background or footnote-type information from the essential facts by exiling this kind of junk to a sidebar. These sections are often flagged with icons that let you know what type of information you will encounter there. You can easily disregard text marked this way. (I discuss the icons used in this book a little later.)

Foolish Assumptions

I'm going to make only two assumptions about you (let's see how close I get): You have a need to create and use PDF files in your work, and you have access to Acrobat 5. Some of you are working on PCs running some version of Windows or Windows NT. Others of you are working on Macintosh computers running one of the later versions of the Mac operating system.

Beyond that, it's anyone's guess what brings you to Acrobat and PDF. Some of you need to know how to convert all your paper documents into PDF files. Some of you need to know how to save your graphics files as PDFs. Others of you need to know how to create PDF form files in which users can submit important data. Still others of you need to know how to create and publish PDF files as eBooks for sale and distribution on the World Wide Web. Regardless of your needs, you will be able to find the information you require somewhere in the pages of this book.

How This Book Is Organized

This book is organized into five parts, the first four of which cover all the basics of reading, making, and managing PDF files. The fifth part, the indispensable Part of Tens, recaps important Acrobat and PDF features, functions, and enhancements. You should not, however, get too hung up about following along with the structure of the book; ultimately, it doesn't matter at all if you find out how to use Paper Capture to convert printed documents to PDF before you find out how to use PDFMaker 5.0 to convert your Word documents, or if you figure out how to archive your PDF documents in a searchable collection before you discover how to create interactive forms for collecting data online. The important thing is that you find the information — and understand it when you find it — when you need to do what needs getting done.

In case you're interested, here's a synopsis of what you find in each part.

Part 1: Presenting Acrobat and PDF Files

Part I looks at what makes PDF files tick and the most common ways of accessing their information. Chapter 1 covers the many purposes of PDF documents in today's business world. Chapter 2 lays out essential information about using the different Adobe programs that enable you to read and print PDF documents. Chapter 3 acquaints you with the interface of Acrobat 5, Adobe's utility for preparing and editing PDF documents.

Part II: The Wealth of Ways for Creating PDF Files

Part II looks at the many ways of making PDF files. Chapter 4 gives you vital information on how to use and customize the Acrobat Distiller to create the PDF document suited to just the purpose you have in mind. Chapter 5 covers the ins and outs of converting Microsoft Office documents (specifically those created with Word, Excel, and PowerPoint) to PDF. Chapter 6 covers capturing paper documents as PDF files primarily by scanning them directly into Acrobat 5. Chapter 7 tells you how to capture Web pages as PDF files. Chapter 8 covers the printing of all or part of your PDF files on printers you have in-house.

Part III: Reviewing, Editing, and Securing PDFs

Part III covers a mixture of techniques for reviewing, editing, and protecting your PDF files. Chapter 9 introduces you to the many ways for annotating the PDF documents that you send out for online review. Chapter 10 covers editing PDF files in Acrobat 5. Chapter 11 tells you how to secure your PDF documents and protect them from further changes. Chapter 12 acquaints you with the different ways you can extract contents in your PDF files for repurposing with the other software programs you use. Chapter 13 gives you the ins and outs of cataloging your PDF files by creating searchable collections that you can distribute across networks on CD-ROM.

Part IV: PDFs as Electronic Documents

Part IV covers the different roles of electronic PDF files. Chapter 14 covers the creation and usage of PDF documents as interactive forms that you can fill out and whose data you can extract. Chapter 15 acquaints you with creating and preparing PDF files as eBooks for sale and distribution on the World Wide Web. Chapter 16 gives you information on how you can turn PDF documents into online presentations by adding multimedia elements, including audio and video clips.

Part V: The Part of Tens

As is the tradition in these *For Dummies* books, the last part contains lists of the top ten most useful facts, tips, and suggestions. Chapter 17 gives you the top ten features in Acrobat 5 (along with references to the chapters in

the book where they are covered in depth). Chapter 18 gives you the Ten
Commandments for converting your Microsoft Office documents into perfect
PDF files. Chapter 19 gives you a list of my top ten third-party (that is, not
developed by Adobe Systems) add-in programs for augmenting and enhancing
the program's already considerable features. Chapter 20 gives you a list of my
top ten online resources for learning even more about Acrobat and PDF files!

Conventions Used in This Book

The following information gives you the lowdown on how things look in this
book — publishers call these the book's *conventions* (no campaigning, flag-
waving, name-calling, or finger-pointing is involved, however).

Keyboard and mouse

Although most of the keyboard and mouse instructions given in the text are
self-explanatory, there are a few important differences between the typical
Windows and Macintosh keyboards and mice that are worth noting here. For
example, keystroke shortcuts in Acrobat 5 and Acrobat Reader 5 on Windows
often use the Ctrl key in combination with one or more letter keys. The
Macintosh, however, substitutes its ⌘ key (called the Command key, the one
with the apple and the cloverleaf icon) for the Windows Ctrl key (rather than
using its Control key). Also, because the Macintosh keyboard has no Alt key,
its Option key is routinely substituted in all shortcuts using the Alt key.

Regarding the mouse, Windows favors a two-button (left- and right-button)
mouse whereas Macintosh favors a single-button mouse. As a result, while you
access shortcut (or context) menus in Acrobat on Windows by clicking the
right mouse button (a technique commonly known as right-clicking), you hold
down the Control (not the ⌘) key as you click the mouse on the Macintosh
(a technique commonly known as Control+clicking).

Other than these common keyboard and mice anomalies, it's pretty much the
same whether you are working with PDFs in Acrobat and Acrobat Reader on a
Windows or Macintosh machine. In the few cases where there are differences
in Acrobat's capabilities across the platforms, I have duly noted them in the
text, usually in the form of a tip or warning (described in the next section).

Special icons

The following icons are strategically placed in the margins to point out stuff
you may or may not want to read.

This icon alerts you to nerdy discussions that you may well want to skip (or read when no one else is around).

This icon alerts you to shortcuts or other valuable hints related to the topic at hand.

This icon alerts you to information to keep in mind if you want to meet with a modicum of success.

This icon alerts you to information to keep in mind if you want to avert complete disaster.

Where to Go from Here

If you've never had any prior experience with PDF files, I suggest that, right after getting your chuckles with the cartoons, you go first to Chapter 1 and find out what you're dealing with. If you're already familiar with the ins and outs of PDF files, but don't know anything about how you go about creating them, jump to Chapter 4, where you find out how to get started entering data and formulas. Then, as specific needs arise (like "How do I annotate PDF documents in Acrobat 5?" or "How do I protect PDF files from further changes?"), you can go to the Table of Contents or the Index to find the appropriate section and go right to that section for answers.

Part I
Presenting Acrobat and PDF Files

The 5th Wave   By Rich Tennant

Here, boy.

MULTIMEDIA

In this part . . .

A dobe's PDF (Portable Document Format) is characterized as a truly universal file format that preserves all of the original document's formatting, including its fonts, graphics, and layout, across a wide array of different computer platforms. This part of the book is where you find out how PDF came to warrant this lofty characterization.

In Chapter 1, you discover the many platforms that support documents saved as PDFs, the many uses for PDF documents in your work, the different classes of PDF files that you will be dealing with, along with a general overview of the process you follow in saving documents as PDF files. In Chapter 2, you get the lowdown on how to use the various PDF reader software programs offered by Adobe Systems, including Acrobat 5, Acrobat Reader, and Acrobat eBook Reader. Chapter 3 rounds out Part I by introducing you to the interface of Acrobat 5, the Adobe program that not only enables you to view and print PDF files but edit them as well.

Chapter 1

The Ins and Outs of PDF Files

I'm so enthusiastic about Adobe PDF files that I think the abbreviation PDF should stand for Pretty Darn Fantastic instead of the more mundane *Portable Document Format.* In PDF files, you not only see the first inklings of a truly paperless office (or as close as we're likely to get), but also the delivery of a truly universal file format, that is, one truly capable of being opened and used on any of the many computer operating systems currently in use.

In this chapter, you get introduced to what makes PDF files so special and how they can be used to your advantage, especially in office environments that mix and match different computer platforms. As part of this process, you also get acquainted with the different versions of PDF files and how they can be tailored to fit the particular needs of those who use the documents.

The Purpose of PDF Files

PDF, as the name Portable Document Format implies, was developed by Adobe Systems as a means for digital file exchange. The main idea behind the file format is to enable all computer users to be able to open, review, and print the documents saved in it. This means that users who work on computers that don't have the software with which the files were originally created can still see the document as it was originally designed and laid out, including all its fonts and graphics.

The key to this digital file interchange is the nifty little software program known as Acrobat (although Adobe originally named it Carousel when it first appeared in 1993). A free form of this software, known as the *Acrobat Reader,* is available from Adobe Systems for all the major personal computing devices and most versions of all the operating systems known to humankind. As of this writing, these forms include

- Microsoft Windows machines with the following versions: Windows 95 (OSR 2.0), Windows 98 SE, Windows Millennium Edition, Windows NT 4.0 (with Service Pack 5), Windows 2000, or Windows XP

- Macintosh computers with version 8.6, 9.0, 9.1, or OS X of the Macintosh operating system

- Palm handhelds with OS 3.0 or later

- Pocket PC computers with Windows CE or Windows 2002

- IBM AIX workstations with IBM AIX 4.2.1

- HP 9000 Series workstations (model 700 or higher) with HP-UX 9.0.3

- SGI workstations with Silicon Graphics IRIX 5.3

- DEC workstations with DEC OSF/1, version 4

- Sun Solaris SPARCStations with Sun OpenWindows 3.0 or later, Motif 1.2.3 or later, OpenLook 3.0, or CDE 1.0 or later

- Computers running versions of Linux including Red Hat Linux 5.1 or Slackware Linux 2.0

All you have to do to get one of these versions is head your Web browser over to the following page on the Adobe Systems Web site

```
www.adobe.com/products/acrobat/readstep2.html
```

and choose your language, your computer platform, and click the Download button. After downloading the Acrobat Reader to the desktop of your computer platform, double-click the icon representing the compressed version of the program to unpack and install it on your computer.

After you install the Acrobat Reader on your computer, you can then open, review, and print the PDF that you get, regardless of what application programs were used in generating its text and graphics, and regardless of the computer platform on which these programs ran. (See Chapter 2 for details on how to access and review PDF files with this software.)

Benefits of Using PDF Files

The most important benefit derived from the use of PDF files is that anyone whose computer is equipped with Acrobat Reader can open, read, and print them. This essentially enables you to concentrate on the software tools that you have at hand and feel are best suited for producing the document without having to worry about whether or not your client or coworker has the same software available to them. This, as you'll soon see, is but one of the many important uses to which you can put your PDF files with the advent of Acrobat 5.

What you designed is what they see

Because you are assured that your PDF files will essentially appear on-screen and print as you originally designed them no matter the computer on which they're opened or the printing device to which they're output, you don't have to hold back on your design, avoiding the use of certain more decorative fonts and/or complex layouts. Figures 1-1 and 1-2 illustrate this situation. In Figure 1-1, you see a PDF file as it appears when opened with Acrobat Reader 5 on a computer running Windows. Figure 1-2 shows the same PDF file as it appears when opened on a Macintosh computer. As you can see, they are both comparable in terms of the appearance of their fonts and their layout.

PDF files in the review cycle

While PDF debuted as a universal file format for viewing and printing documents on various types of computers and printers, thanks to advances to the Acrobat software (and here I'm referring to the full-fledged Acrobat program that you must pay for rather than the freebie Acrobat Reader available for download), you can now make PDF files an integral part of your design review process. After converting a document to PDF, you can disseminate copies of it to each of the people from whom you need feedback or approval before you put it into use. Each of these people can then add their feedback by adding comments or actually marking up the PDF document in Acrobat 5.

You can then collect their feedback and make the necessary changes either to the PDF version of the file in Acrobat 5 or to the original document (prior to PDF conversion) in the program used in its creation. If managers, coworkers, or clients are required to sign off on the document (either in its original or revised form), they can indicate their approval by stamping the document with their approval or by digitally signing off on it as shown in Figure 1-3 (see Chapter 9 for details on how to use PDF files in a review cycle and Chapter 11 for details on how to use digital signatures).

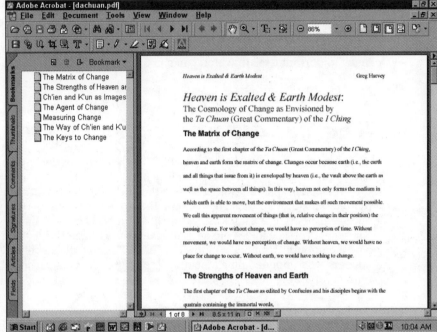

Figure 1-1:
PDF
document
as it
appears in
the Acrobat
Reader 5 on
a computer
running
Windows.

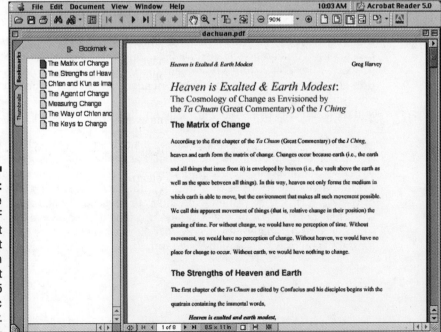

Figure 1-2:
The same
PDF
document
as it
appears in
the Acrobat
Reader 5
on a Mac
computer.

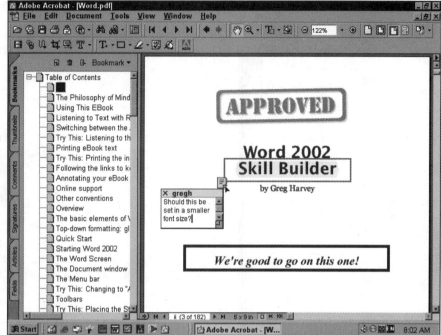

Figure 1-3:
With
Acrobat 5,
you can add
comments
and mark
up text
that needs
revising as
well as give
your stamp
of approval.

Providing forms, both paper and electronic

With the widespread reliance on of the World Wide Web for getting and submitting crucial information, PDF files have taken on another important use, that of providing forms to fill in both online and after printing. Acrobat 5 makes form creation about as easy as it can be.

If you need to make certain paper forms available on your company's intranet or your public Web site so that users can download, print, and then fill them in by hand, you can use Acrobat 5 to scan the paper forms and immediately convert their digital images into PDF files (see Figure 1-4). If you need to be able to search and edit the text in the electronic versions of these forms, you can use the Paper Capture feature — Acrobat's version of OCR (Optical Character Recognition) software — to convert the text image into searchable and editable fonts. (See Chapter 6 for details on scanning paper forms and converting them into PDF files with Acrobat 5.)

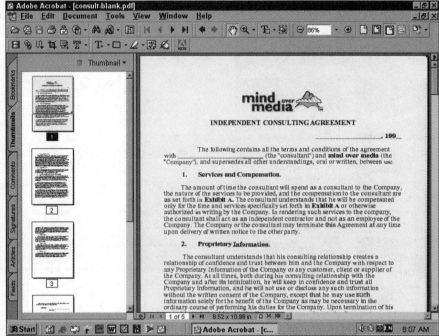

If you need to get feedback or process informational or order forms directly from your company's intranet or its public Web site, you can use Acrobat 5 to design the electronic forms. Acrobat 5 makes it possible to add all types of interactive fields, including text boxes, combo boxes (also known as drop-down list boxes), check boxes, radio buttons, and command buttons (that users can select to do things such as submit their information or clear the form). With the addition of a simple CGI (Common Gateway Interface) script (courtesy of your friendly IT personnel or Internet service provider), you can store the data submitted by way of your PDF forms in text files that your favorite database or spreadsheet program can read and store. (See Chapter 14 for details on creating interactive PDF forms for use online.)

You don't have to use the World Wide Web or a company intranet to be able to fill in electronic PDF forms that you create with Acrobat 5. Users who have Acrobat 5 or Acrobat Reader 5 installed on their computers can open and fill in these electronic forms using this version of Acrobat.

Document archiving

Let's face it: Paper archives are not just bulky and heavy, but they also degrade quickly and are a veritable nightmare to search. For this reason alone, out of all the possible uses for Adobe's Portable Document Format, archiving your documents as PDF files may prove to be the most important to you. Imagine all of your paper contracts, correspondence, company reports, and the like stored as collections on CD-ROMs, which you can retrieve through searches on keywords or vital statistics such as author, client name, or job number.

You can use the Paper Capture feature in Acrobat 5 on the Windows platform to scan and convert such paper documents into searchable PDF files. After you do that, Acrobat makes it easy for you to organize these files into collections (known officially as catalogs), which you can index for truly speedy retrieval using the Acrobat 5 search feature. (See Chapter 6 for details on converting paper documents to PDF and Chapter 13 for details on cataloging and indexing your files prior to storing them on various media.)

The Paper Capture feature in Acrobat 5 for Windows restricts you to scanning and converting paper documents of no more than 50 pages in length. If you know that you must scan and convert documents longer than 50 pages on the Windows platform, you need to purchase the standalone module, Acrobat Capture 3 for Windows NT, 2000, or XP or Acrobat Capture 2.0 for Windows 95/98.

PDF in the prepress workflow

One of the most obvious uses for PDF files is in the prepress workflow, during which documents that require professional printing are checked for potential printing errors and readied for conversion from electronic images to the film or plates used in the final printing of the document using high-end imagesetters (a process known in the industry as *preflight*). Acrobat 5 contains a number of prepress-related printing options along with an overprinting preview and an on-screen color correction feature.

These specialized print options and error-checking features in Acrobat 5 are designed to help professional graphic artists and service bureau personnel in finding and eliminating potentially costly printing problems. Most users not directly involved in this end of the business will have no reason to fool with these printing options or use these specialized preview features. (If, for some unknown reason, you are interested in knowing more about these prepress features, refer to Chapter 8.)

Always check with your service bureau personnel to find out what, if any, prepress options they want you to use prior to sending them your PDF files for preflight. Some houses definitely prefer that you not use *any* of these prepress options, so it is always good to check it out ahead of time.

Quick and easy Web site retrieval

If you are involved with your company's Web design or you are a Web freak who travels frequently and is therefore bereft of a way to stay connected to the Net, you can use Acrobat 5's Web Capture feature to copy and convert to PDF specific Web pages or even entire Web sites that are of interest to you (see Figure 1-5). After you've converted a set of Web pages or an entire Web site into PDF files, you can then browse them from your hard disk with Acrobat or Acrobat Reader without being connected to the Internet.

As both a road warrior and Web enthusiast, you can use this feature to keep up on the latest online information right from the comfort of your portable computer at those times when you're traveling or just waiting to travel.

If you work as a Web designer, the Web Capture feature provides a perfect means for distributing your Web pages for approval to your client or coworkers. If they have Acrobat 5 on their computers, they can even annotate the pages with their suggestions in the form of notes and markups or even give you that final nod of approval using the stamp feature. (See Chapter 7 for details on retrieving and converting Web pages to PDF.)

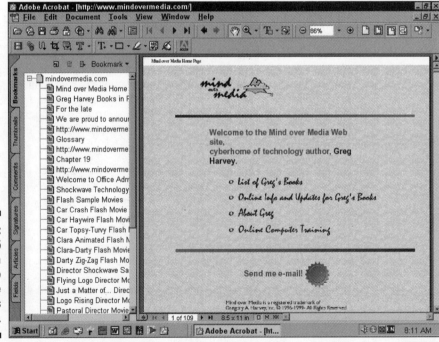

Figure 1-5:
Acrobat 5 makes it a snap to capture Web pages as PDF files.

PDF files as slide shows and multimedia presentations

Another application for PDF files is to use them to create and distribute slide shows and multimedia presentations (see Figure 1-6). Acrobat 5 lets you add interactivity to your slides in the form of hyperlinks, buttons, and slide transitions. You can also use the program to add sound and/or digital movie files to the slides that your users can play back for a true multimedia experience.

To enhance the online slide show or multimedia presentation, Acrobat 5 supports a full-screen mode that the user can invoke with none of the screen clutter normally associated with using Acrobat and Acrobat Reader (full screen mode hides the menus, toolbars, scrollbars, status bar, and in Windows, even the omnipresent Task bar). When a user views your slide show or presentation in full-screen mode, you can set it up so that Acrobat automatically advances through each page after a set time interval using a slide transition of your choice.

If you normally use Microsoft PowerPoint to create your slide shows, you can convert them into PDF files at the touch of a button. You can then use Acrobat 5 to add any extra interactivity and then distribute them for playback on any computer on which the free Acrobat Reader 5 is installed.

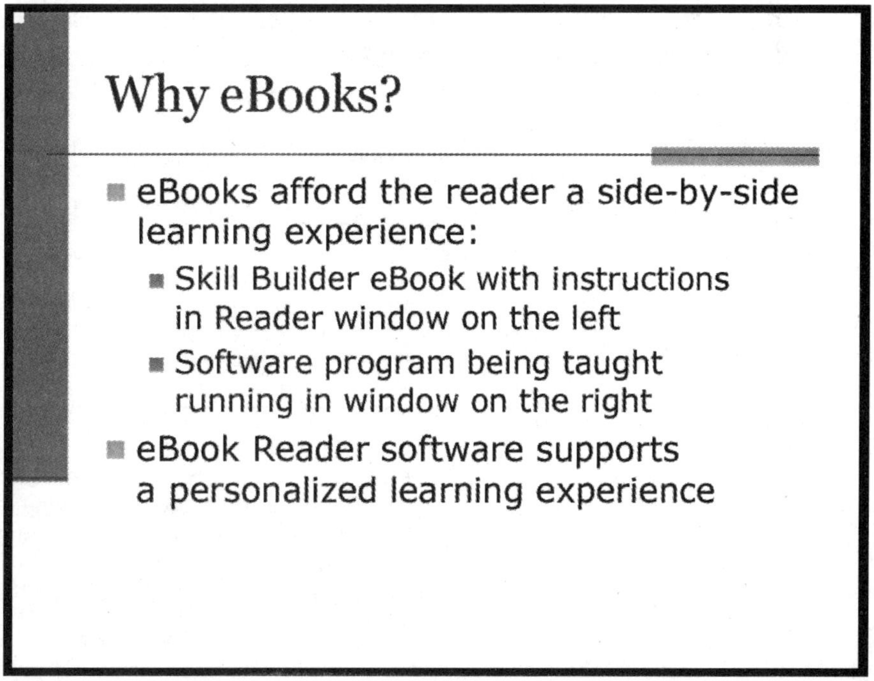

Why eBooks?

■ eBooks afford the reader a side-by-side learning experience:
  ■ Skill Builder eBook with instructions in Reader window on the left
  ■ Software program being taught running in window on the right
■ eBook Reader software supports a personalized learning experience

Figure 1-6:
You can play slide shows saved as PDF files in full-screen mode.

The Different Types of PDF Files

With so many different uses for the Adobe Portable Document Format, it should come as no surprise that PDF files themselves come in a variety of different flavors. In fact, to date, there are four main types of PDF files, each one dependent primarily on where it's going to be seen and how it's going to be used. These four types are

- ✔ **eBook:** Optimized for documents for online reading primarily with the Adobe Acrobat eBook Reader or the latest versions of the Acrobat Reader (versions 4 and 5).
- ✔ **Press:** Optimized for documents intended for output on high-end commercial printers.
- ✔ **Print:** Optimized for documents intended for output on the company's desktop printers.
- ✔ **Screen:** Optimized for documents for online reading with earlier versions of Adobe Acrobat or Acrobat Reader (versions 3 or later).

Table 1-1 shows the most salient characteristics of these four types of PDF files.

Table 1-1		The Four Types of PDF Files		
Type	*Fonts*	*Image Resolution*	*Color Images*	*Compatibility*
eBook	Embedded	150 ppi (pixels per inch)	Converted to RGB	Acrobat 4 or later
Press	Embedded	300 ppi	Unchanged	Acrobat 4 or later
Print	Embedded	300 ppi	Tagged for color management	Acrobat 4 or later
Screen	Not embedded	72 ppi	Converted to RGB	Acrobat 3 or later

As you may suspect from the stats shown in Table 1-1, the Screen PDF is the smallest and most compatible, while at the same time having the lowest graphics resolution. Choose the Screen PDF over eBook when you want to be able to distribute PDF files to users still using version 3 of the Acrobat Reader and when you need to supply the smallest possible file sizes for those with slower download speeds (as with dial-up connections to the Internet). Choose the eBook type when you know your users have the latest version of the Acrobat Reader (especially 5) and when download speeds are not a problem (as when distributing the files on CD-ROM or over an internal network).

The Press PDF file is far and away the largest of the four types. You create this type of PDF only when the final output must be of professional quality and you know that you will eventually hand the file off to a service bureau. Be aware that longer Press PDF files may open very slowly and may even crash your computer. Such files will probably also have to be delivered to the service bureau on a CD-ROM. Choose the Print type over Press for PDF files intended primarily for printing rather than online viewing but where you're sure that the quality of the office printers is sufficient.

Be aware that each of the four major types of PDF files corresponds to a group of settings (referred to as *job options*) that are considered optimal for the particular usage of that type. You can, however, customize these settings to your heart's content, thereby creating your own class of PDF file. (See Chapter 4 for details on the Distiller settings and how to customize them.)

Chapter 2

Accessing PDF Files

• •

• •

As this chapter proves, there's more than one way to open and read a PDF file. You have a choice between using Acrobat Reader or the Acrobat eBook Reader, both of which are free, or, if you've purchased the full-blown Acrobat 5 for creating and editing PDF files, you can, of course, use it as well. As if these weren't enough browsing choices, you can also open and view your PDF files in common Web browsers such as Internet Explorer for Windows and Netscape Navigator on both Windows and Macintosh.

Perusing PDF Files in Acrobat Reader

The most common way to view PDF files is by using Adobe Acrobat Reader. Adobe Systems offers this program as a free download for a wide number of different computer platforms. As of this writing, the most current version of Acrobat Reader is version 5. If this version is available for your computer, you should download and use this latest version of Acrobat Reader.

Acrobat Reader 5 is able to open and read all PDF files created with earlier versions of Acrobat. Be aware, however, that earlier versions of Acrobat Reader cannot open and read PDF files created with the later versions of Adobe Acrobat. As Table 2-1 indicates, each version of Adobe Acrobat creates its own version of PDF files. Later versions of Acrobat can read files created in earlier versions but not vice versa.

Table 2-1	Versions of Acrobat and Their PDF Files	
Acrobat Version	*PDF File Version Created*	*Year Released*
Acrobat 1.0	PDF 1.0	1993
Acrobat 2.0	PDF 1.1	1994
Acrobat 3.0	PDF 1.2	1996
Acrobat 4.0	PDF 1.3	1999
Acrobat 5.0	PDF 1.4	2001

As you note in Table 2-1, you can tell which version of Acrobat produced a particular PDF file version because the sum of the digits in the PDF file version equals the number of the Adobe Acrobat version that created it. For example, you know that a PDF file in version 1.3 was likely created with Acrobat 4 because the sum of its file version numbers, 1 and 3, is 4.

If you're using PDF files on a Windows computer, you can tell what version of PDF file you're dealing with by right-clicking the PDF file icon in Windows Explorer and then selecting Properties on its context menu. Windows opens a Properties dialog box with two tabs: General and PDF Properties. Click the PDF Properties tab to display the file's PDF stats: At the very bottom of the list, the PDF file version is listed. Note that the file version listed will not always tally with the version of Acrobat that created the file because engineering a PDF for backward compatibility is possible.

When creating a PDF file with the Acrobat Distiller in Acrobat 5, you can make it possible for viewers using earlier versions of Acrobat Reader to open your files by setting the Compatibility setting in the Distiller Job Options for an earlier version of Acrobat, specifically either that of Acrobat 3.0 (PDF 1.2) or Acrobat 4.0 (PDF 1.3). By doing this, you ensure your files will reach a wider audience.

Downloading and launching Acrobat Reader 5

The first step to using Acrobat Reader to peruse your PDF files is going to the Adobe Systems Web site and downloading the program. The quickest way to get there is to enter the following URL into your Web browser's Address field and press Enter:

```
www.adobe.com/products/acrobat/readstep2.html
```

This URL takes you to the Download Adobe Acrobat Reader page where all you have to do is enter three pieces of information:

1. The language of the Acrobat Reader (English in most cases)

2. The platform (or operating system) that your computer uses (that is, Windows Me, Windows NT, Windows 2000/XP, Mac 8.6, Mac 9.x, OS X, and so on)

3. The nearest location for downloading (you have a choice between USA and Japan, so this is USA in most cases)

Click the Download button and wait until the Acrobat Reader file is down-loaded on your computer. Then double-click its installer icon to decompress the Reader files and install them on your hard disk (on the Mac, the Acrobat Reader Installer actually downloads the Reader files when you double-click and then installs them on your hard disk).

After installing Acrobat Reader 5 on your hard disk, you can launch the Reader with or without also opening a PDF file. To launch the program without also opening a PDF on the Windows platform, follow these steps:

1. **Click the Start button on the Windows taskbar.**

2. **Highlight Programs (All Programs in Windows XP) on the Start menu.**

3. **Click Acrobat Reader 5.0 on the Programs menu.**

To do this on the Macintosh, follow these steps:

1. **Double-click your hard drive icon on the Mac desktop.**

2. **Double-click the Applications folder on the hard disk.**

3. **Double-click the Acrobat Reader 5.0 file icon in the Applications folder.**

4. **Double-click the Acrobat Reader 5.0 program icon in the Acrobat Reader 5.0 folder.**

After you launch Acrobat Reader, you can then open PDF files for viewing and printing by choosing File⇨Open and selecting the PDF file to open in its Open dialog box.

The easiest way to launch Acrobat Reader and open a PDF file for viewing is to drag a PDF file icon onto an Acrobat Reader shortcut on the Windows or Macintosh desktop. Note that when you install Acrobat Reader 5 on a Windows machine, the installer automatically creates a desktop shortcut called Acrobat Reader 5.0.

To create such a desktop shortcut on the Macintosh (where it's called an *alias*), you open the Acrobat Reader 5.0 folder (located in the Applications folder on your hard disk), click the Acrobat Reader 5.0 icon to select it, press ⌘+M to create an Acrobat Reader 5.0 alias, and then drag this alias icon onto the Macintosh desktop.

Figure 2-1 shows you how the Acrobat Reader 5 window appears on a Windows computer when you launch the Reader and simultaneously open a PDF file within it. Note that in this particular case, the PDF file that opens takes up the full width of the program window up to the Navigation pane, which displays the bookmarks in this document.

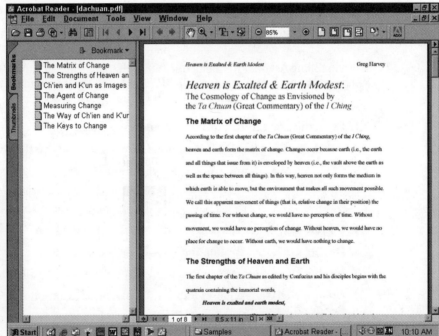

Figure 2-1:
The Acrobat Reader 5 window with the open PDF file used to launch it.

 You can have more than one PDF file open at a time in Acrobat Reader 5. To open multiple files when launching Acrobat Reader 5, Ctrl+click individual PDF file icons or lasso a group of them and then drag the entire selection onto the Acrobat Reader 5.0 desktop shortcut (alias). To do this from the Open dialog box, Ctrl+click or lasso the group before you click the Open button.

The Acrobat Reader 5 window

As you can see in Figure 2-2, the Acrobat Reader window is divided into three areas:

✔ Menu and toolbars at the top of the screen

✔ Document pane with scroll bars to the right and bottom and a status bar to immediate left at the bottom

✔ Navigation pane with two tabs for its two palettes: Bookmarks and Thumbnails

The menu bar contains standard application menus: File through Help. To select a menu and display its items, you click the menu name (or you can press the Alt key plus the underlined letter in the menu name, the so-called *hot key*, in the Windows version). To select a menu item, you drag down to highlight it and then press Enter, or you click it (in the Windows version, you can also select an item by typing its hot key).

The Acrobat Reader 5 toolbars

On the row beneath the menu bar, you see what appears to be a long toolbar with an almost solid row of buttons. As Figure 2-3 indicates, this toolbar is actually six separate toolbars, File through Adobe Online (which is the sole button on its toolbar).

Navigation pane

Toolbars   Menu bar   Document pane

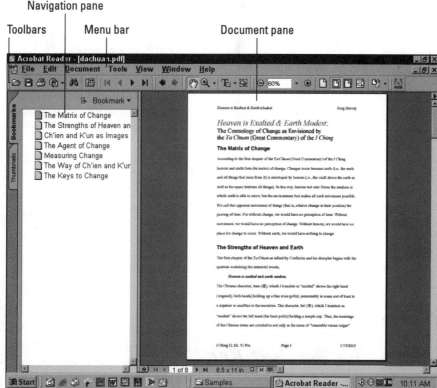

Figure 2-2: The Acrobat Reader 5 window is divided into three areas: menu and toolbars above and Document and Navigation panes below.

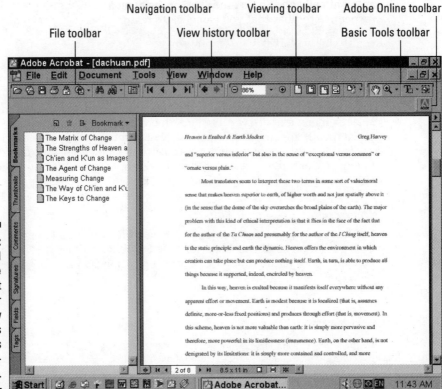

Navigation toolbar   Viewing toolbar   Adobe Online toolbar

File toolbar   View history toolbar   Basic Tools toolbar

Figure 2-3:
The second
row of the
Acrobat
Reader
window
contains
five toolbars
back-to-
back.

Five of the buttons shown in the toolbars in this figure sport downward-pointing shaded triangles. These buttons are as follows:

- The Create Adobe PDF Online button is the fourth from the right in the File toolbar.

- The Zoom In Tool is the second from the right in the Basic Tools toolbar.

- The Text Select Tool is right next to the Zoom In Tool in the same toolbar.

- The Viewing button shows the current page magnification setting as a percentage in the Viewing toolbar.

- The Rotate View Clockwise button is the last button in the Viewing toolbar.

These downward-pointing triangles are actually More Tools buttons that, when clicked, display a pop-up menu with additional related tools. The final item on all these pop-up menus is an Expand This Button option that, when clicked, adds all the buttons on the pop-up menu items to their toolbar. When you expand a toolbar by selecting a button's Expand This Button icon, Acrobat automatically adds a Collapse button (with an arrow pointing left) to the respective toolbar that you can click to restore the original arrangement of a single button with a More Tools button attached.

Note that the Macintosh version of Acrobat Reader 5 replaces the Create Adobe PDF Online button found on the File toolbar in the Windows version with a much more valuable Search button that enables you to do fast text searches using indexes attached to a PDF file. This Search button also has a More Tools button attached to it, with options for displaying the search results in their own dialog box and going to the next and previously highlighted item. Windows users must open their PDF files in Acrobat 5 in order to have access to this valuable search feature.

Table 2-2 lists the buttons on each of these toolbars and describes their functions.

Table 2-2		The Toolbars of Acrobat Reader 5	
Toolbar	*Icon*	*Name*	*Function*
File		Open	Displays the Open dialog box.
		Save a Copy	Displays the Save a Copy dialog box.
		Print	Opens the Print dialog box.
		Create Adobe PDF Online	Connects you to the Create Adobe PDF Online Web service (note that this button is replaced by a Search button on the Mac version of Acrobat Reader). Its More Tools button enables you to select Search Adobe PDF Online.
		Find	Opens the Find dialog box to search for text in the document.
		Show/Hide Navigation Pane	Opens and closes the Navigation pane.

(continued)

Table 2-2 *(continued)*

Toolbar	Icon	Name	Function
Navigation		First Page	Takes you to the beginning of a multipage document.
		Previous Page	Takes you to the prior page in a multipage document.
		Next Page	Takes you to the subsequent page in a multipage document.
		Last Page	Takes you to the end of a multi-page document.
View History		Go to Previous View	Takes you to the last page you visited.
		Go to Next View	Takes you back to the page that was current when you clicked the Go to Previous View button.
Basic Tools		Hand Tool (H)	Selects the hand for selecting links: This tool changes to Arrow when passed over menus and buttons.
		Zoom in Tool (Z)	Zooms in on the area that you draw as a bounding box with magnifying glass icon. Its More Tools button enables you to select a Zoom Out Tool (Shift+Z) for zooming out on an area.
		Text Select Tool (V)	Enables you to select text in the document for copying to the Clipboard. Its More Tools button enables you to choose a Column Select Tool (Shift+V) for selecting text that is set in newspaper columns.

Toolbar	Icon	Name	Function
		Graphics Select Tool (G)	Enables you to select graphics in the document for copying to the Clipboard.
Viewing		Zoom Out	Enables you to decrease the magnification (to see more of the entire document) by set intervals of 25% or less.
	50%	Magnification Level	Displays the current magnification level as a percentage of the actual size (100%). To change the magnification, click the Magnification Level text box, type the new magnification number, and press Enter. To select a preset magnification, click its More Tools button and then click the desired setting on the pop-up menu.
		Zoom In	Enables you to increase the magnification (to see more detail and less of the entire document) by set intervals of 25% or less.
		Actual Size	Resizes the zoom magnification setting to 100%.
		Fit in Window	Resizes the zoom magnification setting so that you see the entire document.
		Fit Width	Resizes the zoom magnification setting so that the width of the document fills the entire Document pane.
		Reflow	Reflows the text of the document to fit its current width and magnification setting in the Document pane so that none of the text runs off the left or right sides of the window.

(continued)

Table 2-2 *(continued)*

Toolbar	Icon	Name	Function
		Rotate View Clockwise	Reorients the current page by rotating it 90 degrees to the right (clockwise). Its More Tools button enables you to select Rotate View Counter-clockwise to reorient the page 90 degrees to the left (counterclockwise).
Adobe Online		Visit Adobe on the World Wide Web	Automatically connects you to the Internet and takes you to the Acrobat 5 section of the Adobe Systems Web site where you can look for updates, news, and product support.

The Acrobat Reader 5 Document pane

The Acrobat Reader 5 Document pane is where your PDF files load for viewing. How much document text and graphics appear in this pane depends upon a number of factors:

Musical toolbars

You don't have to leave the six Acrobat Reader toolbars in the original single-row arrangement. You can move them to new rows or even move them out of the top area of the screen so that they float on top of the Navigation or Document pane. To move a toolbar, you drag it by its separator bar (the slightly raised vertical bar that appears before the first button in each toolbar). As you drag, a dark outline appears at the mouse pointer until you release the mouse button and plunk the toolbar down in its new position. Note that when you release the toolbar in the Navigation or Document pane area, Acrobat reshapes the toolbar so that its buttons are no longer in a single row and gives the toolbar its own title bar. You can move the floating toolbar by this title bar (sans name), but you can't change the shape of the toolbar. To close a floating toolbar, click its close button. To dock a floating toolbar, drag it by its separator bar (right beneath the empty title bar) until its outline assumes a single row shape and then drop it in place.

✔ The size of the pages in the document (displayed in the Page Size indicator in the status bar at the bottom of the Document pane — see Figure 2-4)

✔ The size of your computer monitor

✔ The current zoom (magnification) setting in Acrobat Reader (shown in the Magnification Level button in the Viewing toolbar)

Of these factors, you can change only the current zoom setting either with the buttons in the Viewing toolbar (see Table 2-2) or the options on the View menu. Zoom out to get an overview of the document's layout. Zoom in to make the text large enough to read.

The best way to zoom in on some document detail (be it lines of text or a graphic) is to click the Zoom In tool (or type its hot key, lowercase *Z*) and then use the magnifying-glass pointer to draw a bounding box around the desired text or graphic. When you release the mouse button, Acrobat Reader zooms in on the selected area so that it takes up the entire width of the Document pane.

At the bottom left of the Document pane, you find the status bar, which gives you valuable information about the current PDF file you're viewing and enables you to advance back and forth through the pages and change how the pages are viewed in the Document pane (a single page at a time is the program's default setting). Figure 2-4 helps you identify the status bar buttons.

The Acrobat Reader 5 Navigation pane

The Navigation pane to the left of the Document pane contains two Tab palettes in Acrobat Reader 5: Bookmarks and Thumbnails. The Bookmarks palette normally shows the overall structure of the document in an outline form. Note, however, that not all PDF files that you open in Acrobat Reader 5 have bookmarks because this is a feature the author of the document must decide to include prior to or when actually making the PDF file (see Chapter 4 for more on this topic). The Thumbnails palette shows little representations of each page in the PDF document you're viewing. Note that Acrobat Reader 5 (unlike earlier versions) generates thumbnails for each page in a PDF document whether or not the author embedded them at the time when the PDF was made.

Acrobat Reader 5 offers you several ways to open and close the Navigation pane (which may or may not be displayed automatically when you first open the PDF file for viewing):

✔ Click the Show/Hide Navigation Pane button at the end of the File toolbar

✔ Click the Navigation Pane button at the beginning of the status bar in the Document pane

✔ Press F6

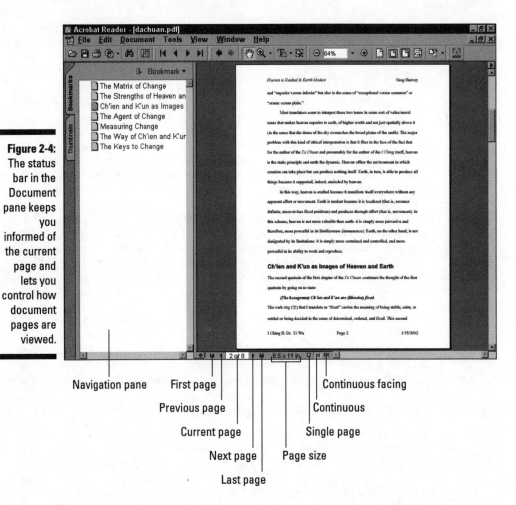

Figure 2-4:
The status bar in the Document pane keeps you informed of the current page and lets you control how document pages are viewed.

Navigation pane — First page — Continuous facing

Previous page — Continuous

Current page — Single page

Next page — Page size

Last page

Note that you can manually resize the Navigation pane to make it wider or narrower. Position the Hand Tool mouse pointer on its border or the double-headed arrow tab to the immediate left of the status bar and then drag right (to make it wider) or left (to narrow it) when this tool changes to a double-headed arrow. Note that Acrobat Reader remembers any width changes that you make to the Navigation pane so that the pane resumes the last modified size each time you use the Reader.

Many times you are tempted to increase the width of the Navigation pane because it isn't wide enough to display all the text in the headings in the Bookmarks palette. Rather than reduce the precious real estate allotted to the Document pane in order to make all the headings visible, you can read a long heading by lingering the Hand Tool mouse pointer over its text. After a second or two, Acrobat displays the entire bookmark heading in a highlighted box that appears on top of the Navigation pane and extends as far as necessary into the Document pane. As soon as you click the bookmark link or move the Hand Tool off the bookmark, this highlighted box disappears.

Using the Bookmarks palette

The Bookmarks palette gives you an overview of the various sections in many PDF documents (see Figure 2-5). Acrobat Reader indicates the section of the document that is currently being displayed in the Document pane by highlighting the page icon of the corresponding bookmark in the Bookmarks palette.

In some documents you open, the Bookmarks palette will have multiple nested levels (indicating subordinate levels in the document's structure or table of contents). When a Bookmarks palette contains multiple levels, you can expand a part of the outline by displaying a heading's nested levels by clicking the Expand button that appears in front of its name. In Windows, Expand buttons appear as boxes containing a plus sign. On the Macintosh, Expand buttons appear as shaded triangles pointing to the right. Note that you can also expand the current bookmark by selecting the Expand Current Bookmark command at the top of the Bookmark pop-up menu (opened by clicking the downward-pointing shaded triangle next to the word *Bookmark* at the top of the palette).

When you expand a particular bookmark heading, all of its subordinate topics appear in an indented list in the Bookmarks palette, and the Expand button becomes a Collapse button (indicated by a box with a minus sign in it on Windows and by a downward-pointing shaded triangle on the Mac). To hide the subordinate topics and tighten up the bookmark list, you click the topic's Collapse button.

You can press F5 to select the Bookmarks palette from the keyboard without having to click the Bookmarks tab itself. Note that if the Navigation pane is closed, pressing F5 opens the pane with the Bookmarks palette selected.

Using the Thumbnails palette

The Thumbnails palette shows you extremely small versions of each page in the PDF document you're viewing in Acrobat Reader (see Figure 2-6). You can use the Navigation pane's vertical scroll bar to scroll through these thumbnails to get an overview of the pages in the current document, and sometimes you can even use them to locate the particular page to which you want to go (especially if that page contains a large, distinguishing graphic).

Note that Acrobat Reader displays the number of each page immediately beneath its thumbnail image in the Thumbnails palette. The program indicates the current page that you're viewing by highlighting its page number underneath the thumbnail. The program also indicates how much of the current page is being displayed in the Document pane on the right with the use of a red outlining box in the current thumbnail (this box appears as just two red lines when the box is stretched as wide as the thumbnail).

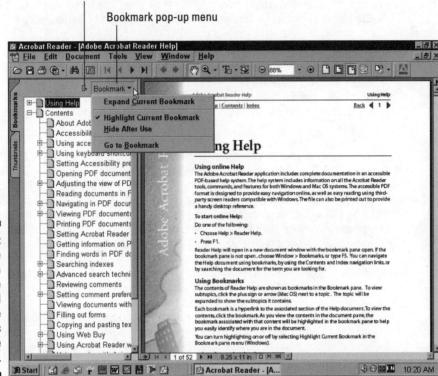

Find Current Bookmark button

Bookmark pop-up menu

Figure 2-5:
The
Navigation
pane
opened
with the
Bookmarks
palette
selected.

You can zoom in and out and scroll up and down through the text of the current page by manipulating the size and position of this red box. To scroll the current page's text up, position the Hand Tool on the bottom edge of the box and then drag it downward (and, of course, to scroll page text down, you drag this outline up). To zoom in on the text of the page in the Document pane, position the Hand Tool on the sizing handle located in the lower-right corner of the red box (causing it to change to a double-headed diagonal arrow) and then drag the corners of the box to make the box smaller so that less is selected. To zoom out on the page, drag the corner to make the box wider and taller. Of course, if you stretch the outline of the red box so that it's as tall and wide as the thumbnail of the current page, Acrobat Reader responds by displaying the entire page in the Document pane the same as if you selected the Fit in Window view.

By default, Acrobat Reader displays what it considers to be large thumbnails (large enough that they must be shown in a single column within the Thumbnails palette). To display more thumbnails in multiple columns in the Thumbnails palette, select the Small Thumbnails menu item on the Thumbnail pop-up menu at the top of the Thumbnails palette.

Thumbnail pop-up menu

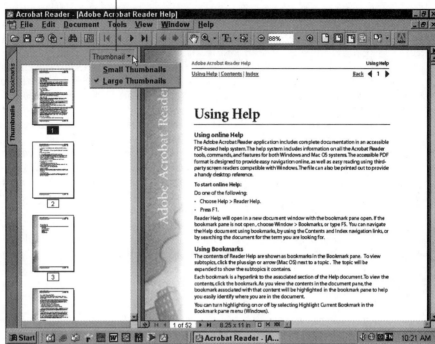

Figure 2-6:
The
Navigation
pane
opened
with the
Thumbnails
palette
selected.

Press F4 to have Acrobat Reader select and display the Thumbnails palette in the open Navigation pane. If the Navigation pane is currently closed, pressing F4 opens the pane with the Thumbnails palette selected.

Using the Article palette

Acrobat 5 supports a feature called *articles* that enables the author or editor to control the reading order when the PDF document is read online. This feature is useful when reading text that has been set in columns, as are many magazine and newspaper articles, because it enables you to read the text as it goes across columns and pages as though it were set as one continuous column (otherwise, you end up having to do a lot zooming in and out and scrolling and can easily lose your place).

To see if the PDF file you're reading has any articles defined for it, choose Window⇨Articles on the Acrobat Reader menu bar. Doing this opens a floating Articles palette in its own dialog box that lists the names of all the articles defined for the document. If this dialog box is empty, then you know that the PDF document doesn't use articles. Note that you can dock this palette on the Navigation pane and add its tab beneath the one for the Thumbnails palette by dragging the Articles tab displayed in the dialog box and dropping it on the Navigation pane.

To read an article listed on the Articles tab, double-click the article name in the list or click its name in the list and then click the Read Article item on its pop-up menu. The first part of the text defined in the article appears in fit-width viewing mode at the Acrobat Reader's default maximum-fit setting, and the mouse pointer changes to a Hand Tool with a down arrow on it. After reading the first section of the article, you continue to the next section either by pressing the Enter key (Return on Mac) or by clicking the Hand Tool pointer. Acrobat Reader indicates when you reach the end of the article by placing a horizontal bar under the arrowhead of the down arrow on the Hand Tool. If you then click the Hand Tool again or press Enter (or Return), Acrobat Reader returns you to the start of the article (indicated by a horizontal bar appearing at the top of the shaft of the down arrow). To return to normal viewing mode after reading an article, click one of the regular viewing buttons on the Viewing toolbar — Actual Size, Fit in Window, or Fit Width — or its corresponding menu option on the View menu (you can even use the View➪ Fit Visible command, which resizes the text and graphics in the document — without page borders — and has no comparable button).

To change the magnification used in reading an article in a PDF file, choose Edit➪Preferences or press Ctrl+K (⌘+K on the Mac), and then select a new magnification setting for the Max Fit Visible Zoom field by clicking it on its associated pop-up menu before you start reading the article.

Navigating PDF documents

Between the buttons on the Navigation toolbar at the top, the navigation buttons on the status bar, the Bookmarks and Thumbnails palettes in the Navigation pane to the left, and the scroll bars on the Document pane to the right, you have a quite a few choices in how you navigate a PDF document in Acrobat Reader. The following list describes the most popular ways to move through the pages:

- ✔ To move a page at a time, press → or ← key or click the Next Page button in the Navigation toolbar or the status bar to move forward or the Previous Page button to move back.

- ✔ To move to the last page in the PDF document, press the End key or click the Last Page button in the Navigation toolbar or the status bar.

- ✔ To move to the first page in the PDF document, press the Home key or click the First Page button in the Navigation toolbar or the status bar.

- ✔ To move to a specific page in the PDF document, drag the scroll button in the Document pane's vertical scroll bar until the page number appears in the ScreenTip; click the Current Page indicator in the status bar, type the page number, and press Enter; or scroll to the page's thumbnail in the Thumbnails palette and click it.

- ✔ To scroll through sections of text (about a half a page at a time), press Page Down (to move forward) or Page Up (to move back).

✔ To scroll continuously through the text, click and hold down the down
(to move forward) and up (to move back) scroll arrows on the vertical
scroll bar in the Document pane.

Changing the page viewing mode

Normally, Acrobat Reader displays a single page of the PDF document at a
time so that when you scroll from the end of one page to the next page, the
next page seems to replace the previous one. You can, if you want, change
the page viewing mode from single to continuous paging, wherein you see a
steady stream of pages as you scroll through the document. To change from
single-page to continuous-page viewing, click the Continuous button on the
right side of the status bar or choose View⏐Continuous from the Acrobat
Reader menu bar.

As part of continuous paging, you can also display facing pages (with verso
or left-hand pages on the left, and recto or right-hand pages on the right). To
display a PDF document with continuous facing pages, click the Continuous -
Facing button on the status bar or choose View⇨Continuous - Facing from
the Acrobat Reader menu bar.

Reading text in full-screen mode

If you're like me and your computer isn't equipped with a mega-monitor, you
may want to make the most of your screen real estate by viewing the PDF
document in full-screen mode. When you switch to full-screen viewing, the
program removes all the screen controls including the menu bar, toolbars,
Navigation pane, status bar, and yes, even the obsequious Windows taskbar.

To view a PDF document in full-screen mode, you press Ctrl+L (⌘+L on the
Macintosh), or you choose View⇨Full Screen from the Acrobat Reader menu
bar. To get out of full-screen mode and return to your regular viewing settings
(replete with menus, toolbars, and so on), press the Escape key (usually
marked Esc on your keyboard).

Note that when viewing a PDF document in full-screen mode, Acrobat Reader
always displays a single page at a time (no matter what page viewing mode
you were using prior to selecting full-screen mode). Because full-screen mode
hides all menus and toolbars, you normally need to rely on keystroke shortcuts to alter the magnification and move through the document text. Here are
some of the more useful keystroke shortcuts for doing just that:

✔ Ctrl++ (Ctrl plus the plus key) to increase magnification and Ctrl+– (Ctrl
plus the minus key) to decrease magnification by 25%

✔ Ctrl+0 to select the Fit in Window view

✔ Ctrl+1 to select the Actual Size view

✔ Ctrl+2 to select the Fit Width view

✔ Ctrl+3 to select the Fit Visible view (this enlarges the document so that it
takes up as much of the screen width as possible)

✔ Page Down or Ctrl+↓ to scroll down the text (and move to the next page in the Fit in Window view) and Page Up or Ctrl+↑ to scroll up the text (to the previous page in the Fit in Window view)

Reading text in the fit-visible viewing mode

Reading a PDF document in full-screen viewing mode is fine as long as you don't mind having to navigate the pages with keystroke shortcuts. If, however, you prefer using the various Acrobat Reader screen controls (including the scroll bars and the navigating buttons on the Navigation toolbar and on the Document window status bar), you're out of luck.

To make online viewing as comfortable as possible while still retaining access to the Acrobat Reader screen controls, try viewing the document text in the fit-visible viewing mode. This viewing mode is very similar to the fit-width mode except that it doesn't retain the space for the document's left and right margins, using this margin space instead to further boost the magnification of the document's text and graphics.

To use this viewing mode, you need to choose View⇨Fit Visible on the Acrobat Reader 5 menu bar or press Ctrl+3 (⌘+3 on the Macintosh because the program does not have a button on the Viewing toolbar).

Reading reflowed text at larger magnifications

As part of the new accessibility features in Acrobat Reader 5, the program is now equipped with a Reflow command that you can use to prevent document text from disappearing off the page at larger magnifications. This feature is a godsend for users with severe vision problems who otherwise wouldn't be able to read the text on the screen at all, and it can be a real boon for the rest of you, particularly when reading a PDF document that uses especially ornate and decorative fonts that can very difficult to decipher given the current screen resolution.

Figures 2-7 and 2-8 illustrate how beneficial reflowing the text can be when doing online reading in Acrobat Reader 5. In Figure 2-7, I selected the Fit Visible command on the Acrobat Reader View menu and then increased the magnification setting to 250%. As you can see, at this magnification you would have to do a lot of horizontal as well as vertical scrolling to read the text. Figure 2-8 shows what happens when you click the Reflow button on the Viewing toolbar. Note how, when this viewing setting is turned on, all the lines of text now fit within the screen width. Although you have to do more vertical scrolling to get through the reflowed text at this magnification, you won't be forced to do any horizontal scrolling at all.

You can turn on the Reflow viewing mode by clicking the Reflow button on the Viewing toolbar, choosing View⇨Reflow on the menu bar, or by pressing Ctrl+4 (⌘+4 on the Mac). While viewing the PDF document with Reflow turned on, you can increase or decrease the magnification settings, and Acrobat Reader 5 will immediately reflow the text to accommodate the increase or decrease in magnification.

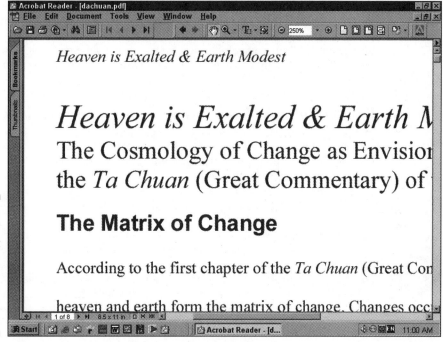

Figure 2-7:
Viewing PDF
document
text in fit-
width mode
at 250%
magnifi-
cation.

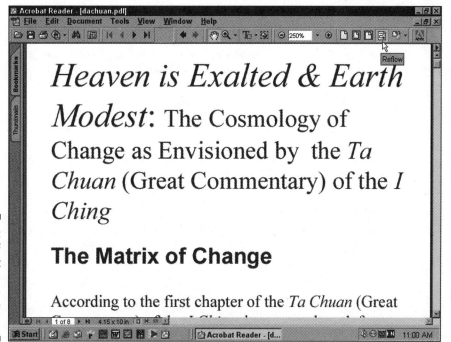

Figure 2-8:
PDF
document
text at 250%
magnifi-
cation after
reflowing.

To get out of Reflow viewing mode, simply select one of the other viewing modes — Actual Size, Fit in Window, Fit Width, or Fit Visible — from the View menu or the Viewing toolbar (remember, Fit Visible is available only on the View menu). When you select one of these other viewing modes, Acrobat Reader automatically reduces the magnification setting to accommodate the text in the mode.

Using bookmarks to locate a particular spot in the document

Instead of just aimlessly scrolling through the PDF text, you may want to find a particular place in the text. If the document has bookmarks, you can often use their links to go right to the spot you want. Simply display the Bookmarks palette in the Navigation pane, expand the topic of interest, and then click the heading at which you want to start reading. When you click a bookmark link, Acrobat Reader displays that heading in the Document pane.

If you scroll through the text of a PDF document in the Document pane and then decide that you want to find your place in the bookmarks, click the Find Current Bookmark button, the one with the arrow pointing toward the tiny sheet of paper located to the immediate left of the title Bookmark at the top of the Bookmarks palette. When you click this button, Acrobat Reader highlights the bookmark in the Bookmarks palette corresponding to the heading closest to your place in the text displayed in the Document pane.

Using Find to locate a particular spot in the document

If your document doesn't have bookmarks (and not all PDF files do), you can use the Find function to search for a heading, key term, or identifying phrase. To search for text with the Find feature, click the Find button in the File toolbar or choose Edit⇨Find from the menu bar to open the Find dialog box. Enter the word or phrase you want to locate in the document in the Find What field of the Find dialog box and then click the Find button or press Enter to search for it in the document. The program then advances to the next occurrence, which it highlights in the text displayed in the Document pane. If no matching text is located, you receive a warning dialog box indicating that this is the case.

To advance to a subsequent occurrence of the search text when the Find dialog box is still open on the screen, click the Find Again button (which replaces the Find button) or press Enter. To find subsequent occurrences after you close the Find dialog box, press Ctrl+G (⌘+G on the Mac). When Acrobat Reader reaches the end of the document, the program displays a warning dialog box indicating that you have searched to the end of the document and asking you if you want to continue the search from the beginning. To continue the search, click OK. To abandon the search, click Cancel or press the Escape key.

Getting a non-tagged PDF to reflow

Note that the Reflow feature works only on tagged PDF documents, which have been prepared with one of the latest versions of an Acrobat Distiller including, of course, the Distiller in Acrobat 5 and PDFMaker 5.0 for Microsoft Office 2000 and XP (see Chapter 15 for more on tagged files). If the PDF file you're viewing isn't tagged, you can tell right away because the Reflow button on the Viewing toolbar is grayed out and not available for use.

To convert such a PDF file to a tagged version for use with the Reflow feature with Acrobat 5, you need to install the Make Accessible Acrobat 5 for Windows plug-in (available as a free download from the Adobe Web site) and then open the file in Acrobat and choose Document⇨Make Accessible on the Acrobat 5 menus (the Make Accessible item is available on the Document menu only when the Make Accessible plug-in is successfully installed.)

To narrow your search by preventing Acrobat Reader from finding matches for your search text within other, longer words (such as the occurrence of *her* in the word *whether*), select the Match Whole Words Only check box in the Find dialog box before you begin the search. To narrow your search to exact case matches, select the Match Case check box. If you want to search backwards from your current position in the PDF document rather than the normal forward, select the Find Backwards check box.

Perusing PDF Files in Acrobat 5

It should come as little or no surprise to learn that viewing PDF files in Adobe Acrobat 5 is no different from viewing them in Adobe Acrobat Reader 5. After all, the free, giveaway Acrobat Reader 5 is simply a trimmed-down version of the full-fledged, must-be-purchased Acrobat 5, lacking all of Acrobat's editing tools (they being what you pay for) but none of the browsing tools.

This means that if you have Acrobat 5 installed on your computer (and I'm assuming that you do or will shortly, otherwise why invest in this book?), you can dispense with Acrobat Reader 5 altogether and use Acrobat 5 as your exclusive PDF editing *and* viewing program. Of course, this means that for details on how to view and browse your PDF files in Acrobat 5, you need to back up and read the earlier information on perusing PDF documents in Acrobat Reader because all of it pertains to using Acrobat 5 to view PDF documents. (For information on using Acrobat 5's editing features to create, edit, and proof PDF files that can then be distributed to readers using Acrobat Reader 5, refer to the chapters in Part II and III of this book.)

Leafing through PDF Files with the Acrobat eBook Reader

Acrobat Reader is not Adobe System's only free PDF browsing program. Its other giveaway software for viewing PDF files is called Acrobat eBook Reader. To download and install this complimentary program, go to the following location on the Adobe Web site and follow the downloading and installation instructions you find there (which are very similar to those for Acrobat Reader 5):

```
www.adobe.com/products/ebookreader
```

You may wonder, why did Adobe go to all the trouble of designing the Acrobat eBook Reader when it already had Acrobat Reader, which was quite capable of opening and displaying PDF documents for viewing and printing? The answer to this question lies in the differences between a regular PDF document and a PDF file as an eBook.

You can think of eBooks as specialized PDF documents that have been designed primarily for online reading to be sold and distributed from secure online servers. As such, they require a software program that optimizes the online reading and download experience for the user (because this download has normally been paid for by him or her), while at the same time enabling electronic publishers and their authors to maintain their copyrights and protect their intellectual property (we have to eat too!). Acrobat eBook Reader is just such an animal (see Chapter 15 for details on creating PDF files as eBooks that are ready for professional publishing).

This is not to say, however, that the Acrobat eBook Reader can only be used for reading eBooks that you purchase from online booksellers such as Barnes&Noble.com and Amazon.com. You can use it, if you wish, to read any PDF document that you produce in-house or receive from other sources. Because the Acrobat eBook Reader costs exactly the same as Acrobat Reader (NOTHING), you can evaluate both programs and make the decision on which to use based on the relative merits of each.

Opening PDF files in the Acrobat eBook Reader

After you've downloaded and installed the Acrobat eBook Reader on your computer, you can launch the program by dragging a PDF file icon onto its desktop shortcut just as you might when using Acrobat Reader 5. You can also launch the program by double-clicking the desktop shortcut or program icon or, if you use Windows, clicking the Start taskbar button, highlighting Programs (All Programs in Windows XP), and then clicking Acrobat eBook Reader.

Figure 2-9 shows you the Acrobat eBook Reader as it appears when you launch the program without also opening a PDF file in it (of course, yours won't sport the same book thumbnails as mine). As you can immediately see in this figure, the interface of the Acrobat eBook Reader is quite different from that of Acrobat Reader 5. The most striking difference is the size of the application itself. Regardless of the computer monitor size, the Acrobat eBook Reader starts up by using only a portion of the screen real estate. The reason for this is that eBooks adhere to a strict page-size standard, one that maintains a strict 4 by 3 aspect ratio wherein page length is always larger than page width by one. It does this to more closely mimic the size and proportion of print books.

Figure 2-9: Adobe's Acrobat eBook Reader Library page showing all PDF and eBook files ready for opening.

The next difference you may notice is that the Acrobat eBook Reader uses Library pages with thumbnail images that identify the PDF and eBook files that you can open for reading. These thumbnails in the Library pages represent all the PDF documents you have opened in the Acrobat eBook Reader and/or all the eBook files that you currently have purchased and downloaded (in a special folder where the Acrobat eBook Reader automatically saves all eBooks that you purchase from online bookstores).

To switch the Library view so that it displays *only* the PDF files you have opened and not the eBooks you've downloaded, you change the Show setting at the top of the Acrobat eBook Reader from the default setting of All to All Documents. When you select the All Documents option from the Show pop-up menu, the Acrobat eBook Reader hides all eBook thumbnails. To hide all PDF documents and display only eBooks that you've downloaded, you select the All Ebooks option on the Show pop-up menu.

 The Acrobat eBook Reader naturally expands the Library pages needed to display thumbnails for all the PDF documents you open or eBooks you purchase (shown in the page indicator at the bottom of the Library page). To access the thumbnails of PDF/eBook files on other Library pages, click the Next Page or Previous Page buttons near the top of the Acrobat eBook Reader Control bar to the immediate right of the viewing area containing the thumbnail images.

Sorting thumbnails

Note that you can not only control which PDF/eBook files appear in the Library pages of your Acrobat eBook Reader with the Show settings, but also control how they're arranged with the Sort settings. To sort the thumbnails in the Acrobat eBook Reader Library, select the sorting key (Author, Title, Date Acquired, or Last Accessed) in the Sort pop-up menu at the top of the Reader. Of course, all of these sorting keys are designed primarily for eBooks where the book's author and title are specifically designated as part of the file (as part of its so-called *metadata*). You can, however, sort the PDF documents you open with the Acrobat eBook Reader by the Date Acquired (the date you first opened the PDF file) and Last Accessed sorting keys.

Opening new files for reading

To open new PDF files for reading with the Acrobat eBook Reader, you click the Open File button near the bottom of the program's Control bar to the right of the area containing the Library thumbnails. Then select the folder and the PDF document you want to peruse and click the Open button.

When you open a PDF file, its first page replaces the Library thumbnails in the Acrobat eBook Reader. To return to the Library to open other PDF files, click the Library button on the program's Control bar. Please note that unlike Acrobat Reader 5 where you can have multiple PDF files open at one time, the Acrobat eBook Reader allows you to open only one PDF file or eBook at a time.

When you open a new PDF document in the Library, the Acrobat eBook Reader automatically closes the document currently open before opening the one you just selected. The good news is that before closing the open file, the Acrobat eBook Reader also routinely marks the last page that you read in the document so that when you next reopen it, that page is automatically displayed in the Reader window.

You can also open Web pages (HTML files) in the Acrobat eBook Reader. To do this, switch the file type from the default of Acrobat PDF files to Web files in the Windows Files of Type pop-up menu (on the Mac, change it to All Files in the Show pop-up menu) and then select the Web page file to open. Note that because Web pages are not formatted to the 4 x 3 aspect ratio used by eBooks, the Acrobat eBook Reader automatically opens them in its fit-width mode, which takes up the entire screen width. Note too, that thumbnails of the Web pages you open in the Acrobat eBook Reader are added to your Library pages like when opening PDF files, except that their thumbnails display only the name of the HTML file rather than rendering a miniature version of the first page, as is the case with PDFs.

Deleting files and quitting

If you need to delete a PDF file from your Library, you can do so by taking these few steps:

1. **If you're currently reading a PDF document or eBook, click the Library button on the Control bar.**

2. **Right-click (Control+click on a Mac) the thumbnail of the PDF file you want to remove from the library to open its context menu.**

3. **Click the Delete option on the context menu.**

   The Delete dialog box at the bottom of the Acrobat eBook Reader opens.

4. **Confirm the removal of the selected file by clicking the Yes button in the Delete dialog box.**

Note that deleting a PDF file from your library only removes the file from your Acrobat eBook Reader Library and does NOT delete the file from your hard disk. If you want to get it off your disk, you have to use your operating system's Delete command.

When you're finished viewing PDF documents and eBooks in your Acrobat eBook Reader, you can close the program by simply clicking the Quit button on its Control bar.

Reading PDF files in the Acrobat eBook Reader

To read a PDF document or eBook that's displayed in one of your Library pages, you need to click its thumbnail to select it (indicated by a highlighted outline surrounding the thumbnail) before you click the Read button in the Control bar. The Acrobat eBook Reader then opens the first page of the document or the page last read (if you previously opened the PDF file in the eBook Reader). The display looks similar to Figure 2-10.

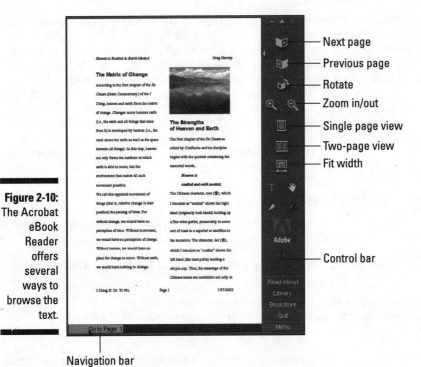

Next page
Previous page
Rotate
Zoom in/out
Single page view
Two-page view
Fit width

Control bar

Navigation bar

Figure 2-10:
The Acrobat
eBook
Reader
offers
several
ways to
browse the
text.

If your Windows computer is equipped with a Text to Speech engine (as is naturally the case if you're running Windows XP), the Read button in the Control bar is replaced by the Read Aloud button. When you click this button, the voice selected in the Text to Speech utility begins reading the text of the PDF document. If you prefer to silently read the text yourself rather than have it read to you, click the Stop button (the square one) in the controls that appear on the left side of the Reader above the Navigation bar. To resume having Text to Speech read aloud at anytime when perusing the text, click the Play button in these controls (the one with the shaded triangle pointing to the right).

Changing the page display

Like Acrobat Reader, the Acrobat eBook Reader enables you to modify the page display to suit the size of your monitor and the size of the text in the document you're reading. To display the document in a two-page spread with the even pages on the left-hand side and the odd pages on the right-hand side (as with a bound book), click the Two-Page button in the central section of the Control bar.

To expand the page to the maximum width for your screen (and toss out the sacrosanct 4 x 3 aspect) in order to make it much easier to read the text, click the Fit Width button on the Control bar. When you select the fit-width viewing option, the Acrobat eBook Reader adds a vertical scroll bar at the right edge of the page display that you can use to scroll up lines of text that are no longer visible.

To magnify the size of the text in any of three viewing modes (single-page, two-page, and fit-width), click the Zoom In button (the magnifying glass with the plus sign in it). Continue to click this button until the text appears the size you want it. Be aware, however, that you can bump up the text size with the Zoom In button to such a degree that some of the text at the beginning and end of the lines floats off the screen and is no longer visible.

When you magnify the text past a certain point in each viewing mode, the Acrobat eBook Reader suddenly adds a vertical scroll bar to right side of the display area (even when you're not in fit-width mode). You can use this scroll bar to vertically scroll lines of text that don't fit in the eBook Reader display area back into view. The Acrobat eBook Reader, however, does not ever sport a horizontal scroll bar no matter how much you magnify the text size with the Zoom In button. This means that you have no way to scroll back into view the text at the beginning and ends of lines that are now beyond the display area.

You can, however, use the Hand Tool to drag the missing text back on the screen. Click the Hand Tool on the Control bar and then use the Hand mouse pointer to drag it back into view. Drag to the left with the pointer to move the page text off the right edge back in view, and drag to the right to move the page text off the left edge back. Click the Hand Tool a second time to stop dragging your document text around the display area. You can also use the Zoom Out button (the magnifying glass with the minus sign to the immediate right of the Zoom In button) to reduce the text magnification until the text is once again small enough so that it all fits within the Acrobat eBook Reader display area.

The Control bar of the Acrobat eBook Reader contains a Sharpen Text button (the one with the letter T) that enables you to adjust how distinct and clear the text appears on your monitor. The Acrobat eBook Reader uses a new font display technology called Adobe CoolType in an attempt to more clearly render fonts on-screen. To do this, in rendering some fonts and some font sizes, the Acrobat eBook Reader mixes blue and red pixels with the normal black to achieve better character depth without making the letters too bold. Depending upon the state of your vision and your monitor, CoolType may make text in some fonts appear fuzzy, as though you were in need of your bifocals.

You can use the Sharpen Text button to select new CoolType display settings that make the text appear more distinct on your monitor. To do this, follow these few steps:

1. **Click the Sharpen Text button on the Control bar.**

   The first of two CoolType Setup dialog boxes appears.

2. **Click the radio button in front of the text sample that appears the sharpest and clearest to your eye.**

3. **Click the Next button.**

   The second of the two CoolType Setup dialog boxes appears.

4. **Again, click the radio button before the text sample that appears the sharpest and clearest to you.**

5. **Click the OK button to close the second of the two CoolType Setup dialog boxes and return to the document whose text is now adjusted to your new settings.**

If you're reading your PDF document or Acrobat eBook on a laptop computer, you can rotate the page 90 degrees so that the aspect ratio of the pages better fits the dimensions of your screen. To rotate the page display 90 degrees clockwise, click the Rotate button. Of course, the idea is that after rotating the PDF document page in this manner, you then turn your notebook 90 degrees counterclockwise so that the page is once again oriented correctly (something you can't very well do with the 50-pound monitor attached to your desktop computer!).

To restore the page to its normal orientation (at least in relation to your keyboard), click the Rotate button a second time. If you prefer having the Acrobat eBook Reader rotate the page counterclockwise rather than clockwise when you click the Rotate button, you can change this in the Preferences:

1. **Click the Menu button on the Control bar.**

2. **Click Preferences on the menu bar.**

   The Preferences dialog box opens.

3. **Click the drop-down button on the right of the Rotation Direction title that currently reads Right-Handed and then click the Left-Handed option on the pop-up menu.**

4. **Click the Close button in the right-hand corner of the Preferences dialog box.**

Paging through the document text

The Acrobat eBook Reader offers you a number of ways to move through the pages of your PDF file or eBook. Here's a list of the ways to move through and to specific pages in the document:

- ✔ Click the Next Page button or press the Page Down key or → key to advance to the next page.

- ✔ Click the Previous Page button or press Page Up or the ← key to redisplay to the previous page.

- ✔ Press the End key to go to the last page of the document.

- ✔ Press the Home key to go to the first page of the document.

- ✔ Position the mouse pointer on the Navigation bar and then use the Go to Page indicator to locate the page you want displayed and click the mouse button.

- ✔ Click the Back button to go back to the page that you viewed just before using the Go to Page indicator.

- ✔ Click the Forward button to return again to the page displayed before you clicked the Back button.

Finding words and phrases

Like Acrobat Reader, the Acrobat eBook Reader has a Find function that you can use to find key words and phrases and highlight them in the text. To use the Find feature, you follow these steps:

1. **Click the Menu button on the Control bar.**

2. **Click the Find button on the menu bar at the bottom of the eBook Reader screen.**

   The Find dialog box opens.

3. **In the Search For field, type the word, words, or phrase as the search text you want to find in the text.**

4. **Click one of the following buttons:**

   - **Find Next:** Click this to try to locate the search text on the current page or in later pages.

   - **Find Previous:** Click this to locate the search text in earlier pages.

   - **Find First:** Click this if you specifically want to locate the first occurrence of the search text.

When the Acrobat eBook Reader locates the first occurrence of the search text in the search direction specified, it closes the Find dialog box and highlights the word, words, or phrase in the text. To locate other occurrences of the search text, click the Next button (to find later occurrences) or Previous button (to find earlier occurrences) that appears on the menu bar. If no other occurrences are found, the Acrobat eBook Reader sounds an alert sound and replaces the Find, Next, and Stop buttons on the menu bar with the normal Navigation bar. If you want to conclude a search session before you reach the last occurrence of the search text, click the Stop button to close the menu and replace it with the Navigation bar.

Using bookmarks to go to a page

Like Acrobat Reader 5, the Acrobat eBook Reader can read all the bookmarks in any PDF document that you open in it. Unlike Acrobat Reader 5, however, the Acrobat eBook Reader also enables you to create new bookmarks in the PDF document so that you can quickly find and return to noteworthy pages anytime you read it.

To use a bookmark to go directly to a particular page, follow these steps:

1. **Click the Menu button on the Control bar.**

2. **Click Bookmarks on the menu bar.**

   The Bookmarks dialog box opens.

3. **Scroll through the bookmark list until you find the bookmark you want and then click the Goto Bookmark button.**

When you click the Goto Bookmark button, the Acrobat eBook Reader takes you directly to the page containing that bookmark.

Keep in mind that not all PDF documents that you open in the Acrobat eBook Reader will have bookmarks. Bookmarks can be automatically created at the time you distill a PDF file, or you can manually create them in Acrobat 5 (see Chapter 9 for details on creating bookmarks).

To create a new bookmark for a page in the Acrobat eBook Reader, follow these steps:

1. **Manually go to the page you want to bookmark so that's displayed in the Acrobat eBook Reader.**

   You can use the Go to Page indicator on the Navigation bar or the Next Page or Previous Page buttons to do this.

2. **Click the Menu button on the Control bar.**

3. **Click Bookmarks on the menu bar.**

   The Bookmarks dialog box opens at the bottom of the eBook Reader.

4. **Click the Add Bookmark button in the Bookmarks dialog box.**

   The Add Bookmark dialog box appears.

5. **Edit the bookmark name in the Bookmark field (the Acrobat eBook Reader automatically grabs the text from the first line of the current page and places it in this field).**

6. **Click the OK button to add the bookmark and close the Add Bookmark dialog box.**

After adding a bookmark, you can use it to go directly to its page by clicking Bookmarks on the eBook Reader menu bar, clicking the bookmark's name in the list, and then clicking the Goto Bookmark button in the Bookmarks dialog box. Note that you can also edit the bookmark description with the Edit Bookmark button or delete unwanted bookmarks with the Delete Bookmark button also located in the Bookmarks dialog box.

Annotating PDF files

In addition to being able to bookmark your PDF files in the Acrobat eBook Reader for quick page access, you can also annotate the text by adding notes and highlighting important words and phrases to make them easy to spot on the page.

You can use the Highlight button on the Control bar (the one that looks like a highlighter) to select the Highlight tool to draw attention to the document:

1. **Click the Highlight button on the Control bar.**

   The mouse pointer changes to a Highlight tool.

2. **Drag the Highlight tool through the text you want to emphasize.**

3. **Click the Highlight button on the Control bar a second time when you're ready to stop highlighting text and want to restore the mouse pointer to its normal Arrowhead shape.**

To remove highlighting from text on the page, drag through the text with the Highlight tool (make sure that you don't let up the mouse button, or you'll end up re-highlighting the text). Note that you can also remove highlighting from all text on the page or all text in the document by right-clicking (Windows) or Control+clicking (Mac) somewhere on the page and then clicking the Clear Page Highlights or the Clear Book Highlights option on the context menu.

The Acrobat eBook Reader supports two kinds of notes: inline notes whose text always shows up on the page (you add these kinds of notes in the margins or in between the lines of text), and hidden notes whose text is hidden until you double-click their note icons (which indicate their place on the page).

To create an inline note, follow these steps:

1. **Click the Annotate button on the Control bar (the one with the pencil).**

   The mouse pointer changes to an Annotate tool.

2. **Right-click (Windows) or Control+click (Mac) the place in the document text where you want the text of the inline note to appear.**

   A rectangular bounding box appears at the place you click.

3. **Type the text of the inline note in the bounding box.**

4. **Click the mouse pointer somewhere outside the bounding box.**

When you click outside the bounding box, it disappears, leaving only the text of the note visible in the text. If you find that the note text is obscuring document text, you can move the inline note. Simply position the mouse pointer over the inline note text until the bounding box reappears. Position the mouse pointer within this bounding box until it changes to a Cross pointer and then drag the bounding box (with note) to its new position. When you move the mouse pointer outside the bounding box, the text of the inline note appears in its new position. Note that you can adjust the borders of the bounding box for an inline note by dragging the borders in the appropriate direction (when you position the mouse pointer on the border of a bounding box, it changes to a double-headed arrow).

To edit or delete the text of an inline note, position the normal Arrowhead mouse pointer somewhere on its text to display its bounding box, and then double-click inside the bounding box to display the insertion point at the beginning of the note text. Use the cursor arrow and Backspace and Delete keys to edit the text. To remove the note, drag through the text, press the Delete key, and then click the mouse pointer somewhere outside of the bounding box (which will then disappear for good).

To create a hidden note, you follow these steps:

1. **Click the Annotate button on the Control bar (the one with the pencil).**

   The mouse pointer changes to an Annotate tool.

2. **Click the place in the document text where you want the text of the hidden note to appear.**

   A Note dialog box appears at the place you click.

3. **Type the text of the hidden note in the Note dialog box.**

4. **Click the Save button at the bottom of the Note dialog box to close it.**

When you close the Note dialog box, only its note icon appears in the document text. To read the text of a hidden note, double-click its note icon to open its Note dialog box. To close the note, click its Close box. While a note's dialog box is open, you can edit its text as needed. To save your changes, be sure to click the Save button at the bottom of the dialog box. To delete a note from the document, click its Delete button in the lower-right corner of its Note dialog box.

Be sure to bookmark the page that you annotate with notes and highlighting if it's not already bookmarked and give it a very descriptive name (such as "Suggested Topics and Revisions"). That way, you can use the bookmark to find the page with your notes when you next peruse the PDF document in the Acrobat eBook Reader. (See the preceding section, "Using bookmarks to go to a page," for details.)

Copying text and printing pages

If the author allows (see the "Checking the PDF file's permissions" sidebar), you can copy sections of text from the PDF file you're viewing and even print out its pages. To copy text, drag the normal Arrowhead mouse pointer through the text to highlight it, and then choose Edit⇨Copy on the Acrobat eBook Reader menu bar or press Ctrl+C (⌘+C on the Mac) to copy the selected text to the Clipboard. After copying it to the Clipboard, you can switch to another program that you have running (such as a word processor or text editor) and then paste it into place in a new document using that program's Paste command (normally, Edit⇨Paste on its menu).

To print pages of the PDF document from the Acrobat eBook Reader, follow these simple steps:

1. **Click the Menu button on the Control bar.**

2. **If the Print command doesn't appear on the menu bar given the current page-view setting you're using, click the Continuation button (marked >) to display the Print option and then click this option.**

   The Print dialog box opens at the bottom of the eBook Reader.

3. **To print a range of pages (permissions permitting), edit the number in the Start Page and End Page fields.**

   By default, the Acrobat eBook Reader lists the current page number as both the start and stop page number.

4. **(Optional) At top of the Print dialog after the heading Output Device, the program lists the name of the printer that it will use to print your pages. To switch to another printer connected to your computer, click the Printer Setup button and select the new printer in the Name field (Format For on the Mac) of the Print Setup dialog box and then click OK.**

5. **Click the Print button to close the Print dialog box and print your page or pages.**

Checking the PDF file's permissions

At the time authors distill their PDF files and eBooks, they can set up security settings that limit you — in the case of eBooks, even completely prevent you — from copying and/or printing document text. To display the copying and printing permissions for a particular PDF file or eBook, open it in the Acrobat eBook Reader or click its thumbnail in your Library pages, and then click the Menu button on the Control bar and Info on the menu bar. Doing this opens the Book Information dialog box at the bottom of the eBook Reader. Click the Permissions button to display the Permissions dialog box that lists both the Copy and Print permissions set by the author for that PDF file or eBook.

Browsing PDF Files in a Web Browser

The last way to read PDF files is with your Web browser. In order for your Web browser to be able to open PDF files, it needs a special PDFViewer plug-in (called, of all things, `nppdf32.dll` on Windows) installed. Note that when you install Acrobat 5 or Acrobat Reader 5 on your computer, this Web browser plug-in is automatically installed.

The only time that you might have to manually futz with the PDFViewer plug-in is when you install a new version of your Web browser after you've installed Acrobat 5 or Acrobat Reader 5 on your computer. If you find that your Web browser isn't able to open PDF files, use your operating system to search for the plug-in (Windows people should search for the file named `nppdf32.dll`, while you Mac people search for the file named PDFViewer). Chances are good that the plug-in file is on your computer and just not in the Plug-ins folder where your Web browser looks.

After you locate the PDFViewer plug-in, you need to copy the file to your Web browser's Plug-ins folder. If you use Internet Explorer on Windows, this folder is in the Internet Explorer folder inside the Program Files folder on your hard disk.

Not all versions of even of the most popular Web browsers support viewing PDF files with the PDFViewer plug-in. For example, although Netscape Navigator versions 4.*x* and 5.*x* use the plug-in and support this feature, the latest version 6.0 does not.

Being able to view PDF files in your Web browser is important because more and more Web sites are offering important updates, white papers, press releases, and even technical manuals in this file format. When your Web browser is able to display the PDF files, you can view them online in the browser without having to go to the trouble of downloading the PDF file on your hard disk and then opening it separately with Acrobat Reader.

Figure 2-11 shows you how Internet Explorer 5 looks when you open a PDF file in it. Note how the Acrobat Reader 5 toolbars are integrated into the normal Internet Explorer 5 user interface, along with the Acrobat Reader Navigation bar complete with the palette tabs for Bookmarks and Thumbnails.

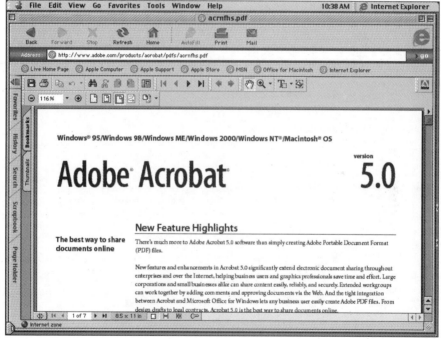

Figure 2-11: Opening an online PDF file for viewing in Internet Explorer 5.1 on a Mac.

Note that if you have Acrobat 5 (the one you have to buy) installed on your computer instead of just the freebie Acrobat Reader 5, the additional toolbars (Basic Tools, Commenting, and Editing) and palette tabs (Comments and Signatures) not found in Acrobat Reader are also added to the Web browser's user interface.

You can save a copy of the PDF document that you're viewing online with the Web browser on your hard disk by clicking the Save button (the one with the disk icon at the very beginning of the very first toolbar). In the Save a Copy dialog box that appears, specify the folder where you want the copy saved and then click the Save button to make the copy. After the PDF document is saved on your disk, you can then open it for reading with the Acrobat 5 Reader, Acrobat 5, or even the Acrobat eBook Reader if you want.

Chapter 3

Getting Acquainted with Acrobat 5

• •

In This Chapter

▶ Finding out ways to start Acrobat 5

▶ Opening and arranging PDF files for viewing and editing

▶ Getting familiar with the Acrobat 5 user interface

▶ Scoping out Acrobat 5's menus

▶ Becoming familiar with Acrobat 5's extra toolbars

▶ Getting online help when you need it

▶ Getting familiar with some of the more important keyboard shortcuts

• •

*Y*ou can think of Acrobat 5 as the full Monty edition of Acrobat Reader 5. Acrobat Reader acts as the free viewer for the PDF files that you prepare with Acrobat 5 (which will put you back just slightly over U.S. $200). As the more full-featured Acrobat product, its user interface, while identical to a great degree with that of Acrobat Reader 5, is still a wee bit more fun-filled and jam-packed than that of Acrobat Reader (which is covered at length in Chapter 2).

In this chapter, you find out what makes Acrobat 5 so special that it's worth a couple hundred bucks. As part of this orientation process, you start to discover all the ways you can use Acrobat 5 to put your PDF files into the hands of all those freeloaders using Acrobat Reader.

Launching Acrobat 5

 When you install Acrobat 5 on a Windows computer, the installer automatically puts a shortcut to the program on the desktop called Adobe Acrobat 5.0. To launch Acrobat 5, double-click this shortcut, or if you have a PDF file you want to edit with the program, drag its file icon onto this shortcut to start Acrobat and open the file for editing. You can also launch the program from the Start menu by clicking the Start button, highlighting the Programs option (All Programs in Windows XP), and then clicking Adobe Acrobat 5.0 on the Programs menu.

 If you plan on using Acrobat regularly, you should add an Adobe Acrobat 5.0 button to the Quick Launch toolbar on the Windows taskbar. That way, you can launch the program from the Windows taskbar with a single click of the Acrobat button even when another application program is running full-screen. To add an Adobe Acrobat 5.0 button to your Quick Launch toolbar, simply drag the Adobe Acrobat 5.0 desktop shortcut to the place on the Quick Launch toolbar where you want the Adobe Acrobat 5.0 button to appear and then release the mouse button.

If you use Acrobat 5 on the Macintosh, you can easily add an Acrobat 5.0 alias on the desktop by following these steps:

1. **Double-click your hard drive icon to open it and then locate the Applications folder in it.**

2. **Double-click the Applications folder to open it and locate the Acrobat 5.0 folder in it.**

3. **Double-click the Acrobat 5.0 folder icon to open it and then locate the Acrobat 5.0 program icon in it.**

4. **Single-click the program icon to select it and then press ⌘+M to create an Acrobat 5.0 alias in this folder.**

5. **Drag the Acrobat 5.0 alias out of the Acrobat 5.0 folder and drop it on the Mac desktop.**

 After creating an Acrobat 5.0 alias on the desktop, you can launch the program by double-clicking the alias icon, or you can launch it and open a PDF file for editing by dragging its file icon and dropping it on this alias icon.

 If you use the Launcher utility on the Macintosh to start your Mac applications, you should add an Acrobat 5 icon to the Launcher so that you can launch Acrobat from it with a single click. To add an Acrobat 5 icon to your Launcher, open it and then drag your Acrobat 5 alias icon and drop it in the Launcher folder.

Opening PDF files for viewing or editing

 Acrobat 5 and the Acrobat Reader 5 enable you to open multiple PDF files at a time. The easiest way to open more than one PDF file is from the Open dialog box, which you can display by choosing File⇨Open on the Acrobat menu, by clicking the Open button (the very first button on the second row of toolbars), or by pressing Ctrl+O (⌘+O on the Macintosh).

In the Open dialog box, first select the folder that contains the PDF files you want to open, and then select the multiple PDF files using one of the following methods:

- ✔ To select a cluster of files, drag a bounding box around the group with the Arrowhead mouse pointer.

- ✔ To select a bunch of files in a single column or row, click the first one to select it and then hold down Shift when you click the last one.

- ✔ To select individual files not all in a cluster, single column, or single row, hold down the Ctrl (Control on the Mac) key as you click each file icon or name.

Figure 3-1 shows the Open dialog box in Windows after selecting several individual PDF files for opening in Acrobat 5. When you click the Open button after selecting multiple files for opening, all of the selected files open in Acrobat in alphabetical order by filename, although only the one whose filename is last in this sequence is actually displayed in Acrobat's document window.

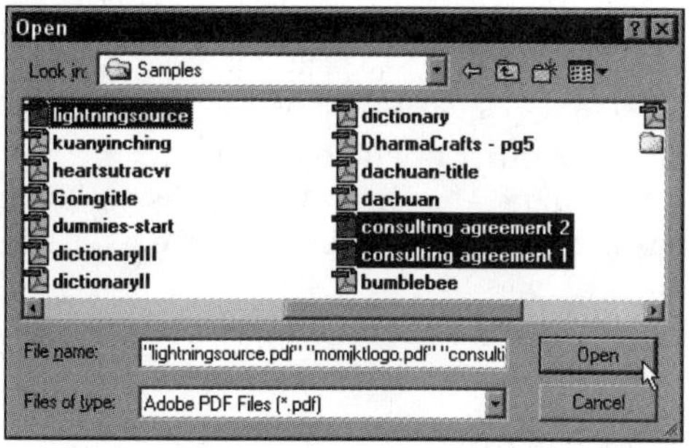

Figure 3-1:
Selecting
multiple PDF
files to open
in Acrobat 5.

To display in the Acrobat document window one of the open files that's currently open but not visible on the screen, select Window on the Acrobat menu bar and then type the number or click the name of that PDF file displayed at the bottom of the Window menu.

Arranging open PDF files in the Acrobat window

When you're working with more than one file in Acrobat, you can use the Tile or Cascade options on the Window menu to display part of all the open files in the Acrobat document window. You have a choice between two Tile options, Horizontally or Vertically. When you choose Window⇨Tile⇨Horizontally, Acrobat arranges the open document windows one on top of the other. When you choose Window⇨Tile⇨Vertically, Acrobat arranges the open document windows side by side.

Generally speaking, vertical tiling is usually more useful than horizontal tiling, given that computer monitors are wider than they are tall, so that when you place them side by side, you can see more of the document's text and graphics. Tiling is very useful when you want to copy text and graphics from one PDF document to another using the drag-and-drop method.

When you choose Window⇨Tile⇨Cascade, Acrobat arranges the open document windows in a cascade. When you cascade the open document windows, the title bars and the tabs of the palettes on the Navigation pane are visible for all the files, although you can only see part of the contents of the first file (that is, alphabetically speaking). To bring a different PDF file to the front, simply click its title bar. The cascade arrangement is useful when you need to see all of the names of the PDF files that are open and you want to copy text and graphics using the Copy and Paste commands.

To end a tiled or cascading window arrangement, click the Maximize button on the active document (the one whose title bar is highlighted and its filename is not grayed out). As soon as you maximize the active PDF document window in Acrobat on Windows, all of the other document windows are automatically maximized as well. In Acrobat on the Mac, however, this is not the case and you must still manually maximize the other document windows when you activate them.

Closing open PDF files

Of course, you can close any document open on the Acrobat screen by clicking its Close button or by choosing File⇨Close on the menu bar (Ctrl+W on Windows and ⌘+W on Mac). When you have multiple files open in a tiled or cascading arrangement in Acrobat, you have to be cognizant of which file is active when you close it, or you can end up closing a file that you still want to use.

To activate a particular document for closing (or editing, for that matter) when ordered in a tiled or cascading arrangement, click its title bar to highlight the title bar and activate the document window (on Acrobat in Windows, you can do this by pressing Ctrl+F6) or by selecting its filename on the Window menu.

Acrobat 5 has a very useful menu command, Window⇨Close All, that you can use to close all of the document windows that you have open at that time. Of course, Acrobat stops and prompts you to save changes to any file in the group it's closing in which you have edits that have yet to be saved.

Getting Comfy with the Acrobat 5 Interface

Because Acrobat Reader 5 is essentially a watered-down version of Acrobat 5, you're already good friends with the basic interface if you've read the sections pertaining to viewing files with the Acrobat Reader 5 in Chapter 2. If you skipped over that material, you may want to give it a quick look before reading the Acrobat 5-specific stuff in the following sections of this chapter.

Acrobat 5, despite its obvious similarity with Acrobat Reader 5 in terms of viewing and navigating PDF documents, offers you a much richer interface with which to work, given its ability to both generate and edit PDF files. In the remaining sections of this chapter, you find important information about the features in the Acrobat 5 interface that make the program the powerful PDF generating and editing tool that it is.

What's good on the Acrobat 5 menus today?

The Acrobat 5 menus (File, Edit, Document, View, Window, and Help) are exactly the same as the Acrobat Reader 5 menus. The items on the Acrobat 5 menus, depending upon the menu, vary greatly from those found on Acrobat Reader. You sometimes find even in cases where the menu items seem to match exactly, that the options offered on the Acrobat 5 menu item are either more numerous, or their functions are tailored specifically to suit the program's editing abilities. The follow sections give you a menu-by-menu description of the most salient Acrobat 5 menu items.

Fun stuff on the File menu

The File menu in Acrobat 5 (shown in Figure 3-2) is home to the common command items for opening, closing, and saving PDF files. Because you can edit PDF files in Acrobat 5, this menu contains a Save option for saving editing changes as well as a Save As command for renaming and saving copies (Acrobat Reader 5 has only a Save as Copy command that enables users to save to disk a copy of the PDF document that they're viewing).

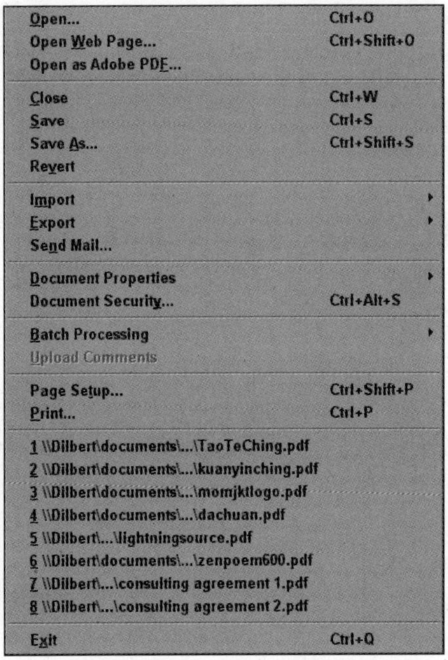

<u>O</u>pen...	Ctrl+O
Open <u>W</u>eb Page...	Ctrl+Shift+O
Open as Adobe PD<u>F</u>...	
<u>C</u>lose	Ctrl+W
<u>S</u>ave	Ctrl+S
Save <u>A</u>s...	Ctrl+Shift+S
Re<u>v</u>ert	
I<u>m</u>port	▶
<u>E</u>xport	▶
Se<u>n</u>d Mail...	
<u>D</u>ocument Properties	▶
Document Secur<u>i</u>ty...	Ctrl+Alt+S
<u>B</u>atch Processing	▶
Upload Comments	
Page Se<u>t</u>up...	Ctrl+Shift+P
<u>P</u>rint...	Ctrl+P
<u>1</u> \\Dilbert\documents\...\TaoTeChing.pdf	
<u>2</u> \\Dilbert\documents\...\kuanyinching.pdf	
<u>3</u> \\Dilbert\documents\...\momjktlogo.pdf	
<u>4</u> \\Dilbert\documents\...\dachuan.pdf	
<u>5</u> \\Dilbert\...\lightningsource.pdf	
<u>6</u> \\Dilbert\documents\...\zenpoem600.pdf	
<u>7</u> \\Dilbert\...\consulting agreement 1.pdf	
<u>8</u> \\Dilbert\...\consulting agreement 2.pdf	
E<u>x</u>it	Ctrl+Q

Figure 3-2:
Examining
the File
menu in
Acrobat 5.

In between the items for opening, closing, and saving files and the standard print (Page Setup and Print) and exiting commands (Exit on Windows and Quit on the Mac), the Acrobat 5 menu contains three special areas:

✔ **Import/Export/Send Mail:** Use the Import command to scan a paper document and save it as a PDF, or to import the comments saved in a special comments file or data saved in a special data file into a form in the PDF file that you have open. The Export command extracts images and saves them in various graphics formats, or saves comments made in a PDF file as a special comments file, or the data entered in a PDF form file in a special form file. Use the Send Mail command to open a new e-mail message in your e-mail program and attach the current PDF file to it.

✔ **Document Properties/Security:** With Document Properties, you set up various and sundry document properties, including a summary, fonts, index, and file metadata. Use the Document Security command to view or change the security settings for the current PDF file.

✔ **Batch Processing/Upload Comments:** You use the Batch Processing command to select or edit one of the many batch processes that enable you to perform particular tasks, such as printing or setting basic security settings for a whole bunch of PDF files at one time. The Upload Comments command enables you to send PDF document comments to a network or Web server when you have it set up to share PDF document review online.

Don't forget the very valuable Revert item on the File menu. You can use the File➪Revert command to dump all the edits that you've made since you last saved your PDF document. When you click the Revert button in the alert dialog box asking you if you want to revert to the previously saved version of the file, Acrobat opens this last-saved version without bothering to save your edits.

Edification on the Edit menu

The Acrobat 5 Edit menu (shown in Figure 3-3) is pretty standard stuff with the usual items for undoing and redoing, copying, cutting and pasting, and finding and searching. You'll find that it differs from the Acrobat Reader 5 Edit menu mainly in its inclusion of additional Preferences menu items, and additional general preference settings that you can set for the PDF document you're editing in the Preferences dialog box.

Undo	Ctrl+Z
Redo Typing	Ctrl+Shift+Z
Cut	Ctrl+X
Copy	Ctrl+C
Paste	Ctrl+V
Delete	
Copy File to Clipboard	
Select All	Ctrl+A
Deselect All	Ctrl+Shift+A
Find...	Ctrl+F
Find Again	Ctrl+G
Search	▶
Properties...	Ctrl+I
Preferences	▶

Figure 3-3: Exploring the Edit menu in Acrobat 5.

Delights on the Document menu

The Document menu in Acrobat 5 (shown in Figure 3-4) contains lots of commands (that have lots of valuable keystroke shortcuts) for quickly navigating through the PDF document you're currently editing, as well as to other documents you have open at the time.

In addition, the Document menu contains an important group of editing commands that affect all the pages in the PDF file that you're editing. These include command items for inserting, replacing, extracting, and deleting pages, as well as commands for cropping and rotating them. They also include items for adding page numbers, setting an action that takes place upon the opening or closing of each page, checking the accessibility of the document (if you have the Make Accessible plug-in installed), and selecting the page reading order that is used by unstructured PDF files (see Chapter 15 for information on Acrobat's structured and tagged files and Make Accessible plug-in).

First Page	Ctrl+Shift+Pg Up
Previous Page	<-
Next Page	->
Last Page	Ctrl+Shift+Pg Dn
Go To Page...	Ctrl+N
Go To Previous Document	Alt+Shift+<-
Go To Previous View	Alt+<-
Go To Next View	Alt+->
Go To Next Document	Alt+Shift+->
Insert Pages...	Ctrl+Shift+I
Extract Pages...	
Replace Pages...	
Delete Pages...	Ctrl+Shift+D
Crop Pages...	Ctrl+T
Rotate Pages...	Ctrl+R
Number Pages...	
Set Page Action...	
Make Accessible	
Select Reading Order...	Ctrl+Shift+C

Figure 3-4: Discovering the Document menu in Acrobat 5.

Treats on the Tools menu

As you can see in Figure 3-5, the Tools menu in Acrobat 5 is a veritable smorgasbord of useful tools. You use its commands to do everything from spell-checking your PDF document to making it secure. Most notable on this menu are the following very important items:

- ✔ **Comments:** For summarizing, filtering, and finding a reviewer's comments in the document.

- ✔ **Compare:** For comparing two documents or two versions within a signed document to see all of the editing changes made after the document was signed.

- ✔ **Paper Capture:** For making scanned files searchable.

- ✔ **Web Capture:** For converting Web pages into PDF files.

- ✔ **Catalog:** For creating a collection of PDF files that can be indexed for fast searching.

- ✔ **Distiller:** For manually creating PDF documents.

- ✔ **Forms:** For adding form fields and using form templates.

- ✔ **Touch Up:** For spot text editing.

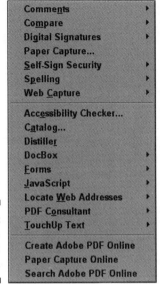

Variations on the View menu

The View menu (shown in Figure 3-6) contains all of the options for changing the page magnification, the way the document pages are displayed (single-page, continuous, or continuous with facing pages) in the Acrobat Document window, as well as options for rotating the pages. This important menu also contains new options for proofing the page layout and colors as well as for previewing how colors will overprint to create traps for misregistration during printing. At the bottom of this menu, you find items for using local fonts (that is, fonts that are installed on the computer on which you're working), and for displaying and hiding a layout grid for aligning graphics and form fields.

Wonders on the Window menu

The Window menu (shown in Figure 3-7) contains the items you need for arranging and selecting document windows for the PDF files you're editing. It also contains items for displaying and hiding the program's menu bar, tool-bars, and many palettes. Note that Acrobat 5 adds two additional toolbars, Commenting and Editing, to the six toolbars (Adobe Online, Basic Tools, File, Navigation, View History, and Viewing) found in Acrobat Reader 5.

The program also adds six additional palettes (Comments, Destinations, Fields, Info, Signatures, and Tags) to the three standard palettes for moving through the PDF document — Articles, Bookmarks, and Navigation. You use these additional palettes to keep track of lots of different types of information that you add to your PDF file.

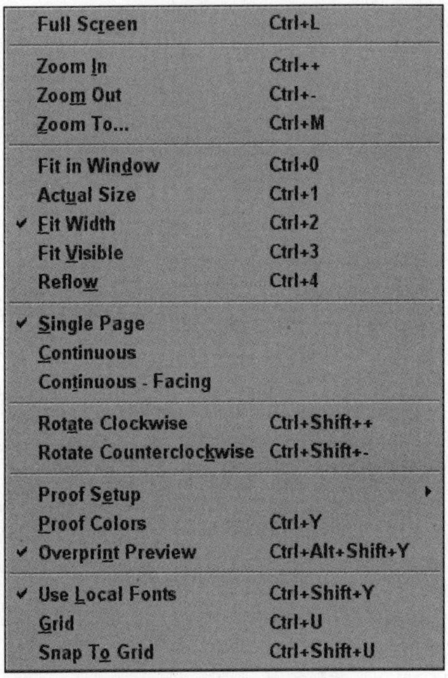

Full Screen	Ctrl+L
Zoom In	Ctrl++
Zoom Out	Ctrl+-
Zoom To...	Ctrl+M
Fit in Window	Ctrl+0
Actual Size	Ctrl+1
✓ Fit Width	Ctrl+2
Fit Visible	Ctrl+3
Reflow	Ctrl+4
✓ Single Page	
Continuous	
Continuous - Facing	
Rotate Clockwise	Ctrl+Shift++
Rotate Counterclockwise	Ctrl+Shift+-
Proof Setup	▶
Proof Colors	Ctrl+Y
✓ Overprint Preview	Ctrl+Alt+Shift+Y
✓ Use Local Fonts	Ctrl+Shift+Y
Grid	Ctrl+U
Snap To Grid	Ctrl+Shift+U

Figure 3-6:
Visiting the
View menu
in Acrobat 5.

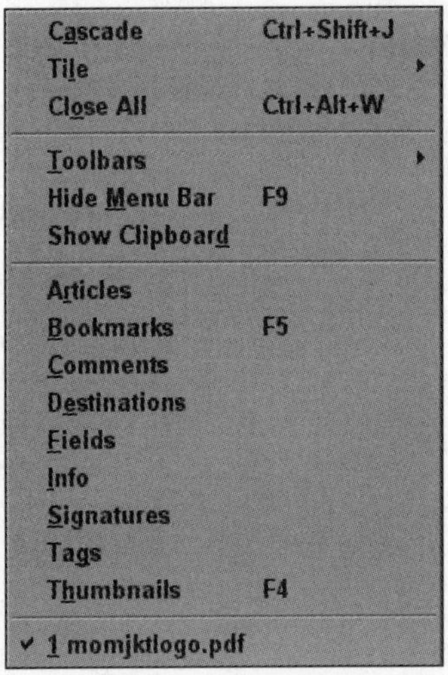

Cascade	Ctrl+Shift+J
Tile	▶
Close All	Ctrl+Alt+W
Toolbars	▶
Hide Menu Bar	F9
Show Clipboard	
Articles	
Bookmarks	F5
Comments	
Destinations	
Fields	
Info	
Signatures	
Tags	
Thumbnails	F4
✓ 1 momjktlogo.pdf	

Figure 3-7:
Walking
through the
Window
menu in
Acrobat 5.

Happiness on the Help menu

The Help menu (shown in Figure 3-8) shows the various options for getting online help with Acrobat 5. The first Help menu item, Acrobat Help, opens a PDF version of the Acrobat Help manual (see the "Getting all the help you need" section later in this chapter for details). The Top Issues, Adobe Online, and Online Registration Help items all launch your Web browser and connect you to the Adobe Systems Web site. Select Adobe Online to check for Acrobat 5 updates that you can install on your computer. Select Top Issues to visit the online support center for Acrobat 5, especially if you're experiencing problems running Acrobat with your hardware. Select the Online Registration option to register your copy of Acrobat 5 (of course, you only need to do this once, right after you first install Acrobat 5 on your computer).

The About Adobe Acrobat Help item displays the program splash screen that shows your version number (which as of this writing should be version 5.0.5), along with your license information, including your serial number (you need to click the splash screen to get rid of it, by the way). The About Adobe Acrobat Plug-Ins Help item displays a list of all the plug-ins (helper utilities that expand Acrobat's functionality in some way) installed in your copy of Acrobat 5. The About 3rd Party Plug-Ins option displays a submenu showing all of the third-party (that is, not made by Adobe Systems) plug-ins installed for your copy of Acrobat 5 (there are only two third-party plug-ins, Acrobat Table/Formatted Text and InterTrust DocBox, installed when you first install Acrobat 5 on your computer).

Figure 3-8: Helping yourself to the Help menu in Acrobat 5.

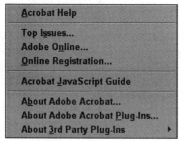

Touring the Commenting and Editing toolbars

Acrobat 5 contains all of the toolbars found in Acrobat Reader 5 plus two, the Commenting toolbar, shown in Figure 3-9, and the Editing toolbar, shown in Figure 3-10 (for complete rundown on the toolbars and buttons that both Acrobat and Acrobat Reader share, see Chapter 2). The buttons on these toolbars are designed to help with common editing tasks (which are totally absent from Acrobat Reader), and you will undoubtedly make much use of them as you work in the program. Refer to Table 3-1 for a brief description of the function of each of these tools.

Table 3-1 **The Commenting and Editing Toolbars of Acrobat 5**

Toolbar	Icon	Name	Function
Commenting		Note Tool	Enables you to annotate text in the PDF document. Its More Tools button enables you to select between the Note Tool, FreeText Tool, Sound Attachment Tool, and File Attachment Tool.
		Pencil Tool	Enables you to mark up text in the PDF document. Its More Tools button enables you to select between the Pencil Tool, Square Tool, Circle Tool, and Line Tool.
		Highlight Tool	Enables you to emphasize text in the PDF document. Its More Tools button enables you to select between the Highlight Tool, Strikeout Tool, and Underline Tool.
		Spell Check Form Fields and Comments	Enables you to spell-check the comments and form fields that you add to a PDF document.
		Digital Signature Tool	Enables you to use the Self-Sign Security software to digitally sign off on a PDF document.
Editing		Movie Tool	Enables you to insert a digital movie for playback in the PDF document.
		Link Tool	Enables you to create a hyperlink in the PDF document.
		Article Tool	Enables you to create articles in the document that designate the order in which portions of the text are to be read using the Article palette in Acrobat Reader 5.
		Crop Tool	Enables you to crop pages in the PDF document.

Toolbar	Icon	Name	Function
		Form Tool	Enables you to add a form field to the PDF document.
		Touch Up Text Tool	Enables you to edit portions of the PDF document. Its More Tools button enables you to select between the Touch Up Text Tool, the Touch Up Object Tool, and the Touch Up Order Tool.

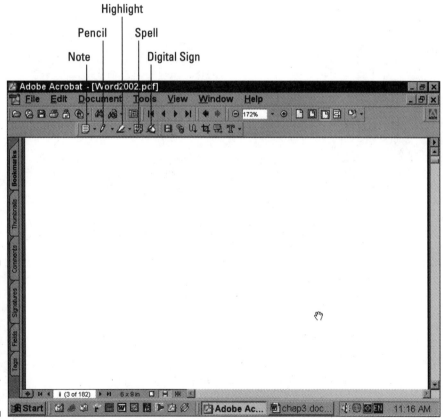

Figure 3-9: You use the buttons on the Commenting toolbar to annotate your document.

Article tool ┌ Crop tool

Link tool   Form tool

Movie tool   Touch Up Text tool

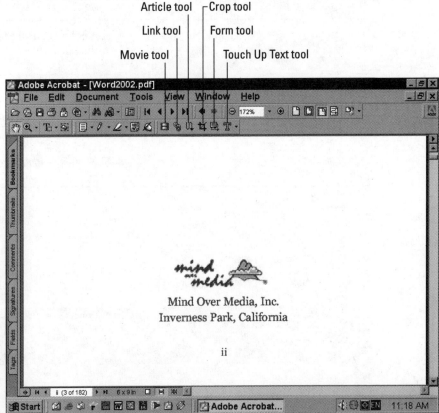

Figure 3-10:
You use the buttons on the Editing toolbar to perform various editing tasks.

Mind Over Media, Inc.
Inverness Park, California

ii

Getting all the help you need

The Acrobat 5 Online Help comes in the form of (what else?) a PDF file full of information in its 287 pages that you can read online or print out for later and repeated reference. To open the Adobe Acrobat Help file for Acrobat 5, choose Help⇨Acrobat Help from the menu bar or press F1 (⌘+? on the Mac).

When the Adobe Acrobat Help file opens, it opens in the Fit Width viewing mode with the Bookmarks tab palette selected in the Navigation pane. Click the Expand button next to Contents to display a list of the various help topics (all of which have their own subtopics) in this document.

To find a help topic by name in the index, click the Collapse button in front of Contents and then click the Expand button in front of Index in the Bookmarks palette to display a list of index pages A through Z. Click the page icon in the

Bookmarks palette of the letter that begins the name of the topic you want to find in the Adobe Acrobat Help file. For example, to find information on using the Find command in Acrobat 5, you click the page icon marked F, and then find the topic you want in the alphabetical list under F.

The page reference listed in the index to each help topic is a hyperlink to that page in the Help text. To go to the page that contains a particular help topic, click its page reference link in the index.

Making quick use of keyboard shortcuts

Acrobat 5 is chock-full of keyboard shortcuts, which is great for a person like me who really likes having access to commands directly from the keyboard (it really bugs me to have to keep taking my hands off the keyboard in order to click menu commands and toolbar buttons). The flipside of the Cheat Sheet card at the very beginning of this book is full of what I consider to be the most important keyboard shortcuts when using Acrobat 5 on a steady basis. Of course, it's designed to rip out of the book so that you can put it up on your bulletin board, or keep it close by your keyboard as you work.

In this section, I only want to say a few words specifically about using the shortcut keys to select the various tools on the Basic Tools, Commenting, and Editing toolbars, which you use extensively in your routine editing of PDF files.

Table 3-2 shows you the shortcut keystrokes for just these three toolbars. Note how all the shortcuts, with the exception of the Spelling Check Form Fields and Comments tool (F7), are letters of the alphabet used alone and in combination with the Shift key (for displaying the hidden tools on the button's pop-up menu). Note too that not all these letters are by any means mnemonic (how'd they get N for the Pencil Tool and S for the Note Tool?).

Table 3-2	Shortcut Keys for the Basic Tools, Commenting, and Editing Toolbars	
Toolbar	**Tool**	**Shortcut Keys**
Basic Tools	Hand	H
	Zoom In	Z
	Zoom Out	Shift+Z
	Text Select	V

(continued)

Table 3-2 *(continued)*

Toolbar	Tool	Shortcut Keys
	Hidden Text Select tools: Column Select, Table Formatted Text Select	Shift+V
	Graphics Select	G
Commenting	Note	S
	Hidden Note tools: Free Text, Sound Attachment, Stamp, File Attachment	Shift+S
	Pencil	N
	Hidden Pencil tools: Square, Circle, and Line	Shift+N
	Spell Check Form Fields and Comments	F7
	Digital Signature	D
Editing	Movie	M
	Link	L
	Article	A
	Crop	C
	Form	F
	TouchUp Text	T
	Hidden TouchUp Text tools: TouchUp Object and TouchUp Order	Shift+T

To select any of the tools on these toolbars (except for the Spell Check Form Fields and Comments tool), type the letter of its shortcut key. Acrobat then selects the tool on the toolbar (indicated by highlighting the button as though it were depressed), and the mouse pointer changes to the shape associated with the tool you selected (for example, a magnifying glass when you select Zoom In or Zoom Out, and an I-beam when you select the TouchUp Text tool).

Note, however, when selecting one of the hidden tools on the same button with a Shift+*letter key* shortcut, that all the hidden tools use the same shortcut. For example, as you see in Table 3-2, although you select the Note tool on the Commenting toolbar by typing S, you select all of its hidden tools — Free Text, Sound Attachment, Stamp, and File Attachment — by pressing Shift+S (uppercase S, if you will).

To tell which of the hidden tools you've selected when typing a Shift-plus-letter key shortcut, watch the icon for the tool's button that appears on its toolbar. Each time you type the shortcut letter while holding down the Shift key, Acrobat 5 selects the next tool on that button's pop menu. As you select the next hidden tool, the program replaces the icon of that button with one associated with that hidden tool.

For example, if you type *S* to select the Note button on the Commenting toolbar and then hold down Shift as you continue to type S, Acrobat will first select the Free Text tool (indicated by a T-with-a-plus-sign icon on the erstwhile Note button), next the Sound Attachment tool (indicated by a speaker icon), next the Stamp tool (indicated by a stamp icon), and next the File Attachment tool (indicated by a thumbtack icon). If you should then press Shift+S yet another time, Acrobat selects the Note tool again (indicated by the normal lined-paged icon with a dog-eared lower-right corner).

Part II
The Wealth of Ways for Creating PDF Files

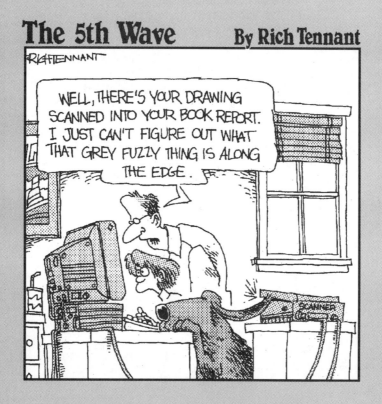

The 5th Wave   By Rich Tennant

WELL, THERE'S YOUR DRAWING SCANNED INTO YOUR BOOK REPORT. I JUST CAN'T FIGURE OUT WHAT THAT GREY FUZZY THING IS ALONG THE EDGE.

In this part . . .

Given the universal nature of the Adobe PDF (Portable Document Format), it should come as little surprise to find out that there are many ways to turn the documents created with the various software programs you use into PDF files. This part of the book introduces you to all the major ways to convert both your electronic and paper documents to PDF files.

In Chapter 4, you encounter the most common ways to turn your electronic documents into PDF files. This chapter includes vital information on the most common ways to convert to PDF, how to customize the settings used in making these conversions, as well as how to automate the conversion process. In Chapter 5, you find out how to turn Microsoft Office documents into PDF files using the PDF Maker 5.0 utility (automatically installed in Word, Excel, and PowerPoint when you install Acrobat 5 on your computer). In Chapter 6, you discover how to convert paper documents into PDF files by scanning them into Acrobat 5. In Chapter 7, you find out how to capture Web pages on your company's intranet or the Internet and save them as PDF files (for later viewing and printing in Acrobat or Acrobat Reader). Finally, in Chapter 8, you find out how to print all or part of the PDF files that you make using these many methods.

Chapter 4

Distilling PDF Files

● ●

In This Chapter

▶ Understanding the common ways to create PDF files

▶ Creating PDF files that fill a variety of functions

▶ Manually distilling PDF files in Acrobat 5

▶ Customizing the Distiller settings

▶ Automating the distilling of PDF files

▶ Using the Adobe PDF Online service to create PDF files

● ●

*O*ne thing is certain, PDF files don't grow on trees, but oftentimes it does seem as though they are produced by every piece of software that you use. The first problem is understanding how exactly to go about producing PDF versions of your files given the software you're using (see Chapter 5 for details on producing PDFs with Microsoft Office programs and Appendix B for details on creating PDF files from a variety of popular Windows and Macintosh graphics and page layout programs). Then, after you do understand the software's procedure, you still have to understand what distiller settings to apply to produce exactly the type of PDF file you want.

In this chapter, you find out how to use the Acrobat Distiller (the Distiller utility included as part of the Acrobat 5 program) to produce the type of PDF files you need. You also discover ways for customizing the basic settings and automating the PDF distillation process.

Common Ways to Create PDF Files

With the advent of Acrobat 5, Adobe Systems has significantly simplified the process of creating PDF files. It used to be in the good old days of PDF production (in other words, when Acrobat 3 was the latest version) that you had little choice but to print a PostScript file from whatever application program you were using to create the file to be converted to PDF. You then had to run this file through the Acrobat Distiller.

Of course, you can still perform this two-part process with Acrobat 5 (which is generally referred to as *manually distilling* the PDF file), and, in fact, the rest of this chapter is devoted to giving you the information you need to create PDF files using this good old-fashioned way. You need to know how to do manual PDF distilling primarily because it gives you the most freedom over the settings that produce exactly the type of PDF file you need. Also, in understanding how to customize the settings in the Acrobat Distiller, you almost always understand how to customize the distilling settings available in your native application software in order to produce precisely the PDF file you require.

Put away that PDFWriter!

Up through version 4 of Acrobat, Adobe distributed a utility called PDFWriter (no longer automatically installed in Acrobat 5) that enabled you to create PDF files from popular application software such as Word, Excel, and PowerPoint in Office 97. Be aware that the PDF files created with the PDFWriter are PDF 1.2 files, meaning that they lack all the current quality and security features offered in the PDF 1.3 (generated by Acrobat 4) and 1.4 files (generated by Acrobat 5).

The PDFWriter is suitable only for the creation of the simplest, text-only PDF documents, completely lacking in interactivity, and please don't use it to produce prepress PDF documents because its 1.2 file format provides no support for embedded EPS graphics (which can really mess up your workflow). Use, instead, either the Acrobat Distiller described in this chapter or, if you're converting Microsoft Office documents, the PDFMaker utility that's automatically installed with Acrobat 5 (described in Chapter 5).

Using Open as PDF in Acrobat 5 for Windows

The Windows version of Acrobat 5 includes a File menu command, Open as Adobe PDF, that you can use to open files saved in the HTML file format (that is, as Web pages), simple text files, as well as a number of common graphics file formats including bitmap (*.bmp or *.rle), CompuServe GIF (*.gif), JPEG (*.jpg, *.jpeg, or *.jpe), PCX (*.pcx), PNG (*.png), and TIFF files (*.tif).

To open one of these file types as a PDF file, follow these steps:

1. **Launch Acrobat 5 and then choose File⇨Open as Adobe PDF from the Acrobat menu bar.**

   The Open dialog box appears.

2. **Open the folder that contains the text, HTML, or graphics file or files that you want to open as PDF files in Acrobat 5 and then click their file icons.**

   To restrict the file listing in a folder to just files of the type you want to open in Acrobat, click the file type in the Files of Type pop-up menu. To select multiple files in the folder you open in the Open dialog box, Ctrl+click each one or, if they're listed sequentially in the list, click the first one and then Shift+click the last one.

3. **Click the Open button in the Open dialog box.**

As soon as you click the Open button, Acrobat opens the selected files as PDF files (indicated by the appearance of the .pdf extension after the original file-name in the Acrobat title bar). To save a file opened as PDF in its new format, choose File⇨Save from the Acrobat menu bar to open the Save As dialog box and then click the Save button. To change the folder where the file is saved, select the new folder on the Save In pop-up menu. To save the file with a new filename, select the File Name field and edit the original filename (leaving the .pdf file extension) before you click the Save button.

Converting HTML files to PDF with the Open as Adobe PDF option on the File menu produces the same type of PDF files as converting Web pages with the File⇨Open Web Page command. Use the Open as Adobe PDF option to convert single HTML files on your local hard disk. Use the Open Web Page option when you want to download and capture extensive pages on Web sites (see Chapter 7 for details).

Converting graphics files to PDFs with the Open as Adobe PDF option on the File menu does not produce the same quality PDF graphics files as distilling them from their native application or manually distilling them with the Acrobat Distiller. Reserve this method for Windows graphics that you can't convert into PostScript files or that you intend to use only in online PDF documents or files that will be printed only on in-house printers. Never use this quick-and-dirty method to produce PDF files that you intend to send out for professional printing because they lack the encoded PostScript necessary to produce the quality prepress demands.

Using the Acrobat 5 Distiller

You use the PDF file Distiller that launches from within Acrobat 5 to convert only two kinds of files: those saved as PostScript files (usually printed to PostScript using the application's Print command) or those saved in the EPS (Encapsulated PostScript) files. This means that before you can use the Acrobat Distiller, you must have the files you want to convert saved in one of these two file formats.

Assuming that you have your files readied in these formats, you perform the following general steps to turn them into PDFs:

1. **Launch the Acrobat 5 program.**

2. **Choose Tools⇨Distiller from the Acrobat menu bar to launch the Distiller.**

   The Acrobat Distiller program window appears, as shown in Figure 4-1.

3. **From the Job Options pop-up menu, select the name of the job option that uses the desired distilling settings.**

   (See the following sections, "To every PDF there is a purpose. . . ." for details on the default job options, and "Making job options of your very own" for details on creating customized job options.)

4. **Choose File⇨Open from the Acrobat Distiller menus or press Ctrl+O (⌘+O on the Mac).**

   The Acrobat Distiller - Open PostScript File dialog box opens.

5. **In the Acrobat Distiller - Open PostScript File dialog box, open the folder that contains the PostScript or EPS file you want to convert to PDF, and then click the file icon and the Open button.**

   If you're distilling an EPS (Encapsulated PostScript) file rather than a plain old PostScript file, don't forget to select EPS files rather than the default PostScript files in the Files of Type (Show on the Mac) pop-up menu.

   The Acrobat Distiller - Specify PDF File Name dialog box appears.

6. **If you want, edit the default filename (which is the original filename plus the .pdf file extension) and/or the folder to hold the resulting PDF file in the Save In field and then click the Save button.**

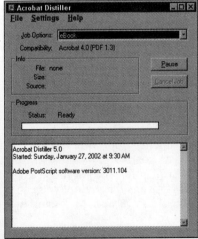

Figure 4-1:
The Acrobat
Distiller
program
window as it
appears
when you
launch it in
Acrobat 5.

As soon as you click Save in the Acrobat Distiller - Specify PDF File Name dialog box, the Acrobat Distiller begins distilling the selected PostScript file. The program displays the progress of the file distillation in the Progress bar in the middle of the Acrobat Distiller window. If you discover that you're distilling the wrong file, click the Cancel Job button. If, for any reason, you need to pause the distilling job, click the Pause button in the Acrobat Distiller. When you're ready to complete the job, click the Resume button (which replaces Pause as soon as you pause the job).

After the Acrobat Distiller finishes the job, it displays the destination of the resulting PDF file, the name of the source PostScript file, and the time it took to do this distillation job in a list box at the bottom of the Acrobat Distiller window (see Figure 4-2).

Figure 4-2:
Statistics
on the
completed
distilling job
appear in
the list box
at the
bottom of
the Acrobat
Distiller
program
window.

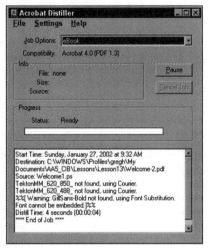

Upon completion of a distilling job, the Acrobat Distiller window remains open so that you can repeat this process and distill more PostScript files if you wish. When you're finished distilling files, close the Acrobat Distiller by clicking its Close box or by choosing the File⇨Exit (Quit on the Mac) command from its menus. After closing the Acrobat Distiller, you can open the distilled PDF file and check out the results in Acrobat 5 by using its File⇨Open command.

To every PDF there is a purpose. . . .

The four preset job options in the Acrobat Distiller represent what Adobe considers to be the optimal distilling settings for creating the basic types of PDF files:

✔ **eBook:** This is the default preset job option that is automatically used in distilling your file unless you select one of the other preset options or one of your own design. Use this job option to generate PDF files that are to be read online but whose image quality needs to be of a higher quality than that of Screen option (described later in this list). This job option converts all colors to RGB, downsamples images to 150 dpi, and provides Acrobat 4 (PDF 1.3 file) compatibility.

✔ **Press:** Use this job option to generate prepress PDF files that are intended for high-end printing by a professional printer or service bureau. This job option leaves all colors unchanged, downsamples images to 300 dpi but provides high-quality JPEG compression, and embeds all fonts used in the source document. Of the four presets, this job option produces PDF files of the largest file size. When converting especially large and graphically complex documents, you may end up generating enormous PDF files that are impossible to deliver to your service bureau (in such cases, you have to split the document up into separate files that, once distilled, you can successfully send).

✔ **Print:** Use this job option to generate PDF files for printing on in-house laser printers or for storing on CD-ROM. This preset is perfect for generating comps or proofs to distribute for client review. This job option, like the Press preset, leaves all colors unchanged, although it does tag them for color management, downsamples images to 300 dpi, and embeds all document fonts in the resulting PDF file.

✔ **Screen:** Use this job option to generate PDF files to be posted on your online Web site on the Internet, a corporate intranet, or a network server for online reading or for quick downloading. This job option converts all colors to RGB, downsamples images to 72 dpi, and optimizes files for page-at-a-time viewing by providing Acrobat 3.0 (PDF 1.2) file compatibility. Of the four presets, this job option produces PDF files of the smallest file size.

You can use any of these four default job options as is or as the starting point for creating customized job options that take into consideration special online display or printing parameters that you need to meet.

When deciding between the two preset job options designed primarily for online viewing (that is, Screen versus eBook) or between the two preset job options designed primarily for printing (Print versus Press), you need to balance the need for quality in the PDF file against the need for file economy. You know the old saw, "You get what you pay for." The more information in the resulting PDF file, the richer the content and the bigger the document.

The Acrobat Distiller retains the distilling settings last used even after you close the program so that they are in effect the next time you use the Acrobat Distiller. This means that if, for example, you distill a file using the Press job option, Press will be selected as the new default preset (instead of the original eBook default). This makes it imperative that you check the Job Options field each time you open the Acrobat Distiller before you set about distilling files with it. Otherwise, you may end up wasting time distilling a huge file ready for professional printing with the Press preset when you only needed to generate a small, compact file for your Web site with the Screen preset.

Automatically displaying your distilled file in Acrobat

Normally, when you manually distill a PDF file with the Acrobat Distiller, the program does not automatically display the new PDF file in Acrobat 5. If you want to automatically check out the results of each distillation you perform with Acrobat Distiller, you need to select the View PDF When Using Distiller check box option in the Acrobat Distiller - Preferences dialog box.

To open this dialog box, shown in Figure 4-3, choose File⇨Preferences on the Acrobat Distiller menus or press Ctrl+K (⌘+K on the Mac). Then click the View PDF When Using Distiller check box to put a check mark in it before you click the OK button. After selecting this check box, upon the completion of each PDF distillation you perform with the Acrobat Distiller, Acrobat will automatically close the Acrobat Distiller window and display the newly distilled PDF in its Document window.

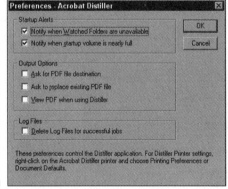

Figure 4-3:
Changing the Output options in the Acrobat Distiller - Preferences dialog box.

As you see in Figure 4-3, the Output check box options in the Acrobat Distiller - Preferences dialog box also include an option called Ask to Replace Existing PDF File. Select this option to make sure that the Acrobat Distiller always prompts you if you are about to inadvertently replace an existing PDF file with the one you've just distilled with the Acrobat Distiller. Note that the Distiller program won't allow you to check both the Ask for PDF File Destination and the Ask to Replace Existing PDF File check boxes in the Acrobat Distiller - Preferences dialog box at the same time. When you click the Ask for PDF File Destination check box, the program immediately grays out the Ask to Replace Existing PDF File check box. The assumption is that if you have the Acrobat Distiller prompt you for the destination of the new PDF, you will notice any filename conflict in the process of selecting the file's destination folder.

Making job options of your very own

The best way to go about creating your own job options for distilling PDF files is to select the preset job option with the settings closest to the ones you want to customize in the Acrobat Distiller and then make appropriate changes to individual settings. For example, to create a custom job option for distilling PDF files for pamphlets with a special trim size and binding that will be professionally printed by a service bureau using a particular typesetter, you would start by selecting Press in the Job Options pop-up menu in the Acrobat Distiller. Then you would open the Press - Job Options dialog box by choosing Settings⇨Job Options on the Acrobat Distiller menus or pressing Ctrl+J (⌘+J on the Mac).

Changing the General options

When you first open the Job Options dialog box in the Acrobat Distiller, this dialog box opens with the General tab selected (similar to the one shown in Figure 4-4). Note that the particular settings selected on the General tab (and the four other tabs in the Job Options dialog box, for that matter) reflect the optimal values assigned to whatever preset job option is selected at the time you open the dialog box (this being the Press job option in the example shown in Figure 4-4).

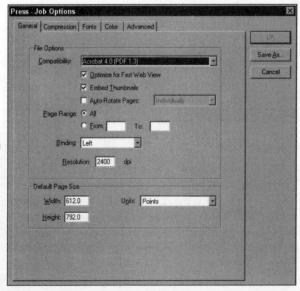

Figure 4-4:
The options
on the
General tab
of the
Press - Job
Options
dialog box.

You then begin customizing the values for whatever settings need changing in your custom job option. On the General tab, these settings include

- ✔ **Compatibility:** Specifies the PDF file version for the final distilled document and thereby its level of Acrobat Reader compatibility. You have a choice between Acrobat 5.0 (PDF 1.4), Acrobat 4.0 (PDF 1.3), and Acrobat 3.0 (PDF 1.2). When creating a job option for distilling prepress PDFs, stay with the default value of Acrobat 4.0 (PDF 1.3) unless your service bureau specifically tells you that it can handle PDF 1.4 files or if you need the highest level of file encryption (PDF 1.4 files support 128-bit file encryption — the highest level of security available). Don't select Acrobat 3.0 (PDF 1.2) unless you are creating a custom job option for online files that requires Acrobat Reader 3.0 compatibility to reach the widest possible audience.

- ✔ **Optimize for Fast Web View:** When selected, specifies that the distilled PDF file be structured so that individual pages are downloaded for faster viewing in the user's Web browser (a process known affectionately as *byte serving*), and that text and line art in the source file be compressed. Keeping this check box option selected has no adverse affects on prepress PDF files (nor any particular benefit).

- ✔ **Embed Thumbnails:** Creates thumbnail images and embeds them as part of the distilled file for use in navigating the file's text in Acrobat Reader. Note that Acrobat Reader 5 automatically creates thumbnails whether or not this option is selected. Users of earlier versions of Acrobat Reader will not have them unless this option is selected. Be aware, however, that embedding thumbnails does increase the PDF file size, especially for documents with many pages.

- ✔ **Auto-Rotate Pages:** When selected, automatically rotates the pages of the distilled PDF file to match the orientation of the text. This setting can be applied Individually to pages or Collectively by File.

- ✔ **Page Range:** Specifies the range of pages in the source document to be distilled in the final PDF file. The default setting is the All radio button. To set a range of pages, click the From radio button and then enter values in the From and To fields.

- ✔ **Binding:** Specifies how pages and thumbnails are displayed in the Acrobat Reader when the two-page and continuous page viewing options are selected. This setting has no effect on the printed binding edge. You have a choice between Left (the default), used for all European languages, and Right for this setting.

- ✔ **Resolution:** Specifies the print resolution to be used in the distilled PDF file when this setting is *not* specified by PostScript commands in the source file. Most of the time, you can leave the default 2400 dpi (dots per inch) setting as is. If you change the value to match that of the printer with which the PDF file will be printed, you must enter a value in its field that is between 72 and 4000.

✔ **Default Page Size:** Specifies the size of the pages in the final PDF document when this information is not specified by the PostScript commands in the source file. By default, the Width and Height values for the Default Page Size are displayed in points. When modifying the page size values in the Width and Height fields, be sure to select the appropriate units (Picas, Inches, or Centimeters) in the Units pop-up menu.

Changing the Compression options

The settings on the Compression tab of the Job Options dialog box (similar to the one shown in Figure 4-5) determine in large part both the quality and the size of the distilled PDF file. As you can see in Figure 4-5, the Compression settings for a job option fall into four broad categories: Color Images, Grayscale Images, Monochrome Images, and Text and Line Art.

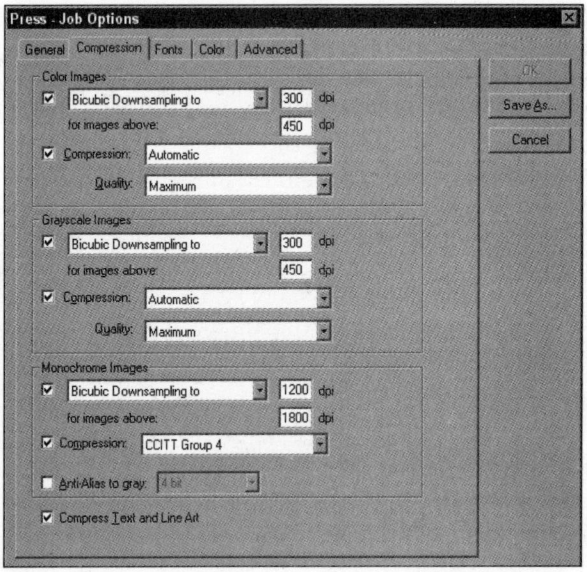

Figure 4-5: The options on the Compression tab of the Press - Job Options dialog box.

Note that when modifying the Color Images, Grayscale Images, and Monochrome Images settings, you have the ability to change the type of downsampling and the rate, as well as the type of compression (and in terms of color and grayscale images, the quality as well). *Downsampling* refers to a process of applying a mathematical algorithm to a bunch of pixels in the images to determine how to combine them into fewer (but larger) pixels at a new resolution. *Compression* refers to the applying of a mathematical algorithm to the pixels in your images in order to eliminate redundant pixels. There are two types of compression: *lossless,* which results in no loss of image integrity, and *lossy,* which removes pixels from the image that can't be retrieved and thus does result in some degradation of the image quality.

In terms of the type of downsampling, you have the following choices:

- ✓ **Bicubic Downsampling To** (the default), which uses a weighted average to come up with a new pixel color value at a new resolution. This type of downsampling takes the longest but gives the best results for high-end images with fine color gradations.

- ✓ **Average Downsampling To,** which averages the color pixel values in a particular area to replace them with a new color value at a new resolution

- ✓ **Subsampling To,** which uses the color pixel value of a pixel at the center of a particular region as the replacement value for the pixels in that region

When using any of these types, you must specify a threshold value that tells the Acrobat Distiller which images to downsample and gives the lowest image resolution to which they can be resampled.

In terms of the type of compression for color and grayscale images, you have a choice among the following options:

- ✓ **Automatic** (the default), which leaves the decision as to which type of compression (JPEG or ZIP) to apply to the images in the distilled file to Acrobat Distiller

- ✓ **JPEG,** a lossy compression scheme in which image data is analyzed in 8 by 8 pixel blocks and redundant pixels are permanently removed

- ✓ **ZIP,** a lossless compression in which the image size is reduced while the image integrity is preserved

When you choose Automatic or JPEG compression, you can set the Quality setting to Maximum (the default), High, Medium, Low, or Minimal. Note that the higher the setting on this list (with Maximum at the top), the better the image quality and the less the compression and the larger the final file size. The lower the setting on this list (with Minimal at the bottom), the lower the image quality and the higher the compression and the smaller the file size.

When you choose ZIP compression, you can choose between 8-bit (the default) and 4-bit. Always select the type that is equal to or greater than the bit depth of your images or you will lose image integrity (note that 4-bit images have 16 colors or shades of gray and 8-bit images have 256 or more colors or shades of gray).

For monochrome (that is, black and white) images in the source file, you can choose between ZIP (the default), two types of CCITT (Consulting Committee on International Telephony and Telegraph) developed for compressing FAX transmissions, and Run Length (or RLE for Run-Length Encoding) developed for compressing images with large separate areas of black and white. All of these Monochrome compression settings are of the lossless type that are pretty comparable in terms of size and quality, so in most cases, you can stay with the ZIP default.

The last setting that you can change for Monochrome Images is the Anti-Alias to Gray setting. Select this check box to have the Acrobat Distiller smooth jagged lines on text and black-and-white images (also known as *jaggies*). When you check this option, Acrobat Distiller lets you select the bit depth for the anti-aliasing (that is, the levels of gray to be generated): 4-bit (the default) for 2 levels, 8-bit for 4 levels, or 8-bit for 256 levels of gray.

When experimenting with the Compression settings, be sure that you do *not* deselect the Compress Text and Line Art check box because this applies the lossless ZIP compression (resulting in no loss of information) to the text and line art that always helps make the final PDF file a little smaller.

Changing the Fonts options

The options on the Fonts tab of the Job Options dialog box (shown in Figure 4-6) enable you to determine which fonts are embedded in the distilled PDF file. By default, all presets except for Screen automatically check the Embed All Fonts check box. When this option is checked, Acrobat Distiller includes all the fonts used in the source document as part of the final PDF file. This is essential when creating a custom job option for distilling prepress PDF files because nothing can mess up your artwork or upset your service bureau more than delivering PDF files without the necessary fonts.

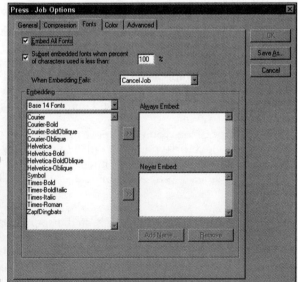

Figure 4-6:
The options on the Fonts tab of the Press - Job Options dialog box.

To help cut down on the bloat caused by embedding fonts in the final PDF file, the Fonts tab has a Subset Embedded Fonts When Percent of Characters Is Less Than check box that, when checked, tells Acrobat Distiller to embed only the characters in a font that are actually used in the source document. This means that if your source document only uses 15 characters in Bodoni Bold, only the PostScript commands for generating those 15 characters and not for the entire character set are included in the final PDF file.

The percentage field to the immediate right of this Subset Embedded Fonts check box enables you to set the threshold percentage at which the entire character set is embedded. The 100% default setting means that the only time that all the characters are embedded is when they are all needed (and you should leave this percentage at 100% whenever you use the Subset Embedded Fonts option).

Directly beneath the Embed All Fonts and Subset Embedded Fonts check boxes, you find a When Embedding Fails combo box that tells Acrobat Distiller what warning to display or action to take if, for some reason, font embedding fails while distilling a PDF file (usually because the font is not installed on the computer on which the job option is being used).

If you intend to create prepress PDF files with the custom job option you're building, be sure to select Cancel Job on the When Embedding Fails pop-up menu so that no prepress PDF file can be created without the necessary fonts. If you don't mind if Acrobat or Acrobat Reader has to do some font substitution in the final file, you can select the Ignore option on the When Embedding Fails pop-up menu. If you want to be informed each time font embedding fails during a distilling job, select the Warn and Continue option instead.

If you prefer to handpick which fonts are to be embedded during the PDF file distilling and which are not, you use the Embedding section of the Fonts tab instead of the Embed All Fonts option. To indicate which fonts to embed, select the location of the fonts in the pop-up menu attached to the combo box located directly under the heading Embedding (by default, this is set to Base 14 Fonts, which displays all the fonts installed with Acrobat 5). Then click the name of each font you want to specify in the list box on the left to select it and then click either the double greater-than button (>>) to the left of the Always Embed list box to add the font there or the one to the left of the Never Embed list box to put it there.

To ensure that font embedding doesn't fail when distilling a file with your custom job option, make sure to list all the possible locations where fonts are installed on your system (including networked disks, if fonts are stored on a special volume). To do this, choose Settings⇨Font Locations on the Acrobat Distiller menu (upon closing the Job Options dialog box) or press Ctrl+L (⌘+L on the Mac), and then use the Add button in the Acrobat Distiller - Font Locations dialog box (see Figure 4-7) to select and add all the font folders on your computer system that should be used in font embedding.

Font Substitution 101

If you don't embed certain fonts in the final PDF document, then the Acrobat Distiller does the best it can at font substitution using what's known as the Multiple Master typeface. In font substitution, Acrobat Distiller matches serif fonts with serif fonts and sans-serif with sans-serif and tries to pick available substitute fonts whose use have little or no impact on the line and page layout of the final document. It does an okay job with substituting straightforward, non-decorative fonts and a less-than-stellar job with substituting those highly decorative or script-type fonts with which you just love to embellish your documents.

Not all fonts you install on your computer give you the *license* (that is, the legal right) to embed them in the PDF files you distill. For example, Adobe lets you embed the fonts you license from it without impunity. Agfa/Monotype, on the other hand, does not. You need to check the license that came with the fonts you installed. Also, when you intend to send the PDF file out to a service bureau or professional printer, check with those folks because they may have special standing licenses that cover the fonts you're using in a document they're printing so that you can embed the fonts without violating the law!

Figure 4-7:
Specifying
all the font
folders
on the
computer
system to
aid in font
embedding.

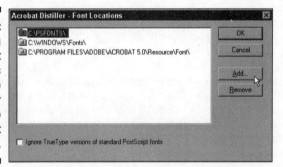

You may be wondering how you tell which fonts have been embedded and which, if any, have been substituted when viewing a PDF file in Acrobat 5. To check on which fonts are embedded in the PDF document you're viewing, open the Document Fonts dialog box by choosing File⇨Document Properties⇨ Fonts on the Acrobat menu bar or by pressing Ctrl+Alt+F (⌘+Option+F on the Mac). When you select this command, a Document Fonts dialog box (similar to the one shown in Figure 4-8) opens, listing all fonts that are embedded in the file.

Figure 4-8:
Examining
the
embedded
fonts in a
PDF file that
you're
viewing in
Acrobat 5.

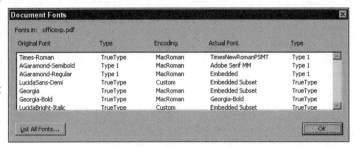

The easiest way to spot substitute fonts in the file you're viewing in Acrobat is to toggle off the View➪Use Local Fonts command (Ctrl+Shift+Y on Windows or ⌘+Shift+Y on the Mac). When you turn this setting off, Acrobat Distiller ignores the local fonts on your computer and then displays the substitute fonts. Any fonts that the program can't substitute are indicated with bullets, and, of course, if all the fonts are embedded in the file, the PDF document is not affected by turning this setting off.

Changing the Color options

The Color tab on the Press - Job Options dialog box (shown in Figure 4-9) enables you to specify how colors are managed in the distilling process and, most importantly, whether or not you want the colors in the source document converted into what graphic designers call another *color space* (that is, converted to the RGB — or Red, Green, Blue — model used by computer monitors to display colors).

Color 101

Color and color management are about the most obtuse of topics (they must give PhDs in the field). In a nutshell, monitors produce colors additively using the RGB, or Red, Green, and Blue, model (just like your color TV), and color printing produces colors subtractively using the CMYK model that combines Cyan, Magenta, Yellow, and BlacK inks. The problem lies in rectifying the large gamut of colors in the RGB model with the more limited and quite different range of

the CMYK model. Enter ICC (International Color Consortium) color management, which profiles the range of colors that every device involved in the displaying and printing of colors can produce so that colors are displayed or printed consistently across all devices. To learn more about the wonderful world of color and color management, go to www.adobe.com/print/prodzone and then follow the links to the articles on color and color management.

As you would expect, when building a custom job option using either the Screen or eBook preset, the Acrobat Distiller automatically selects Convert All Colors to sRGB in the Color Management pop-up window. This is because both of these presets are optimized for on-screen viewing instead of printing. When you build a custom job option using the Press preset, the Leave Color Unchanged option is automatically selected so that no CMYK colors are changed during file distillation.

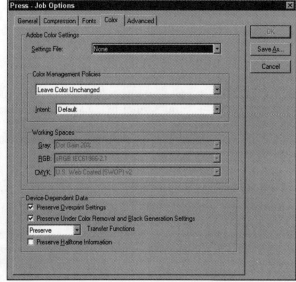

Figure 4-9:
The options on the Color tab of the Press - Job Options dialog box.

The rest of the options on the Color tab of the Job Options dialog box should be approached with great caution. Always check with your service partners before making modifications to these settings, such as selecting a color management settings file from the Settings File pop-up menu (None is the default setting for all four presets), selecting one of the tag options in the Color Management pop-up (Tag Everything for Color Management or Tag Only Images for Color Management), or, for heaven's sake, fooling with any of the Device Dependent options.

Changing the Advanced options

As the name implies, the Advanced tab of the Job Options dialog box (shown in Figure 4-10) contains a bunch of check box options, most of which, I'm happy to report, you won't ever have to monkey with. In case you're the least bit curious, Prologue.ps and Epilogue.ps, just as their names imply, are the beginning and ending files in between which is sandwiched the file with the PostScript codes that actually produce the text and images in your document. DSC, by the way, is an acronym for Desktop Color Separation files. These are the types of files created by QuarkXPress, and they must be converted into a PostScript or EPS file before distilling or else the Acrobat Distiller will burp something silly.

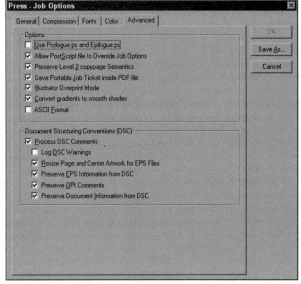

Figure 4-10:
The options
on the
Advanced
tab of the
Press - Job
Options
dialog box.

Saving your custom job option

When you finish making your modifications on the various tabs of the Job Options dialog box, you are ready to save your custom job option. Click the Save As button on the right side of the Job Options dialog box and then edit the default filename in the Save Job Options As dialog box. Be careful not to modify the .joboptions file extension in Acrobat Distiller for Windows and don't change the folder where it's saved (it needs to be in the Settings folder; otherwise, the Acrobat Distiller won't know where to find it).

After editing the filename, click the Save button and then click the Close button in the Job Options dialog box to close it and return to the Acrobat Distiller window. The name of the custom job option you just defined now appears in the Job Options pop-up menu, along with the four presets, so that you can select it anytime you need to in distilling your PDF files.

To access a custom option that you need to delete, copy, or share with a coworker, go to your computer's operating system and open the Settings folder found inside the Distiller (misspelled Distillr on Windows) folder within the Acrobat 5.0 folder and find the job options file there.

Setting security settings for the new PDF file

Whenever you create a PDF file with the Acrobat Distiller, you can restrict access to its contents by assigning a password to it, and, further, control what other Acrobat and Acrobat Reader users can and cannot do with it by restricting the file permissions. To add these kinds of securities to a file in Acrobat Distiller, choose Settings⇨Security on the Acrobat Distiller menus or press Ctrl+S (⌘+S on the Mac) to open the Acrobat Distiller - Security dialog box (shown in Figure 4-11). You do this after you designate which job options to use but before you specify which source file to distill.

Figure 4-11: Modifying the options in the Acrobat Distiller - Security dialog box.

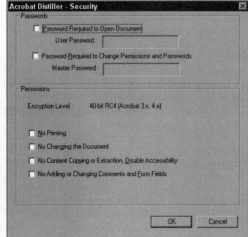

To prevent anyone who doesn't know the secret password from even being able to open the final PDF document, click the Password Required to Open Document check box and then enter the password in the User Password field. To prevent anyone who has the password for opening the document from changing the password and/or the permissions you set for the file, click the Password Required to Change Permissions and Password check box and enter a password in the Master Password field (make sure you don't assign the same password here that you assigned for opening the PDF file).

When setting the permissions for the file, you have the following choices:

- ✔ **No Printing** to prevent users from printing any part of the PDF document in either Acrobat 5 or Acrobat Reader 5

- ✔ **No Changing the Document** to prevent users from editing its contents in Acrobat

- ✔ **No Content Copying or Extraction, Disable Accessibility** to prevent users in Acrobat 5 or Acrobat Reader 5 from copying parts of the document to the Clipboard or extracting graphics (in Acrobat — see Chapter 12 for details). This option also disables accessibility features like Reflow that can make reading easier (see Chapter 2 for more information).

- ✔ **No Adding or Changing Comments and Form Fields** to prevent users in Acrobat 5 from making any further changes to comments and form fields that are in the PDF file

Automated PDF files — would you watch this folder for me?

Acrobat 5 makes it easy to automate the distilling of PostScript files (the print-to-disk kind and the EPS kind). All you do is set up folders in your operating system and then tell the Acrobat Distiller to keep an eye on them (such folders are thereafter known as *watched folders*). Whenever you copy a PostScript file into the In subfolder (automatically created along with an Out subfolder) within one these watched folders, the Acrobat Distiller utility automatically distills the PostScript file into PDF as soon as the program looks at the contents of the watched folder and determines the file's ready for distilling.

When setting up watched folders, you determine which job options to use in distilling the PostScript files you place there. This means that you can set up an eBook watched folder to which you assign the eBook job option or one of your custom job options based on its settings, as well as a Press watched folder to which you assign the Press job option or one of its variants. Then, to distill a PDF file using the eBook settings, you just drop the PostScript file into the eBook watched folder, and to distill a PDF file using the Press settings, you drop it into the Press watched folder.

To set up watched folders on your hard disk, follow these steps:

1. **In your operating system, create and name the folder you want watched.**

2. **Launch Acrobat 5, and then launch the Acrobat Distiller by choosing Tools➪Distiller on the Acrobat menu bar.**

3. **Choose Settings➪Watched Folders on the Acrobat Distiller menus or press Ctrl+F (⌘+F on the Mac).**

   The Watched Folders dialog box appears (see Figure 4-12).

4. **Click the Add button, and then in the Browse for Folder dialog box that opens, select the folder that you created and click OK.**

   After the Browse for Folder dialog box closes, the folder you selected is displayed in the list box of the Watched Folders dialog box.

5. **Click the folder you created to select it.**

6. **Click the Load Options button to display the Load Job Options dialog box. Click the name of the job options to be applied to the files distilled in this folder and then click the Open button.**

7. **If you want to modify any of the settings in the job option you selected for the watched folder, click the Job Options button and modify the settings as desired.**

8. **If you want to assign a password to the file or change the file permissions, click the Security button and assign these settings in the Security dialog box.**

   (See "Setting security settings for the new PDF file" earlier in this chapter for details, and be sure to jot down your password and store it in a safe place.)

9. **To add another watched folder, click the Add button again and then repeat Steps 5 through 8.**

10. **By default, the Acrobat Distiller checks the watched folders you define every ten seconds to see whether or not they contain a new file to distill. To modify this interval (usually to lengthen it), click the Check Watched Folders Every field and enter the number of seconds there.**

11. **By default, the Acrobat Distiller automatically moves all PostScript files that it distills in your watched folders into a folder marked Out (the PDF versions, however, remain in the watched folder). To have the PostScript files deleted after they're distilled, select Deleted on the PostScript File Is pop-up menu.**

12. **To have the Acrobat Distiller automatically clear processed files in the watched folders that are so many days old, click the Delete Output Files Older Than check box and then enter the number of days (10 by default) in the Days field.**

13. **After you finish adding watched folders and setting up their parameters, click OK.**

    The Watched Folders dialog box closes.

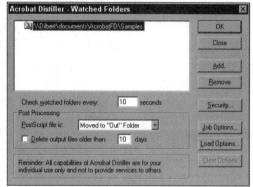

Note that watched folders are not designed to serve as the clearing house for all your PDF distilling across the entire corporate network. If your company needs to set up just such a clearing house, look into purchasing Adobe's Acrobat Distiller Server that is made for just that kind of bulk processing using watched folders.

Making Acrobat Distiller your printer

You don't have to launch the Acrobat Distiller in order to use it and its job options (including the custom job options described earlier in the "Making job options of your own" section) to distill your PDF files. In fact, with certain application software, you don't even need to create a print-to-file PostScript or Encapsulated PostScript file in order to do the distilling. All you have to do is select the Acrobat Distiller as your printer in the program's Print dialog box.

Figure 4-13 illustrates this process using Microsoft Excel 2000 on Windows. Here, I selected Acrobat Distiller as the printer from the Name pop-up menu in the Excel Print dialog box. To select the type Job Options (called Conversion Settings in Microsoft programs), I click the Properties button in the Print dialog box and then click the Adobe PDF Settings tab in the Acrobat Distiller Properties dialog box. Here, I can change the job options to use (eBook in this example) in the Conversion Settings pop-up menu and even edit these job options by clicking the Edit Conversion Settings button — see Chapter 5 for details).

After selecting the job options/conversion settings to use and clicking the OK button to close the Acrobat Distiller Properties dialog box, I have only to click the OK button in the Print dialog box to run the Acrobat Distiller. Prior to distilling the file, the Acrobat Distiller opens a Save PDF File As dialog box that enables me to rename and to relocate the new PDF file if I wish (otherwise the new file carries the same filename as the original Excel workbook file with a .pdf extension and is automatically saved on the desktop of my computer). Then, after I click the Save button, the Acrobat Distiller completes the distilling, finally opening the converted PDF file in Acrobat 5.0!

Figure 4-13:
Making the
Acrobat
Distiller the
printer in
a program
like Excel
causes the
Acrobat
Distiller
utility
to run in a
background
as it creates
the PDF file.

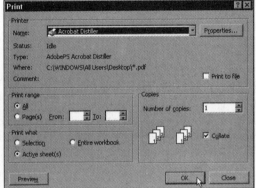

PDF Files Courtesy of Adobe PDF Online

Adobe Systems offers a subscription service currently available only in the United States and Canada called Create Adobe PDF Online that you can use to distill your source files. This subscription service costs $9.99 a month or $99.99 a year for creating an unlimited number of PDF files (you can also sign up for a trial subscription to this service that lets you create up to five PDF files for free).

You can submit a wide variety of different file formats to be converted to PDF including HTML pages, Microsoft Office files, and a whole bunch of graphics formats, including all those created by Adobe's many graphics and page layout programs (basically all the file formats supported by Acrobat 5). Note, however, that you can't submit native QuarkXPress files for converting (you need to convert them to PostScript files as you do with any other unsupported file format). You can get a complete list of all the file formats supported by the Create Adobe PDF Online service by visiting its Web site.

To sign up for this service or try it out free, go the following Web address:

```
createpdf.adobe.com/
```

Note that this online service puts a size limit of 100MB on the files that you can upload for distilling and these files must take no longer than 15 minutes to convert. When submitting a file for distilling as shown in Figure 4-14, you can select any of the four preset job options (eBook, Press, Print, or Screen), and you can also specify file permissions (although you can't customize the settings of the presets or assign password protection to the file). When submitting a file for distilling, you can also specify whether to have the final PDF file e-mailed to you or displayed in your Web browser.

Figure 4-14: Using the Create Adobe PDF Online subscription service to create PDF files.

Chapter 5

Converting Microsoft Office Documents

*A*crobat 5 makes it a snap to convert Microsoft Office documents created and saved in the Word, Excel, or PowerPoint file formats to PDF files so that they can partake of all the benefits offered by this universal file format. When you install Acrobat 5 on a Windows or Macintosh computer on which these Microsoft Office applications (Office 2000 and XP on Windows and Office 98 and 2001 on Macintosh) have already been installed, Acrobat 5 enhances the Word, Excel, and PowerPoint interface by adding a one-touch button (called Convert to Adobe PDF) to the Office toolbars as well as an Acrobat menu to the Office menus.

As you discover in this chapter, you can use this Convert to Adobe PDF button and the additional Acrobat menu to convert your native Microsoft Office documents into PDF documents in just a flash. The best thing about this enhanced PDF conversion functionality is that you retain the ability to use any of the preset job options (eBook, Press, Print, and Screen) for distilling as well as all the custom job options you create. Even more importantly, you can have the paragraph styles used in your Word documents automatically converted into bookmarks in the resulting PDF documents, and on the Windows platform, you can have your Word documents automatically converted into tagged PDF documents so that their text can reflow when viewed in Acrobat 5 or Acrobat Reader 5.

Using PDFMaker in Microsoft Office for Windows

With the release of Acrobat 5, gone are the days of having to select the Acrobat Distiller as the name of your printer in the Word, Excel, or PowerPoint Print dialog box in order to convert the native Office document file format into PDF (although you can still make perfectly good PDF files that way). Figure 5-1 shows the two sets of controls that are automatically added to the Microsoft Word, Excel, and PowerPoint 2000 and 2002 interfaces when you install Acrobat 5 on your computer.

If you install Acrobat 5 on a computer on which Office 2000 or Office XP are already installed but neither the Acrobat menu nor the PDFMaker toolbar appear in the Word, Excel, and PowerPoint interface, you probably need to update Acrobat 5 to version 5.0.5 (the most current version as of this writing). The 5.0.5 update is available as a free download from the Adobe Web site at www.adobe.com/acrobat. Installing this upgrade usually takes care of the missing PDFMaker tools and Acrobat menu as well as ensures full Windows XP compatibility.

All you have to do in order to convert the current document open in Word, Excel, or PowerPoint into a PDF document is follow these three simple steps:

1. **Choose Acrobat⇨Convert to Adobe PDF from the Office application's menu bar or click the Convert to Adobe PDF button on the PDFMaker 5.0 toolbar.**

   The Save PDF File As dialog box appears.

2. **Edit the filename of the converted PDF file in the Name field and select the folder in which to save it on your hard disk.**

   If you don't edit the filename, PDFMaker gives the new PDF file the same name as its Office counterpart but with the .pdf filename extension.

3. **Click the Save button.**

PDFMaker does the rest. As it converts the open document in the Office application to PDF, it keeps you informed of its progress in converting the document's text and graphics in a progress bar in an Acrobat alert dialog box that appears. As soon as PDFMaker finishes the document conversion indicated on the progress bar, this Acrobat alert dialog box disappears.

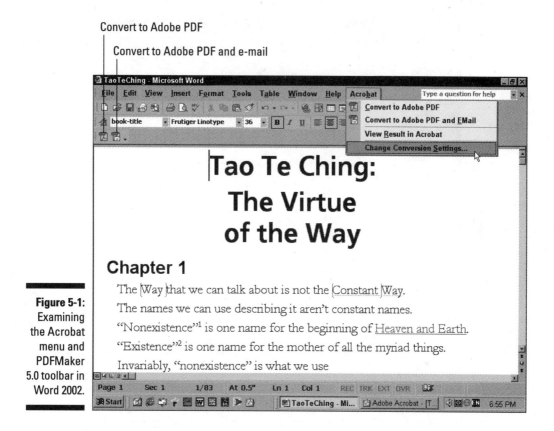

Convert to Adobe PDF

Convert to Adobe PDF and e-mail

Figure 5-1:
Examining
the Acrobat
menu and
PDFMaker
5.0 toolbar in
Word 2002.

To view the PDF document you just converted, launch Acrobat 5 and then select the newly converted PDF file as the one to open (or better yet, open the PDF file's folder in the My Documents or the My Computer window and then just drag its file icon onto the Acrobat 5.0 desktop shortcut). Figure 5-2 shows the Word document (that first made its appearance in the background of Figure 5-1) as it looks in Acrobat 5 after its conversion to PDF.

Automatically viewing the converted PDF in Acrobat

If you'd like to view the converted PDF file automatically in Acrobat 5 as soon as the PDFMaker completes the Office-to-PDF file conversion in your Office application, turn on the View Result in Acrobat option by choosing Acrobat⇨ View Result in Acrobat from the program's menu bar before you invoke the Convert to Adobe PDF button or select the Convert to Adobe PDF item on the Acrobat menu.

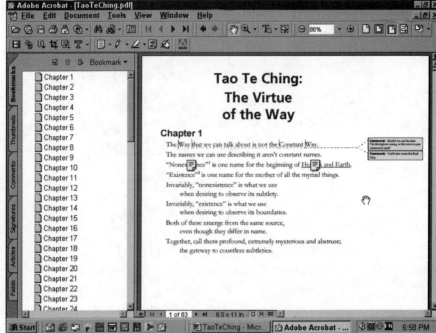

Figure 5-2:
PDF version
of the Word
document
converted
by
PDFMaker
as it opens
in Acrobat 5.

When the View Result in Acrobat option is turned on (indicated by a check mark in front of the View Result in Acrobat item on the Acrobat menu), PDFMaker does not display the Save PDF File As dialog box prompting you for the final PDF filename and folder location prior to performing the conversion. Instead, this utility converts the current Office document and then automatically launches Acrobat 5 (if it's not already running in the background) in which it displays the converted PDF file as the current document in the Acrobat Document window.

Note carefully that because the PDFMaker does not prompt you for the PDF filename and folder location prior to conversion, the converted PDF file displayed in Acrobat 5 is untitled (meaning also that it is unsaved!). This means that it's up to you save the PDF file using the File⇨Save menu command, the Save button on the Files toolbar, or the Ctrl+S keystroke shortcut (⌘+S on the Mac) before you close Acrobat and return to your Office application program.

This unsaved condition for the newly converted PDF file, of course, can work to your advantage if your intention is primarily to evaluate the results in light of the PDFMaker conversion settings used in creating the new file. Because the converted PDF file is unsaved, you can dump the file by consciously choosing not to save it before leaving Acrobat and returning to the Office program should you find that the conversion settings did not result in the quality you desired. Then, after you're back in the Office application, you can tweak the conversion settings (see "Customizing the PDF conversion settings," later in this chapter, for details) and then use the PDFMaker to try the Office-to-PDF conversion again.

Keep in mind that the View Result in Acrobat option remains turned on in the Microsoft application until you intentionally turn it off. Because this menu item is a toggle option, you turn it off just as you turned it on by choosing Acrobat⇨View Result in Acrobat on the Office application program's menu bar (which removes the check mark from the menu item). With this menu item toggled off, the PDFMaker goes back to prompting you for the filename and folder location before making the conversion and then automatically saving the converted PDF file in that location without you ever leaving your Microsoft application program.

Converting and e-mailing PDF files

When converting an Office document to PDF, the PDFMaker offers you the option to automatically send the converted file as an attachment to a new e-mail message. You can use this option to quickly send a PDF version of an important Office document to a coworker or client who needs the information delivered in the cross-platform PDF format.

To convert the document currently open in Word, Excel, or PowerPoint into a PDF document and immediately send it off attached to a new e-mail message, make sure that the View Result in Acrobat option on the Acrobat menu bar is turned off (if this option has a check mark in front of it, select it again on the Acrobat menu to remove the check mark to turn it off) and then follow these steps:

1. **Choose Acrobat⇨Convert to Adobe PDF and Email from the Office application's menu bar or click the Convert to Adobe PDF and Email button (the second button) on the PDFMaker 5.0 toolbar.**

   The Save PDF File As dialog box appears.

2. **Edit the filename of the converted PDF file in the Name field and select the folder in which to save it on your hard disk.**

   If you don't edit the filename, PDFMaker gives the new PDF file the same name as its Office counterpart but with the .pdf filename extension.

3. **Click the Save button to convert the file and then launch your e-mail program.**

4. **Fill in the e-mail addresses of the recipient(s) in the To and Cc fields as required and then describe the contents of the message in the Subject field in the message header before writing a memo to the recipient(s) in the body of the message.**

5. **Click the Send button to send the e-mail message to the designated recipient(s) complete with the attached PDF document and then return to your Microsoft Office program.**

Customizing the PDF conversion settings

PDFMaker enables you to change and customize the distilling settings used in any of your Office-to-PDF file conversions (PDFWriter supports no customizing of distilling settings whatsoever). To customize the distilling settings, you choose Acrobat⇨Change Conversion Settings from the Office application program's menu bar to open the Acrobat PDFMaker 5.0 for Microsoft Office dialog box.

Figure 5-3 shows this dialog box as it appears in Microsoft Word with its five tabs: Settings, Security, Office, Bookmarks, and Display Options. Note that the Acrobat PDFMaker 5.0 for Microsoft Office dialog box that opens when you choose Acrobat⇨Change Conversion Settings from the Microsoft Excel or PowerPoint menus has only the four tabs: Settings, Security, Office, and Display Options. A separate Bookmarks tab is unique to Microsoft Word because it alone supports paragraph styles that can be converted into book-marks in the resulting PDF file. You should also be aware that the particular options offered on the Office tab and Display Options tab vary according to which application program (Word, Excel, or PowerPoint) you happen to be in. Only the options offered on the Settings and Security tabs are uniform in all three Office application programs.

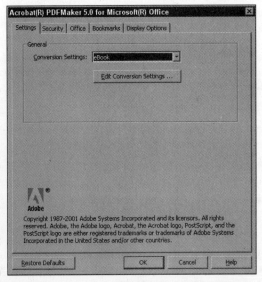

Figure 5-3:
Opening the
Acrobat
PDFMaker
5.0 for
Microsoft
Office dialog
box in
Microsoft
Word.

The Settings tab

The Settings tab of the Acrobat PDFMaker 5.0 for Microsoft Office dialog box enables you to change the job options (now called *conversion settings* in PDFMaker). As when using Acrobat Distiller to create your PDFs, the default preset job option is eBook when you first open the Acrobat PDFMaker 5.0 for Microsoft Office dialog box. You can use the Conversion Settings pop-up menu to select one of the other preset job options (Press, Print, or Screen) or to select any of the custom job options that you create.

To customize one of the preset job options and thereby create a new custom job option, select the preset that uses settings closest to the ones you want in the custom job option in the Conversion Settings pop-up menu and then click the Edit Conversion Settings button to open the Job Options dialog box for the select preset.

The Job Options dialog boxes that PDFMaker opens in your Microsoft Office program contain the same tabs (General, Compression, Fonts, Color, and Advanced) with the same options as the Job Options dialog boxes that the Acrobat Distiller opens when you select its Settings➪Job Options menu command. As is true in the Acrobat Distiller, the particular values and settings that are selected on the individual tabs of the Job Options dialog box depend upon which preset you select when you open the dialog box with the PDFMaker's Edit Conversion Settings button (refer to Chapter 4 for detailed information on how to modify these settings).

After customizing the settings on the tabs of the Job Options dialog box, you save these settings by clicking the Save As button and then naming the custom job options. As with the Acrobat Distiller, any custom job options you save are automatically added to the PDFMaker's Conversion Settings pop-up menu as soon as you close the Job Options dialog box.

The Security tab

The Security tab in the Acrobat PDFMaker 5.0 for Microsoft Office dialog box contains options that enable you to password-protect the converted PDF file (so that only the people you give the password can open the file) and set the file permissions (which control how the document can be edited and whether or not it can be printed). The options on this tab are identical to the ones found in the Acrobat Distiller - Security dialog box (refer to Chapter 4 for details on how to go about setting the password and file permission options).

The Office tab

The Office tab in the Acrobat PDFMaker 5.0 for Microsoft Office dialog box contains a bunch of almost entirely check box options that enable you to control what Office-specific information is carried over to the new PDF documents you'll be generating. These options are arranged into three groups: General, Features (called Word Features in Word, Excel Features in Excel, and, surprise, surprise, PowerPoint Features in PowerPoint), and Document Tag.

Figure 5-4 shows the Office tab as it appears when you open the Acrobat PDFMaker 5.0 for Microsoft Office dialog box in Microsoft Word. As you might expect, the Features area on this tab contains the most options, with a number of settings for converting very specific word processing features into PDF equivalents. The check box options in the General and Document Tag sections shown in this figure are identical in all three versions (Word, Excel, and PowerPoint) of the Acrobat PDFMaker 5.0 for Microsoft Office dialog box.

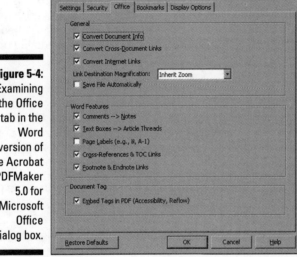

Figure 5-4: Examining the Office tab in the Word version of the Acrobat PDFMaker 5.0 for Microsoft Office dialog box.

The options in the General features section of the Office tab include:

- ✔ **Convert Document Info** to convert the document-specific information (such as the Title, Subject, Author, and Keywords information found on the Summary tab of the document's Properties dialog box) to metadata in the new PDF file that can be indexed and searched (see Chapter 13 for information on searching)

- ✔ **Convert Cross-Documents Links** to convert all links to external documents found in the source Office document to working hyperlinks in the new PDF document

- ✔ **Convert Internet Links** to convert all internal hyperlinks to other parts of the source Office document to working hyperlinks in the new PDF document

- ✔ **Save File Automatically** to have PDFMaker automatically save the Office document you're converting to PDF without prompting you to do so as part of the conversion process

The Document Tag section of the Office tab contains the single check box option, Embed Tags in PDF (Accessibility, Reflow), which is checked by default. When this option is selected, users who view the PDF document in Acrobat 5 or Acrobat Reader 5 can use the View⇨Reflow menu command or the Reflow button on the Viewing toolbar to keep the text reflowing on-screen so that it remains visible at all times no matter how high you set the magnification (see Chapter 2 for details).

Keep this option selected for all the PDF files you convert unless they are specifically targeted *only* to users of Acrobat Reader 4 and earlier.

The Word Features on the Office tab

The Word Features section of the Office tab on the Acrobat PDFMaker 5.0 for Microsoft Office dialog box contains the following options:

- ✔ **Comments⇨Notes** to convert all comments added to the Word document into notes in the resulting PDF document

- ✔ **Text Boxes⇨Article Threads** to convert all notations made in the text boxes found in the Word document into articles that control the way the text is read in Acrobat 5 or Acrobat Reader 5 (see Chapter 2 for more information)

- ✔ **Page Labels (e.g., iii, A-1)** to carry page numbers added to the Word document over to the converted PDF document

- ✔ **Cross-References & TOC Links** to convert all cross-references and any table of contents found in the Word document into active hyperlinks in the resulting PDF document

- ✔ **Footnote & Endnote Links** to convert all footnotes and endnotes in the Word document into active hyperlinks in the resulting PDF document

The Excel Features on the Office tab

The Excel Features section of the Office tab on the Acrobat PDFMaker 5.0 for Microsoft Office dialog box contains the following options:

- ✔ **Entire Workbook** to convert the tables and lists of data on the worksheets in the entire Excel workbook into pages in the resulting PDF document

- ✔ **Active Worksheet Only** to convert the tables and lists of data on just the current worksheet in the Excel workbook into pages in the resulting PDF document

- ✔ **Create Bookmarks** to convert all the hyperlinks found in the worksheet(s) into active hyperlinks in the resulting PDF document

The PowerPoint Features on the Office tab

The PowerPoint Features section of the Office tab on the Acrobat PDFMaker 5.0 for Microsoft Office dialog box contains a single Create Bookmarks check box option, which is checked by default. When this option is selected, the PDFMaker converts all the hyperlinks found in the slides of the PowerPoint presentation into active hyperlinks in the resulting PDF document.

Changing the settings on the Bookmarks tab

The Bookmarks tab (shown in Figure 5-5) is unique to the Word version of the Acrobat PDFMaker 5.0 for Microsoft Office dialog box. Its options enable you to convert the headings and paragraph styles found in the original Word document into bookmarks in the resulting PDF document. It also enables you to set the magnification level for the bookmark destination text that controls how that part of the PDF document appears when opened by the user in Acrobat or Acrobat Reader.

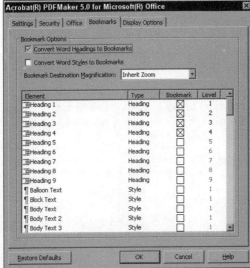

Figure 5-5: Examining the Bookmarks tab in the Word version of the Acrobat PDFMaker 5.0 for Microsoft Office dialog box.

The Bookmarks tab contains the following options:

✔ **Convert Word Headings to Bookmarks** to automatically convert all Word Heading styles used in the original document to bookmarks in the final PDF document. When this box is checked (as it is by default), all Heading styles used in the document are selected in the list box below. To restrict bookmark conversion to just particular heading levels, remove the check marks from the check boxes for all the Heading styles you don't want used in this list.

✔ **Convert Word Styles to Bookmarks** to automatically convert all styles (not just the heading styles) used in the original Word document to bookmarks in the final PDF document. When you select this check box, the check boxes for all the styles used in your document are selected in list box below. To restrict bookmark conversion to just particular levels, remove the check marks from the check boxes for all the individual styles you don't want used in this list.

✔ **Bookmark Destination Magnification** to control the magnification level for the bookmark destinations (that is, the pages in the PDF text that appear when a user clicks their associated bookmark in the Bookmarks palette). By default, they inherit the zoom magnification that the user selects for viewing the rest of the PDF document text. To set them to a specific viewing option, select the desired option — Fit Page, Fit Width, Fit Height, or Fit Visible — in the pop-up menu of the related combo box whose value currently reads Inherit Zoom.

Changing the settings on the Display Options tab

The Display Options tab contains important settings that control how the converted PDF document appears when the user opens it, as well as how the various links and notes that are carried over appear in the final PDF file. Figure 5-6 shows the Display Options tab as it appears when you open the Acrobat PDFMaker 5.0 for Microsoft Office dialog box in Microsoft Word. Note that the Excel and PowerPoint versions of the tab have identical options in their Document Open Options and Link Appearance sections. However, both lack the Comments section shown at the bottom of Figure 5-6; the Comments section is unique to the Word version of the Display Options tab.

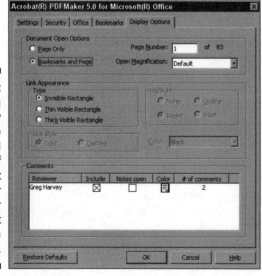

Figure 5-6: Examining the Display Options tab in the Word version of the Acrobat PDFMaker 5.0 for Microsoft Office dialog box.

The settings in the Document Open Options section of the Display Options tab enable you determine how the PDF document appears when the user opens it in Acrobat or Acrobat Reader. These options include:

- ✔ **Page Only** to open the PDF document without the Navigation pane displayed

- ✔ **Bookmarks and Page** to open the PDF document with the Navigation pane displayed and the Bookmarks palette selected

- ✔ **Page Number** to determine which page is automatically opened in the PDF reader (usually page 1). To open a page with some other number, enter that value in the Page Number field.

- ✔ **Open Magnification** to set the initial magnification of the PDF document when the user opens it in Acrobat or Acrobat Reader. Default is the initial setting so that the PDF document opens in whatever magnification is set as the default for the user's version of Acrobat or Acrobat Reader. To change this setting, select a new value (25, 50, 75, 100, 125, 150, 200, 400, 800, 1600, Fit in Window, Fit Width, or Fit Visible) in the Open Magnification pop-up menu.

The Link Appearance options control how the hyperlinks that you carry over to the converted PDF file appear in the user's version of Acrobat or Acrobat Reader. These options include:

- ✔ **Type** to choose between Invisible Rectangle (the default), Thin Visible Rectangle, and Thick Visible Rectangle as the appearance for the hyperlinks in the PDF document text. When Invisible Rectangle is selected, links are not marked at all in the text (the user detects a link when the mouse pointer changes to a hand-with-pointing-index-finger as the pointer passes over it), and the other appearance options — Highlight, Line Style, and Color — are all unavailable. To display a thin box around each link, click the Thin Visible Rectangle radio button. To display a thick box around each link, click the Thick Visible Rectangle radio button.

- ✔ **Highlight** to determine how the thin or thick visible rectangular links appear when clicked. Select one of the four highlight radio buttons: None, Invert (the default), Outline, or Inset.

- ✔ **Line Style** to determine the line style, Solid (the default) or Dashed, used in displaying thin or thick visible rectangular links in your PDF document.

- ✔ **Color** to choose a color other than black for the lines used in displaying thin or thick visible rectangular links in your PDF document. Select a new color by selecting its name (Blue, Cyan, Green, Magenta, Red, Yellow, or White) on the Color pop-up menu.

Converting Office 2001 files on the Mac

If you're using Microsoft Office 98 or 2001 on the Macintosh under system 9.x or OS X, you have access only to a single PDFMaker button on the PDFMaker 5.0 toolbar in Word, Excel, and PowerPoint after you install Acrobat 5.0.5 on your computer; you can use this button to convert Office documents to PDF files. You do not, however, have access to an Acrobat menu as you do on computers running Windows. This means that you have no way to change the conversion settings as described in this section. To select a new job option (Screen, eBook, Press, or Print) for converting your Office file, you need to open the Print dialog box (⌘+P), choose Create Adobe PDF in the Printer pop-up menu, and then choose the desired option in the Job Options pop-up menu before you click the Save button.

The Comments list box, which appears only when converting a Word document to PDF, enables you to determine how reviewers' comments in the Word document appear in the final PDF document. You can make the following changes to the settings for individual reviewers in the Comments list box:

✔ To omit comments by a particular reviewer in the list, click the check box in the Include column for that reviewer to remove its check mark.

✔ To display the converted notes for a particular reviewer so that his or her comments are displayed in the PDF document without the user having to double-click their icons in Acrobat, click the check box in the Notes Open column for that reviewer to add a check mark to it.

✔ To change the color associated with a particular reviewer, click the note icon in the Color column for that reviewer until it appears in the desired color.

Remember that you can add to the notes, links, and bookmarks that are carried over from the original Word document in the converted PDF document using the annotation features in Acrobat 5 — see Chapter 9 for details.

Chapter 6

Capturing Paper Documents

●●

●●

*A*crobat 5 makes it easy to turn your paper documents into PDF files that you can share with clients and coworkers via e-mail or post for viewing on your company's intranet or Web site on the Internet. Capturing paper documents as PDF files also provides a perfect way for you to electronically archive important documents such as contracts, reports, and financial statements.

Then, after you've scanned these documents in as PDF files, if you're a Windows user, you can use Acrobat's Paper Capture feature within Acrobat to turn them from graphic files to fully searchable text (if you're a Mac user, you do this using Adobe's free [for you] Paper Capture Online service). That way, even after you catalog them and store them on media such as CD-ROM or removable disk media, you still retain the ability to search their text. As you find out in this chapter, all you need to turn almost any of your paper documents into PDF documents is a scanner connected to your computer and a little know-how about using the Acrobat 5 Paper Capture feature.

Scanning Paper Documents in Acrobat 5

To capture paper documents as PDF files, you first scan them using the import scan feature in Acrobat 5. The steps for doing this are quite straightforward:

1. **Turn on your scanner and position the first sheet of the document correctly on its glass.**

2. **Launch Acrobat 5, and if you want to add the pages you're about to scan to a particular PDF document, open that document in Acrobat.**

3. **Choose File⇨Import⇨Scan on the Acrobat menu bar.**

   The Acrobat Scan Plug-In dialog box opens, which is similar to the one shown in Figure 6-1.

4. **In the Scanner area of the dialog box, select the name of your scanner and the driver it uses (if the device listed is not the one you want to use, select its name and driver in the Device pop-up menu) and indicate whether the device should scan one side (the default) or both sides of the paper.**

   Select Double-sided in the Format pop-up if you need to scan both the front side and backside of the pages.

5. **If you have a PDF document open in Acrobat at the time you choose File⇨Import⇨Scan, you have a choice in the Destination area of the Acrobat Scan Plug-In dialog box between Open New PDF Document and Append to Current Document. Note that if you have no PDF document currently open, the Append to Current Document radio button is the only available choice. If a PDF document is currently open, Acrobat selects the Append to Current Document radio button by default, and you must remember to click the Open New PDF Document radio button if you want to avoid adding the scanned pages to the end of the current document.**

6. **Click the Scan button.**

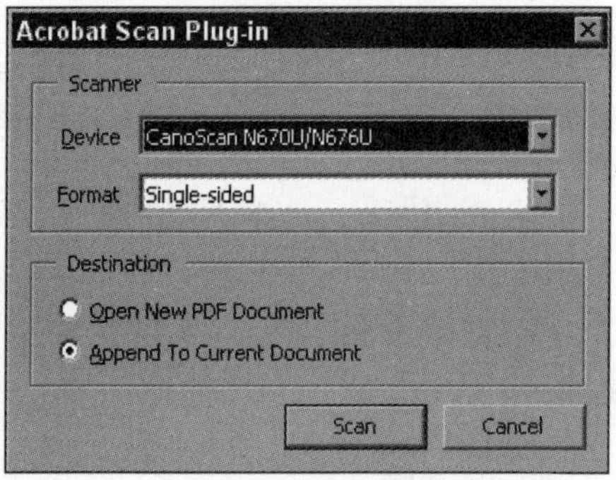

Figure 6-1:
Select the
scanner,
page format,
and
destination
in the
Acrobat
Scan
Plug-In
dialog box.

When you click the Scan button in the Acrobat Scan Plug-In dialog box, the scanning software used by your particular brand of scanner opens its own dialog box in which you can select the scanning settings and often preview the scanned page. Figure 6-2 shows the controls in the ScanGear dialog box used by my Canon scanner that opens when I click the Scan button in the Acrobat Scan Plug-In dialog box.

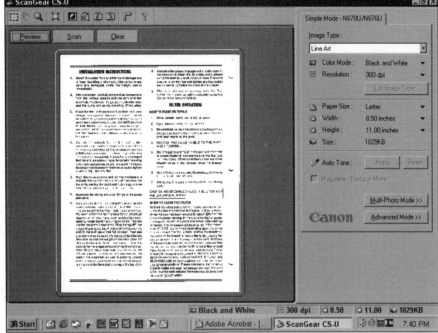

Figure 6-2:
Select the scanning settings with the software installed for your type of scanner.

When choosing the scanning settings, you want to select the lowest resolution quality for the type of document that stills gives you an acceptable image in the final PDF file. The reason for this is the higher the resolution, especially when dealing with color images, the larger the file, and at high resolutions with lots of colors, you can end up with an enormous document.

When selecting the scanning settings, keep these tips in mind:

✔ When scanning black-and-white images and text-only documents, you must set the resolution between 200 and 600 dpi (dots per inch). When scanning color images and text, you must select a range between 200 and 400 dpi. This is because the Paper Capture plug-in that recognizes the text in a scanned document and converts it to searchable and editable text can only process documents scanned in these ranges.

✔ For most documents, scanning at a resolution of 300 dpi produces the best paper captures. If, when using the Paper Capture plug-in, you find that the document contains many unrecognized words, or if the document has a lot of very small text (9 points or smaller), try scanning at a higher resolution (up to 600 dpi).

✔ Scan in black and white whenever possible.

✔ When scanning color or grayscale pages containing large type, try scanning at a resolution of 200 dpi for faster processing with Paper Capture.

✔ Avoid using dithering or halftone scanner settings. These improve the appearance of photographic images but make it difficult for the Paper Capture plug-in to recognize text.

✔ When scanning text printed on colored paper, increase the brightness and contrast by approximately 10%. If your scanner supports color filtering capability, select a filter that drops out the background color.

✔ If your scanner has a manual brightness control, use it to get the letters as clean as possible. If some of the thicker characters in the document are touching when scanned, try again using a higher brightness setting. If some of the thinner characters are too separated in the scan, try a lower brightness setting next time.

After selecting your scanning settings in your scan software (and previewing the page if your scan software offers this feature), start scanning the page by clicking the Scan button (or its equivalent). When your scanner finishes scanning the page, Acrobat displays another Acrobat Scan Plug-In dialog box (similar to the one shown in Figure 6-3) that prompts you to get the next page ready for scanning or to signal that you're done scanning.

Figure 6-3:
Click the
Next button
to scan the
backside of
the first
page or the
next page
in the
document.

When this dialog box appears, you take one of the following three actions depending upon what type of document you're scanning:

✔ If you're scanning a single-page document, click the Done button in this Acrobat Scan Plug-In dialog box.

✔ If you're scanning a double-sided document, turn the paper over in the scanner and then click the Next button.

> ✔ If you're scanning single-sided pages but your paper document contains multiple pages, replace the first page with the second page and then click the Next button.

When you click the Done button, Acrobat closes the Acrobat Scan Plug-In dialog box and displays the page you just scanned in the Acrobat Document window. When you click the Next button, Acrobat closes the Acrobat Scan Plug-In dialog box and returns you to your scanning software where you can start scanning the backside of the page or the next page by clicking its Scan button.

For a multipage document, you continue the process of clicking the Next button in the Acrobat Scan Plug-In dialog box, replacing the current page with the next page on the scanner, and then clicking the Scan button in your scanner software. When you finish scanning the last page in your document, click the Done button in the Acrobat Scan Plug-In dialog box to see the first page of your new PDF document displayed in Acrobat.

Making scanned documents searchable and editable

When you scan a document directly into a PDF file (as described in the preceding section), Acrobat captures all the text and graphics on each page as though they were all just one big graphic image. This is fine as far as it goes, except that it doesn't go very far because you can neither edit nor search the PDF document (because, as far as Acrobat is concerned, the document doesn't contain any text to edit or search, just one humongous graphic). That's where the Paper Capture plug-in in Acrobat 5 for Windows comes into play: You can use it to make a PDF that you can either just search or both search and edit.

For some unknown reason, some of the first copies of Acrobat 5 for Windows shipped without the Paper Capture plug-in (I know this personally because my copy of Acrobat 5 was missing this all-important plug-in). If you find, like me, that your Tools menu in Acrobat 5 is missing the Paper Capture item, you need to download and install the Paper Capture plug-in from the Adobe Web site at www.adobe.com/products/acrobat. Note that the Paper Capture plug-in has a 50-page document limit. If you need to process PDF documents over 50 pages in length, you need to look into purchasing Adobe Acrobat Capture, a full-blown version of the Paper Capture plug-in that can handle longer documents.

To use Paper Capture, all you have to do is choose Tools⇨Paper Capture to open the Paper Capture Plug-In dialog box (shown in Figure 6-4), select the page or pages to be processed (All Pages, Current Page, or From Page x to y), and then click the OK button; the Paper Capture utility does the rest. As it processes the page or pages in the document that you designated, a Paper Capture Plug-In alert dialog box keeps you informed of its progress in preparing and performing the page recognition. When Paper Capture finishes doing the page recognition, this alert dialog box disappears and you can then save the changes to your PDF document with the File⇨Save command.

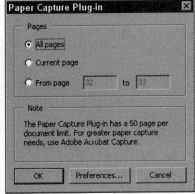

Figure 6-4:
Selecting the pages to process in the Paper Capture Plug-In dialog box.

When doing the page recognition in a PDF document, the Paper Capture plug-in offers you a choice between the following three Output Style options:

- ✔ **Formatted Text & Graphics** to make the text in the PDF document both editable and searchable. Select this setting if you not only want to be able to find text in the document but also possibly make editing changes to it.

- ✔ **Searchable Image (Exact)** to make the text in the PDF document searchable but not editable (this is the default setting). Use this setting if you're processing a document that needs to be searchable but should never be edited in any way, such as an executed contract.

- ✔ **Searchable Image (Compact)** to make the text in the PDF document searchable but not editable and to compress its graphics. Select this setting if you're processing a document whose text requires searching without editing and that also contains a fair number of graphic images that need compressing. When you select this setting, Paper Capture applies JPEG compression to color images and ZIP compression to black-and-white images.

To select a different output style setting, click the Preferences button in the Paper Capture Plug-In dialog box to open the Preferences dialog box (similar to the one shown in Figure 6-5). This dialog box not only enables you to select a new output style in the PDF Output Style pop-up menu but also to designate the primary language used in the text in the Primary OCR Language pop-up menu (OCR stands for Optical Character Recognition, which is the kind of software that Paper Capture uses to recognize and convert text captured as a graphic into text that can be searched and edited).

If your PDF document contains graphic images, you can tell Paper Capture how much to compress the images by selecting the maximum resolution in the Downsample Images pop-up menu. This menu offers you three options in addition to None (for no compression): Low (300 dpi), Medium (150 dpi), and High (72 dpi). The Low, Medium, and High options refer to the amount of compression applied to the images, and the values 300, 150, and 72 dpi (dots per inch) refer to their resolution and thus their quality. As always, the higher the amount of compression, the smaller the file size and the lower the image quality.

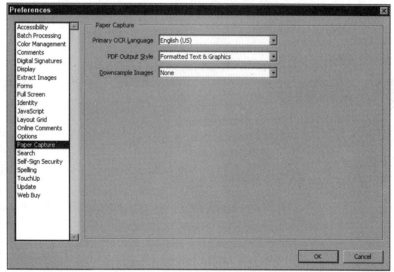

Figure 6-5: Modifying the Paper Capture settings in the Preferences dialog box.

After processing the pages of your PDF document with the Paper Capture plug-in, use the Find feature (Ctrl+F on Windows and ⌘+F on the Mac) to search for words or phrases in the text to verify it can be searched. If you used the Formatted Text & Graphics output style in doing the page recognition, you can select the TouchUp Text Tool by clicking its button on the

Editing toolbar or by typing T, and then click the I-beam pointer in a line of text to select the line with a bounding box (see Chapter 10 for more on editing with this tool) to verify that you can edit the text as well. Always remember to use File➪Save to save the changes made to your document by processing with Paper Capture.

Correcting Paper Capture boo-boos

Although the OCR (Optical Character Recognition) software used by Paper Capture, for example, has become better and better over the years, it's still far from perfect. After processing a scanned PDF document using the Formatted Text & Graphics output style, you need to check your processed document for words that Paper Capture didn't recognize and therefore wasn't able to convert from bitmapped graphics into text characters.

To make this check and correct these OCR errors, you follow these steps:

1. **Choose Tools➪TouchUp Text➪Show Capture Suspects from the Acrobat menus.**

   The program flags all the unrecognized words in the text by putting a red rectangle around each of them.

2. **Choose Tools➪TouchUp Text➪Find First Suspect from the Acrobat menus or press Ctrl+H (⌘+H on the Mac) to highlight the first unrecognized word in the text.**

   Acrobat shows a magnified view of the unrecognized word in the Capture Suspect dialog box, which is similar to the one shown in Figure 6-6.

3. **In the Capture Suspect dialog box, choose one of the following options:**

   • To accept the word displayed and convert it from a graphic into text, click the Accept (TAB) button or press the Tab key.

   • To edit the suspect word in the document itself, type over the high-lighted characters in the suspect word and then click the Accept (TAB) button or press the Tab key to make the change and go to the next suspect.

   • To ignore an unrecognized word and not convert it to text, just click the Next (Ctrl+H) button or press Ctrl+H (⌘+H on the Mac) to move right on to the next suspect.

4. **Repeat Step 3 until you've checked and corrected all the unrecognized words in the processed document.**

5. **Click the Close button in the upper-right corner of the Capture Suspect dialog box to close it, and then choose File➪Save to save your corrections to the PDF document.**

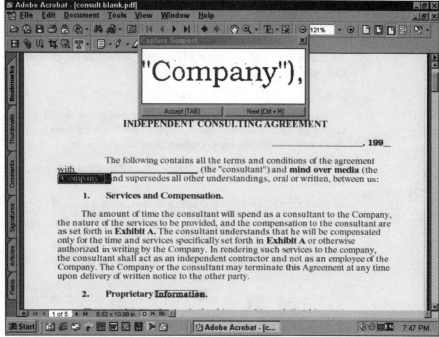

Figure 6-6:
Finding the
first
unrecog-
nized word
in the
processed
text.

Importing Previously Scanned Documents into Acrobat

If you already have a scanned document or an electronic fax saved on your hard disk in a graphics format such as TIFF or BMP (the Tagged Information File Format and Bitmap format are most commonly used for saving scanned images), you can open the file in Acrobat 5 and then process its pages with the Paper Capture plug-in (as described in the previous section). To open the scanned graphic file in Acrobat, you follow these steps:

1. **Choose File⇨Open as PDF from the Acrobat menus to display the Open dialog box.**

2. **Open the folder that contains the graphics file containing the scanned image and then click its file icon.**

   If the graphics file is saved in a graphics format other than TIFF, select this file format in the Files of Type pop-up menu (the Show pop-up on the Mac) so that its file icon is displayed in the Open dialog box.

3. **Click the Open button.**

   The scanned graphic is displayed in the Document window in Acrobat.

 4. **To save the graphics file as a PDF file, choose File⇨Save from the Acrobat menus, and then edit the filename and the folder in which you want to save it (if you desire) before clicking the Save button.**

 5. **To make the text in the new PDF file searchable, choose Tools⇨Paper Capture from the Acrobat menus.**

    The Paper Capture Plug-In dialog box opens.

 6. **To modify the Paper Capture settings before using it to process the pages of your PDF document, click the Preferences button to open the Preferences dialog box. Otherwise, skip to Step 11.**

 7. **Select the language of the text in the Primary OCR Language pop-up menu.**

 8. **In the PDF Output Style pop-up menu, select one of the following:**

    - To be able to both search and edit the text, select Formatted Text & Graphics.

    - To make the document text searchable only, select the Searchable Image (Exact) setting.

    - To make the text in a document containing many images searchable, select Searchable Image (Compact) instead.

 9. **To compress the graphics in the PDF document, select the amount of compression [Low (300 dpi), Medium (150 dpi), or High (72 dpi)] in the Downsample Images pop-up menu.**

 10. **Click OK to close the Preferences dialog box and return to the Paper Capture Plug-In dialog box.**

 11. **Click OK in the Paper Capture Plug-In dialog box to begin the page processing.**

 12. **Choose File⇨Save from the Acrobat menus a second time to save your changes.**

After processing the pages of a scanned image that you've saved as a PDF document with Paper Capture, if you used the Formatted Text & Graphics output style, you use Acrobat's Show Capture Suspects and Find First Suspect commands on the Tools⇨TouchUp Text menu to locate and eliminate all OCR errors in the text as described in the preceding section, "Correcting Paper Capture boo-boos."

Using the Paper Capture Online Service

Those of you who use Acrobat 5 on the Macintosh have to rely on Adobe's Paper Capture Online service for page-processing your scanned documents or fax transmittals to make them searchable or both searchable and editable.

Fortunately, as an Acrobat 5 user on the Mac, you are eligible for free, unlimited use of the Paper Capture Online service.

To set up your free subscription to this online service, launch Acrobat 5 and then choose File⇨Tools⇨Paper Capture Online. Acrobat then launches your Web browser, connects you to the Internet, and takes you to the page on the Adobe Web site where you can sign up and get your login and password.

After you've subscribed to the service, you can then upload as many scanned files (of no more than 50 pages in length) as you want and process them online with Paper Capture as follows:

1. **Use your Web browser to go to** `createpdf.adobe.com` **and then sign in by entering your login and password in the Login and Password fields.**

   The Create Adobe PDF Online page appears.

2. **Click the Paper Capture link.**

   A page appears where you specify which file to process and what settings to use.

3. **In the section called Create a Searchable PDF, select the file to process by clicking the Browse button, selecting its file icon in the Choose File dialog box, and clicking the Open button.**

4. **If your document contains text in a language other than English, select the language in the Primary OCR Language pop-up menu.**

5. **By default, the Paper Capture Online service selects Formatted Text & Graphics as its default output style (saved under the name Standard) to make the processed file both searchable and editable. To edit these settings, click the Edit Settings button, click the New button, and select the new settings using the tab options on the Edit Settings page. Then click the Save button and enter a descriptive name for the new settings in the dialog box that appears and click OK. After creating new settings, make sure that their name is selected in the Available Settings list before you click the Done button.**

6. **If you want to password-protect the PDF document or set restrictions on the file permissions, click the Set Security Options link and then enter the password for opening and/or changing the password and permissions, select the file attributes you want to restrict, and click the Set button.**

7. **Select the desired method for having the processed file returned to you in the Delivery Method pop-up menu.**

   Your choices are Wait for PDF Conversion in Browser, E-Mail Me a Link to My New PDF, or E-Mail Me My New PDF as an Attachment.

8. **Click the Create PDF button at the bottom of the page to upload your file and have it processed according to your wishes.**

When the Create Adobe Acrobat Online service finishes uploading your document, it displays a Confirmation screen that gives you an identification number and that indicates how the processed file will be delivered to you. Depending upon your settings, the service then delivers the processed PDF file to you either by displaying it in your Web browser (assuming that you use one that supports the plug-in for displaying PDF files) or in an e-mail message as a link or a file attachment.

Chapter 7

Capturing Web Pages

· ·

· ·

*W*hen you first hear that Acrobat 5 can capture Web pages as PDF files, you may wonder why on Earth anyone in her right mind would want to do such a thing. After all, Web browsers are not only perfectly capable of displaying any and all Web pages in their native HTML (Hypertext Markup Language) format but are also much more widespread than Acrobat and Acrobat Reader. And, of course, this is true as long as you're connected to the Internet. The moment you get disconnected from the Internet, all Web browser access to their content shuts off (unless your browser is capable of caching the pages on your hard disk and you know how to set this up).

In this chapter, you discover how easy it is to capture Web pages as PDF files that you can browse at any time on any computer equipped with a copy of Acrobat or Acrobat Reader. Because the Web pages are PDF files, not only can you browse them when you don't have Internet access handy, but you can also annotate them and distribute them as you would any other PDF document. This makes internal Web site design reviews a real joy because it's easy to send the PDF versions of the Web pages to clients and coworkers for approval, as well as elicit feedback from them right on the pages themselves if they're using Acrobat 5.

One of the best reasons for capturing a Web site in PDF format is to be able to browse its contents when you're traveling and at other times when you can't go online. This feature is also a godsend when you need to give a presentation or conduct a training session that involves the use of Web material because you still have access to the Web content (internal links and all) even if you lose your Internet connection or are not able for one reason or another to go online. When viewing Web pages in Acrobat or Acrobat Reader, you can use the Full Screen view to get rid of all the distracting menus, toolbars, and so on (see Chapter 2 for details) because you will be using the site's own links and navigation controls to move from page to page. You control what page transitions are used and how to navigate from page to page in full-screen mode by opening the Preferences dialog box (Ctrl+K on Windows and ⌘+K on the Mac) and then clicking Full Screen in the list of preferences.

Opening Web Pages as PDF Files

To be able to capture Web pages (and even entire Web sites) as PDF files for viewing in Acrobat or Acrobat Reader, all you need is Internet access, Acrobat 5, and the Web site's URL (Uniform Resource Locator). Before you can use Acrobat to capture Web pages, you must have your computer correctly configured for accessing the Internet. If you already get online with a popular Web browser such as Microsoft Internet Explorer or Netscape Navigator, Acrobat should be able to detect these settings and use them for Web capture. If you find that you can't capture Web pages as described in this section, open the Internet Properties dialog box from within Acrobat by choosing Edit➪ Preferences➪Internet Settings and then seek help from your ISP (Internet service provider) or IP personnel in getting your Internet settings correctly configured in Acrobat.

The steps for capturing the pages are easy as can be:

1. **Choose File➪Open as Web Page, or choose Tools➪Web Capture➪ Open Web Page from the Acrobat menu bar, or press Ctrl+Shift+O (⌘+Shift+O on the Mac).**

   The Open Web Page dialog box (similar to the one shown in Figure 7-1) appears.

2. **In the URL field, type or paste in the URL address of the site whose Web pages are to be downloaded.**

   If you're converting a local HTML document to PDF (that is, one that's saved on your hard disk or local area network rather than on the Internet), click the Browse button. Then open the folder, select the document's file icon in the Select File to Open dialog box, and then click the Select button.

3. **In the Settings area of the Open Web Page dialog box, select the Get Entire Site radio button to capture all the Web pages on the site.**

   • To capture only the Web site's start page, leave the Levels radio button selected with 1 in its field to the immediate right.

   • To capture all the pages linked to the start page, increase the value in the Levels field to 2 (to get all the pages linked to all the pages linked to the start page, increase the Levels value to 3, and so on).

- To restrict the Web page capture to only pages found on the same Web site or on the same Web server, click the Only Get Page Under Same Path and Stay on Same Server check boxes as well.

4. **Click the Download button to begin capturing the designated Web pages as PDF files.**

If you select the Get Entire Site radio button, the Potentially Large Download Confirmation alert dialog box automatically appears, warning you that you may have bitten off more than your computer can chew. If you're sure that you have the patience (or a lightning-fast download connection), have sufficient hard disk space, and are not attempting to download the Library of Congress Web site, click the Yes button to proceed with the potentially large download of the entire site.

Figure 7-1:
Using the
controls in
the Open
Web Page
dialog box
to capture
Web pages
as PDF files.

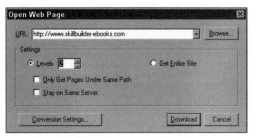

As soon as you click the Download button or the Yes button in the Potentially Large Download Confirmation alert dialog box, Acrobat begins downloading and converting the designated Web pages and displays the Download Status dialog box, which keeps you informed of the progress of the first part of the downloading process.

As the Web pages start arriving on your hard disk, the Download Status dialog box disappears as quickly as it appeared, and the first page of the Web site appears in Acrobat's Document pane. The Navigation pane with the Bookmarks palette selected is also automatically displayed in the Acrobat window. The Bookmarks palette illustrates the hierarchical relationship of the pages you downloaded (see Figure 7-2) as it continues to display the names of the pages on each level as they are successfully downloaded.

If Acrobat is not able to download the complete contents of all the pages on the levels you designated for download, it displays a dialog box called There Were Errors that lists all the files that it could not find or otherwise success-fully download. After reviewing this list of files, click the OK button in the There Were Errors dialog box to close it.

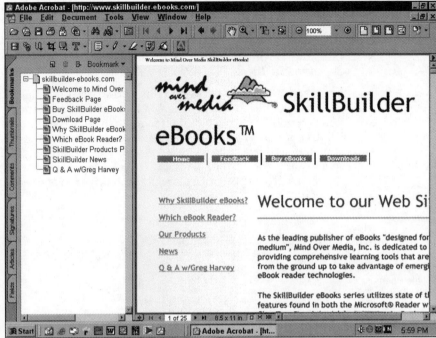

Figure 7-2:
Captured
Web pages
display their
linked
structure
in the
Bookmarks
palette.

After all the Web pages you asked for on a particular Web site are delivered to your hard disk, you still need to save the pages as a single PDF file so that you can access them in Acrobat or Acrobat Reader without being connected to the Internet. To do this, choose File⇨Save from the Acrobat menus and then give the new PDF file a name, select the folder in which you want to save it, and click the Save button.

Browsing captured Web pages in Acrobat or Acrobat Reader

After you download Web pages and save them as PDF documents, you can browse their contents in Acrobat 5 or Acrobat Reader 5 just as you would any other PDF file. You can go from page to page by clicking the page bookmarks on the Bookmarks tab or the page thumbnails on the Thumbnails tab of the Navigation pane, or you can use the buttons on the Navigation and View History toolbars (see Chapter 2 for more specific information on all the ways to navigate a PDF document).

Following Web links in Acrobat 5

In addition to using the normal navigation controls found in Acrobat 5 and Acrobat Reader 5, because you're dealing with Web pages you can use their own navigation controls, usually in the form of various navigation buttons and hyperlinks, to move from page to page. Be aware, however, that unless you've captured the entire Web site, you will often come upon buttons and links to pages that haven't yet been downloaded and aren't currently part of the PDF file. If your computer has access to the Internet at the time you're viewing the file, you can still follow its Web links and even download its Web pages and add them to the PDF document.

When browsing the file in Acrobat 5, you can tell when you're on a link to a page that you haven't downloaded as part of the PDF file because the program adds a plus sign (+) to the mouse pointer using the Hand-with-pointing-index-finger, and a ScreenTip showing the page's URL address appears. In Acrobat Reader 5, the program adds a W (for Web) to the mouse pointer along with the ScreenTip showing the page's URL.

The first time you click a link to a Web page that hasn't been captured in Acrobat 5, the program displays the Specify Weblink Behavior dialog box, shown in Figure 7-3. To have Acrobat 5 download the Web page in Acrobat and add it to the current PDF file, leave the In Acrobat radio button selected and then click OK. To have Acrobat launch your Web browser to display the page there and, therefore, not add the Web page to your PDF document, click the In Web Browser radio button instead before clicking OK.

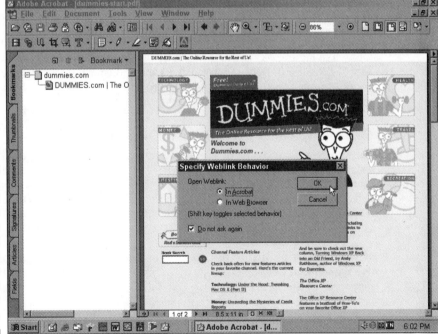

Figure 7-3:
Indicating how to open the Web page attached to the link in the Specify Weblink Behavior dialog box.

Note in Figure 7-3 that the Do Not Ask Again check box is automatically selected in the Specify Weblink Behavior dialog box. This means that the next time you click a link in the PDF file, Acrobat will either automatically download and display the page in Acrobat (if the In Acrobat option is selected) or in your Web browser (if the In Web Browser option is selected) without prompting you to decide between using the In Acrobat and In Web Browser option in the Specify Weblink Behavior dialog box.

If you want to be prompted each time you click a link to a page that hasn't yet been downloaded, click the Do Not Ask Again check box to deselect it. Even if you don't deselect this check box, you can still switch between the In Acrobat and In Web Browser options using the Shift key when you click a link (that's what the `Shift key toggles selected behavior` message in the Specify Weblink Behavior dialog box is trying to tell you). So, for example, if you leave the In Acrobat radio button selected the first time you follow a hyperlink to have the page added to the PDF file in Acrobat, but decide at the next link that you only want to browse the page with your Web browser, you accomplish this by holding down the Shift key as you click that hyperlink.

Browsing Web links in Acrobat Reader 5

When you follow Web links in a Web-captured PDF file with Acrobat Reader 5, the program always opens the associated Web pages in your Web browser (only Acrobat 5 has the ability to capture Web pages and save them in PDF files). You can then surf the Web site by following its links as you would when browsing any other Web site.

Figure 7-4 shows you what happened when I clicked the Money button (shown in Figure 7-3) in the Dummies PDF file after opening this file in Acrobat Reader 5. Because Acrobat Reader doesn't let you capture Web pages, it opens the Money page linked to this button in my Web browser, which just happens to be Internet Explorer 6.

Creating Web links in a standard PDF file

You can have Acrobat 5 convert all complete URL addresses (that is, ones that follow the full format that includes http:// in the address) entered in a standard PDF file (that is, one not created with the Web Capture feature) into active hyperlinks by choosing Tools⇨Locate Web Addresses⇨Create Web Links from URLs in Text from the Acrobat menus. This opens the Create Web Links dialog box, shown in Figure 7-5.

To have Acrobat scan all the pages of the document for URLs to convert to live Web links, click the OK button. To have the program convert the URLs on just some of the pages in the PDF document, click the From radio button and enter the page number of the first and last page in the From and To fields, respectively.

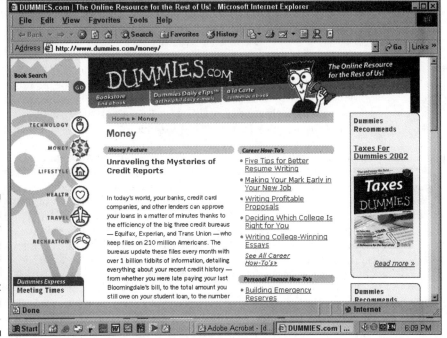

Figure 7-4:
The Money page on the Dummies site opened in Internet Explorer in Windows.

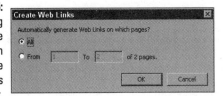

Figure 7-5:
Converting URLs to live Web links in the Create Web Links dialog box.

After Acrobat 5 has converted the URLs on the specified pages of the PDF file to active links, you can follow the links by clicking them with the Hand-with-pointing-finger mouse pointer. Note that when following the Web links you add in this manner, Acrobat uses the Web link behavior that's in effect at that time. This is indicated by the icon that's added to the Hand-with-index-finger mouse pointer: The appearance of a plus sign (+) means the page will be downloaded and added to the PDF file, whereas a W indicates that the page will open in your Web browser.

Browsing captured Web pages in Acrobat eBook Reader

You can also browse Web pages captured and saved as PDF files in the Acrobat eBook Reader. When you open one of these PDF files with this program, it automatically displays the first page you captured in the Reader, while simultaneously adding a thumbnail of this page to your Library pages (see Chapter 2 for details on opening and browsing PDF files in the Acrobat eBook Reader).

The best way to browse captured Web pages in the Acrobat eBook Reader is to view them in the Fit Width mode. To do this, you click the Fit Width button on the Reader's Control bar (this is the button in the middle of the bar with the page icon that has two arrows pointing away from each other underneath it). To maximize the screen view even further, hide the Control bar until you position the mouse pointer over the scroll bar at the right side of the screen. To do this, click the Menu button on the Control bar and then click Preferences on the menu bar. In the Preferences dialog box, click the Auto Hide Control Bar check box before you click its Close button.

When you follow Web links to pages that haven't yet been saved as part of the PDF file in the Acrobat eBook Reader, the program opens the pages right within the Acrobat eBook Reader itself. Unlike when browsing such links in Acrobat Reader 5, the eBook Reader never opens the linked pages in your Web browser.

Modifying the Web capture preferences

When you download and save Web pages as PDF files in Acrobat 5, the program uses a set of default capture settings that you can modify. To change the Web capture settings, choose Edit⇨Preferences⇨Web Capture on the Acrobat menus to open the Web Capture Preferences dialog box, shown in Figure 7-6.

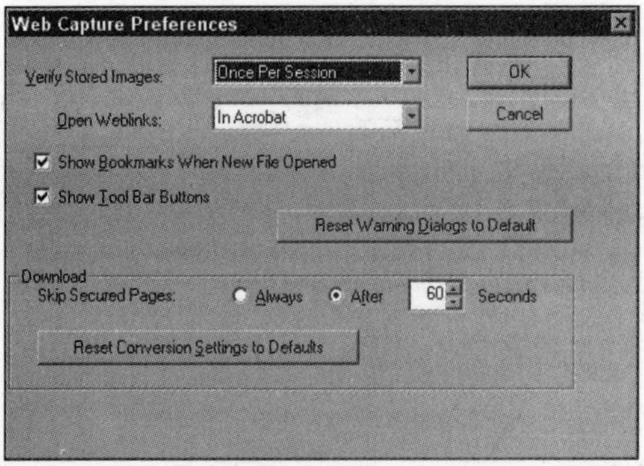

Figure 7-6:
Examining
the options
in the Web
Capture
Preferences
dialog box.

Web Capture Preferences

Verify Stored Images: Once Per Session   OK

Open Weblinks: In Acrobat   Cancel

☑ Show Bookmarks When New File Opened
☑ Show Tool Bar Buttons

Reset Warning Dialogs to Default

Download
Skip Secured Pages: ○ Always ● After   60 Seconds

Reset Conversion Settings to Defaults

You can modify the Web capture default settings by changing any of the following options:

- ✔ **Verify Stored Images** to tell Acrobat how often to check online for updates to the images on the Web pages that you've captured in your PDF files. When the default setting, Once Per Session, is selected, Acrobat automatically checks for updates just once when you first open the PDF file (provided that you have Internet access at that time). You can change this setting by selecting either Always (for continuous checking) or Never on its pop-up menu.

- ✔ **Open Weblinks** to indicate whether Acrobat should download and save new Web pages in Acrobat when you click their Web links or simply display the pages in your Web browser. Note that the Specify Weblink Behavior dialog box inherits the setting you select here as its default (which you can override by holding down the Shift key when you click a Web link).

- ✔ **Store Bookmarks When New File Opened** to tell Acrobat whether or not to display the Navigation pane with the Bookmarks palette selected when you first open a PDF file with the captured Web pages. Deselect this check box when you don't want to give up valuable viewing real estate in the Document window to the Navigation pane. Note that Acrobat creates bookmarks for the downloaded Web pages whether or not this check box option is selected.

- ✔ **Show Tool Bar Buttons** to tell Acrobat whether or not to display the Open Web Page button on the File toolbar in Acrobat, which you can use instead of the File⇨Open as Web Page or the Tools⇨Web Capture⇨ Open Web Page menu commands to download and save Web pages in a PDF file.

- ✔ **Reset Warning Dialogs to Default** to turn on any alert dialog boxes that you may have disabled by deselecting their Do Not Show Again check boxes.

- ✔ **Skip Secured Pages** to indicate whether or not Acrobat should skip over the downloading of password-protected Web pages on the site you're capturing. Select the Always radio button to have the program immediately skip over all such pages. Select the After radio button and specify the number of seconds in the associated field to have the program stop and prompt you for the site's password dialog box for the number of seconds specified, only to then automatically skip the downloading of that page and continue downloading other pages if you don't respond to the prompt.

- ✔ **Reset Conversion Settings to Defaults** to reset all the Conversion settings to their original values (see the section immediately following for information on changing the Conversion settings).

Modifying the Web capture Conversion settings

Before capturing Web pages from a Web site, you can modify the Conversion settings that tell Acrobat how to treat their content in the new PDF file. To do this, you click the Conversion Settings button on the bottom-left side of the Open Web Page dialog box. Clicking this button opens the Conversion Settings dialog box, shown in Figure 7-7.

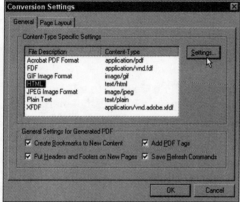

Figure 7-7: Examining the options on the General tab of the Conversion Settings dialog box.

The General tab is divided into two areas: Content-Type Specific Settings and General Settings for Generated PDF. In the Content-Type Specific Settings area, you see a list box listing all the types of text and graphics files that are downloaded and converted in the new PDF file. The only settings that you can modify in this list are the HTML and Plain Text settings. When you click either one of these types, the Settings button to the right of the list box becomes active.

When you click the Settings button when HTML is selected in the list box, Acrobat opens an HTML Conversion Settings dialog box where you can control the default layout, colors, and fonts displayed in the Web pages you capture. Don't mess with any of these settings if your purpose is to do a design review of the Web pages you're about to capture, because these changes could prevent you from experiencing the pages as the designers intended.

The General Settings for Generated PDF area contains the following four check box options:

✔ **Create Bookmarks to New Content:** Acrobat automatically creates bookmarks for each Web page you download, using the page's title as the bookmark name. Note that if a page doesn't have a title, Acrobat uses the page's URL address as the bookmark name.

✔ **Add PDF Tags:** Acrobat creates and stores a hierarchical structure in the PDF file that tells special screen-reading software for the visually impaired how to sequence the various Web page elements for reading at large magnification. The support for screen readers is part of Acrobat 5's new group of Accessibility features designed to enhance the usability of the software for people with disabilities (see Chapter 17 for more on Acrobat's Accessibility features).

✔ **Put Headers and Footers on New Pages:** Acrobat creates page headers and footers that display the title of each Web page in the header at the top of the page and the URL of the page in the footer at the bottom.

✔ **Save Refresh Commands:** Acrobat saves a list of the URLs for all the pages captured in the PDF file that it can use to later check for updated content. You must have this Conversion option selected when you capture Web pages if you want Acrobat to be able to automatically download new versions of the Web pages when it detects updated content (see "Refreshing updated content," later in this chapter, for more on refreshing Web content).

Adding Web Pages to a PDF File

If the need arises, you can always add Web pages to an existing PDF file, whether or not that PDF document already contains captured Web pages. To capture Web pages and add them to the PDF currently displayed in the Acrobat document window, choose Tools⇨Web Capture⇨Append Web Page from the menu bar to open the Append Web Page dialog box. Here, you enter the URL of the Web page you want to append and specify the number of page levels to include before clicking the Download button (this dialog box contains the same options as the Open Web Page dialog box — see the section "Opening Web Pages as PDF Files," at the beginning of this chapter, for details). When you click the Download button in the Append Web Page dialog box, Acrobat downloads the specified pages, automatically adding them to the end of the PDF file.

Adding linked pages to a PDF file

Another way to add Web pages to a PDF file that contains captured Web content is through the Web links displayed in the Select Page Links to Download dialog box. For this method, you view all the Web links on a particular Web page in the PDF document and then select the ones for the additional pages you want to append to the current PDF file as follows:

1. **In the Acrobat 5 Document window, display the Web page whose links you want to use for downloading new pages.**

2. **Choose Tools⇨Web Capture⇨View Web Links from the Acrobat menu bar.**

   The Select Page Links to Download dialog box (similar to the one shown in Figure 7-8) opens.

3. **Click the URLs in this list for all the Web pages you want to add to the current PDF file.**

   To select multiple individual URLs, Ctrl+click them. To select a continuous range of URLs, click the first one and then Shift+click the last one in the range. To select all the URLs for downloading, click the Select All button.

4. **Click the Download button to add the Web pages for the selected URLs to the current PDF file.**

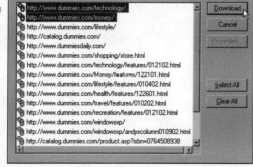

Figure 7-8:
Selecting
the URLs to
download
in the
Select Page
Links to
Download
dialog box.

Refreshing updated content

Some Web sites, especially those that cover current affairs or the news, frequently update the content of some or all of their pages. If your purpose in capturing Web pages is to keep up-to-date on the information offered by a site, you will need to refresh the pages on a regular basis to ensure that your file has the most recent content.

To refresh the content of the captured pages in your PDF file, you choose Tools⇨Web Capture⇨Refresh Pages from the menu bar. Doing this opens the Refresh Pages dialog box, shown in Figure 7-9. Click the Refresh button to have Acrobat check all the pages in the Refresh Commands list for updates.

Figure 7-9:
Checking
Web pages
for updated
content with
the Refresh
Pages
dialog box.

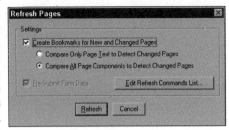

By default, the program compares the text of the captured pages with their counterparts online. If Acrobat detects any discrepancies between the two, it automatically updates the downloaded page in the PDF file by replacing it with a copy of the latest page on the Web site. If you want Acrobat to compare all elements on the Web pages when looking for the ones that need refreshing instead of just comparing the text, click the Compare All Page Components to Detect Changed Pages check box in the Refresh Pages dialog box before you click the Refresh button.

If you want to exclude certain pages from the Refresh Command list, click the Edit Refresh Commands List button to open the Refresh Commands List dialog box. This dialog box lists all the pages marked for refreshing. To skip particular pages in the refresh operation, click the Clear All button and then click the URLs for all the pages you do want refreshed to highlight them before you click OK.

Keep in mind that you can't add new URLs to the list displayed in the Refresh Commands List dialog box: You can only tell Acrobat which ones to ignore when refreshing the pages. The only way to add a URL to the Refresh Commands list is to capture its Web page when the Save Refresh Commands check box option has been checked in the Conversion Settings dialog box!

Chapter 8

Printing PDF Files

● ●

In This Chapter

▶ Printing with the standard print settings

▶ Modifying the print settings

▶ Looking at the high-end, prepress printing settings

▶ Getting online printing tips

● ●

*A*crobat may offer the promise of a paperless office, and PDF may be the quintessential electronic file format, but despite it all, you will find times when the one and only thing you want to do with the program is print out the PDF documents you open in it. In this chapter, you discover all the ways to print all or just part of a PDF file with your in-house printers as well as how to customize the print settings to print just selected pages and to accommodate the printing of oversized pages.

Printing PDF Files

Printing PDF documents in Acrobat 5 or Acrobat Reader 5 is very similar to printing documents in any other Windows or Macintosh application program that you use. If you just need a printout of the document's pages using the standard Print options, you follow these simple steps:

1. **To change the general print settings such as the paper size or to change the printing orientation from the default of portrait mode (where text runs parallel with the short edge of the paper) to landscape mode (where text runs parallel with the long edge), choose File⇨Page Setup from the Acrobat or Acrobat Reader menu bar or press Ctrl+Shift+P (⌘+Shift+P on the Mac) to open the Page Setup dialog box where you modify these options and then click OK.**

   The actual options and controls available in the Page Setup dialog box vary according to the actual printer selected as your default.

2. **Choose File➪Print from the Acrobat or Acrobat Reader menu bar or press Ctrl+P (⌘+P on the Mac).**

   The Print dialog box opens, as shown in Figure 8-1.

3. **If you have more than one printer installed on your system, you can select a new printer to print the PDF document. On Windows, you switch printers by selecting the name of the printer in the Name combo box. On the Macintosh, you do this by selecting a new printer on the Printer pop-up menu.**

4. **Specify which pages you want to print by doing one of the following:**

   - To print all the pages in the current PDF document, leave the All radio button selected.

   - To print only the page currently displayed in Acrobat or Acrobat Reader, click the Current Page radio button.

   - To print a continuous range of pages in the document, click the Pages radio button and enter the first page to print in the From field and the last page to print in the To field.

5. **To print all annotations made to the text on the designated pages, leave the Comments check box selected. To print only the text and graphics on the pages, without the notes, click the Comments check box to remove its check mark.**

   See Chapter 9 for details on adding notes and marking up text and to find out how to summarize the comments in a document and then save them in a separate file that you can print.

6. **Click the OK button to begin printing the pages of your PDF file.**

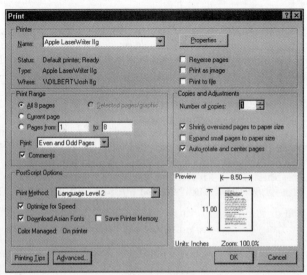

Figure 8-1: Opening the Print dialog box in Acrobat 5 to print the current PDF document.

Playing with the PostScript options

If you have a PostScript printer on Acrobat or Acrobat Reader for Windows, you can modify the PostScript Options in the Print dialog box. Use the Print Method combo box to select the level of PostScript (1, 2, or 3) best suited for your printer (some older laser printers don't understand levels of PostScript). When the Optimize for Speed check box is selected, Acrobat sends the fonts used on each page in the PDF document to the printer as needed. When the Download Asian Fonts check box is selected, Acrobat downloads Asian Fonts used but not embedded in the PDF document to the laser printer if they are not already installed on it. Select the Save Printer Memory check box to have Acrobat download all the fonts for a given page before that page is printed to save on printer memory.

In the upper-right corner of the Windows version of the Print dialog box, you find three check box options — Reverse Pages, Print as Image, and Print to File:

- Select the Reverse Pages whenever you want Acrobat to print the pages backward starting with the last page and ending with the first page in the designated range.

- Select the Print as Image option to have Acrobat print the text and graphics on each page as though they were all bitmapped graphics. Use this option only when the fonts aren't embedded in the PDF document and your printer doesn't have them available to have the text on each printed page look as much like on-screen PDF versions as possible.

- Select the Print to File option only when you want to create a file for a type of printer that you don't actually have available on your computer system. You can then send or take the print file to a computer that has the targeted printer connected to it but doesn't have the Acrobat or Acrobat Reader program installed. When you drag the print file on the printer icon, it prints the PDF document with all the printing options you specified in Acrobat.

Printing selected pages on Windows

Sometimes, you don't need to print all the pages in a PDF document or even a continuous range of pages. If you're using Acrobat 5 or Acrobat Reader 5 on Windows, you can print individual, nonconsecutive pages in the document (the printing capabilities of the Macintosh operating system don't support this feature). To do this, you need to select the individual pages before you open the Print dialog box by following these steps:

1. **Click the Thumbnails tab in the Navigation pane to bring its palette to the front. If the Navigation pane is closed, press F4 to open and select the Thumbnails palette.**

2. **To see all the thumbnails for the pages you want to select for printing, you may need to switch to small thumbnails and widen the Navigation pane:**

   - To switch to small thumbnails, click the Thumbnail button at the top of the palette and then click Small Thumbnails near the bottom of its pop-up menu.

   - To widen the Navigation pane until all the thumbnails are displayed (or all the ones with pages you want to print), position the mouse pointer on the border between the Navigation and Document panes and then, when the mouse pointer becomes a double-headed arrow, drag the border to the right until the Navigation pane is wide enough to display all the thumbnails.

3. **Ctrl+click (Control+click on the Macintosh) the thumbnails for all the individual pages you want to print to select them in the Thumbnail palette.**

4. **Choose File⇨Print from the Acrobat or Acrobat Reader menu bar or press Ctrl+P (⌘+P on the Mac).**

   The Print dialog box opens with the Selected Pages radio button selected (as shown in Figure 8-2).

5. **Click OK to begin printing only the selected pages in the PDF document.**

To print just a graphic on the page, click the Graphics Select tool (G) on the Basic Tools toolbar and use it to draw a bounding box around the image. After selecting the image in this manner, right-click (Control+click on the Mac) to display the image's shortcut menu where you click the Print option to open the Print dialog box.

Printing oversized documents on Windows

Some of the PDF documents that you want to print are too large to fit even the largest paper sizes that your printer can handle. As you can see in Figures 8-1 and 8-2, Acrobat handles this in the Windows Print dialog box by automatically selecting the Shrink Oversized Pages to Paper Size check box. This option automatically scales down the text and graphics on each page to fit the paper size selected for your printer.

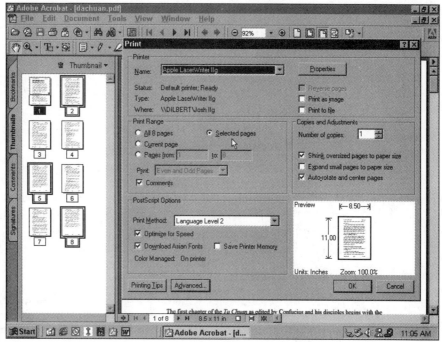

The program also automatically selects the Auto-Rotate and Center Pages
check box option. When this option is selected, Acrobat routinely rotates
PDF documents that are wider than the selected paper size while at the same
time centering the text and graphics that do fit. When this check box option
is selected in conjunction with the Shrink Oversized Pages to Paper Size
option, Acrobat shrinks the text and graphics on each page so that they all fit
and are centered on the page.

If you have a PostScript printer installed on your system, you can print oversized pages in your PDF documents using a system called *tiling*. When you
print oversized pages by tiling, Acrobat or Acrobat Reader divides each oversized page into sections, each of which is printed on a single page of paper.
You can then fit the tiled pages together to see how the oversized page will
appear when printed with a printer that can handle the oversized page.

The first step to doing this type of printing is to deselect the Shrink Oversized
Pages to Paper Size and the Auto-Rotate and Center Pages check box options
in the Print dialog box. When you deselect these options, instead of displaying
the entire document centered in the Preview area in the lower-right corner of
the Print dialog box, it now shows only the upper-left portion of the first oversized page (this represents, in essence, the first section to be printed when
the page is tiled).

After turning off the Shrink Oversized Pages to Paper Size and the Auto-Rotate and Center Pages options, you then click the Advanced button in the lower-left corner of the Print dialog box. Doing this displays the Print Settings dialog box, which is similar to the one shown in Figure 8-3. To set up tiling in the Print Settings dialog box, follow these steps:

1. **Click the Automatic radio button to have Acrobat calculate how best to tile the oversized page.**

   As soon as you select the Automatic radio button, the Overlap, Emit Slug, and Tile Marks options become available.

2. **Click the Overlap field and enter a value that represents the amount you want the printing on adjacent tiles to overlap each other so you can more easily align them with each other. Enter a decimal value for this overlap distance of anywhere between 0.125 and 0.25 inches.**

   You need this overlap distance because laser printers have to maintain a minimum of blank space on the page where they grab and pull the paper. The exact value you enter depends on your particular printer and the page size your tiles use.

3. **By default, Acrobat selects the Emit Plug check box, which instructs your printer to print a single-line description (the slug) on each tiled page that identifies the filename, print date, and row and column in the grid of tiled pages. Deselect this check box only if you're sure that you can figure out how the tiled pages fit together without this information.**

4. **If you want Acrobat to print registration marks on each tiled page, change the default setting of None in the Tile Marks combo box by selecting Western Style on its pop-up menu.**

   This gives you the crosshatched registration marks universally used in North American and European printers.

5. **Click OK in the Print Settings dialog box to close it and return to the Print dialog box, and then click OK in the Print dialog box to begin printing the tiled pages.**

Using the prepress printing settings

In addition to the Tiling options, the Print Settings dialog box in Windows (see to Figure 8-3) also contains a section called High End Features. As their name implies, these features are used only when preparing a PDF document for professional printing with high-end imagesetters. Don't mess with these prepress settings without the advice and consent of your favorite service bureau people.

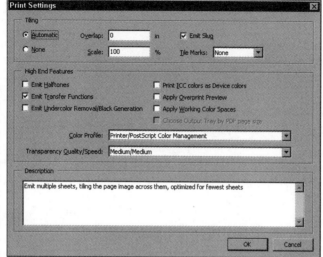

Figure 8-3:
Using the
Tiling
options in
the Print
Settings
dialog box
to print an
oversized
document.

When you click the name of any check box option in the High End Features, Acrobat displays a brief description of that option in the Description list box at the bottom of the Print Settings dialog box. Just be mindful that when clicking the name of an option to get a brief explanation of its function, you also end up either entering or removing a check mark from its check box. If you're just exploring the options to learn more about their use, be sure that you don't inadvertently select an option you don't really want to use.

Troubleshooting Printing Problems in Windows

You can use the Print Tips button in the Windows version of Acrobat 5 and Acrobat Reader 5 to go online to the Adobe Web site to get a slew of suggestions on how to troubleshoot the most common printing problems with Acrobat. This area of the Adobe support knowledge base is particularly helpful if you're having trouble printing a PDF file on a PostScript printer. The Web page includes instructions on how to enable the PostScript error handler for your printer depending upon which version of Windows you're using so you can track the specific errors that printing the PDF file is causing. It also contains a link to another page on the Adobe Web site that tells you what these PostScript errors really mean and gives you some suggestions on how to get around them.

Part III
Reviewing, Editing, and Securing PDFs

The 5th Wave   By Rich Tennant

DAD ADDS MULTIMEDIA SOUND AND GRAPHICS TO THE TRADITIONAL CAMPFIRE GHOST STORY.

In this part . . .

After you've converted your electronic and paper documents to PDF files, you're ready to explore the many Acrobat 5 features for reviewing, editing, organizing, and making them secure. Part III introduces all of these kinds of important, post-production features.

In Chapter 9, you find out how to use Acrobat 5 to annotate your PDF files so that coworkers and clients alike can review them online, and you can summarize their feedback. In Chapter 10, you discover the types of PDF document editing that you can perform in Acrobat 5. Chapter 11 introduces you to the ways to secure your PDF files from unwanted changes. It also gives you the lowdown on how to use digital signatures in Acrobat 5 to sign off on changes as well as prevent future changes. Chapter 12 covers the ways you can repurpose the contents of your PDF files by extracting the text and graphics for uses with the other software programs you commonly use. Finally, Chapter 13 rounds out Part III by giving you vital information on how to catalog and archive your PDF files by building searchable PDF document collections that you can distribute on CD-ROM or your company's network or intranet.

Chapter 9

Annotating PDF Files for Review

· ·

· ·

*O*ne of the most important groups of features in Acrobat 5 is the annotation features that enable you to mark up and add comments to a PDF document. These features facilitate the review process by enabling all the different people on a design team to give you their feedback in a consistent and timely manner. The annotation features in Acrobat 5 also assist in the approval process by enabling you to get feedback and eventually the final okay from clients and key personnel in house.

In this chapter, you discover the many ways to annotate a PDF document, including adding bookmarks to make it easier to navigate the document you're reviewing as well as attaching comments (in many different formats including text notes, sound notes, and attached files) and marking up text and graphics. You also become familiar with the ways to collect and summarize review comments for a particular PDF file in anticipation of making the final edits (as described in Chapter 10).

The Ins and Outs of Bookmarks

Bookmarks are the links that appear on the Bookmarks palette in the Navigation pane in a PDF document. They are most often used to take you directly to different sections within the document. Bookmarks can take you to different pages in the document or even different views of a page.

Bookmarks can also link you to different documents (PDF and non-PDF) on your computer as well as to Web pages on the Internet. As if this weren't enough, bookmarks can also perform certain actions in the PDF document such as submitting a form's data, playing a sound or movie, or selecting a particular menu item (see Chapters 14 and 16 for information on working with PDF forms and adding interactivity to PDF files).

To use a bookmark to jump to a particular page or page view, to open a new document or Web page, or to execute a command or perform a specified action, all you have to do is click the name or icon of the bookmark in the Bookmarks palette of the Navigation pane. If you want, you can have Acrobat automatically close the Navigation pane whenever you click a bookmark by selecting the Hide After Use setting on the Bookmark pop-up menu. This option is particularly useful for bookmarks that open pages in the document that are displayed in the Fit Width or Fit Visible page views and require maximum screen area for legibility.

The only trouble with the Hide After Use setting is that you must keep manually opening the Bookmarks palette by clicking its tab or pressing F5 each and every time you use a bookmark in order to use any of the others on the palette. This can become quite tedious in a complex PDF document with many sections where you rely on bookmarks in order to be able to review and comment on the diverse material. For this reason, restrict the Hide After Use setting to situations where you don't expect to do a lot of navigation from the Bookmarks palette. To turn off the Hide After Use setting, just click the pop-up button attached to the Bookmarks palette menu and click the Hide After Use item to remove the check mark from it.

Generating automated bookmarks

When you use the PDFMaker plug-in to convert documents created with Microsoft Word for Windows to PDF, you can specify that the document heading and other styles, cross-references, and footnotes automatically be converted into bookmarks in the final PDF file (see Chapter 5 for details). Also, when capturing Web pages, Acrobat can automatically generate bookmarks for each page that you capture (see Chapter 7 for details).

When the Add PDF Tags option is selected during conversion, the bookmarks automatically generated from Word documents with the PDFMaker 5.0 and from Web pages in Acrobat 5 are saved as a special type called *tagged* bookmarks. Tagged bookmarks keep track of the underlying structure of the document (such as heading levels and paragraph styles in Word documents and HTML tags in Web pages) by tagging these elements.

You can use the elements stored in any tagged PDF document or captured Web page to automatically generate bookmarks for any particular element in the document (for details on creating a tagged PDF file or converting a non-tagged PDF file, see Chapter 15). To generate automatic bookmarks for a tagged file, click the Bookmarks palette menu's pop-up button and then click New Bookmarks from Structure on the menu to open the Structure Elements dialog box, which is similar to the one shown in Figure 9-1. Note that the New Bookmarks from Structure menu item is grayed out if the PDF document you're working with isn't tagged.

Figure 9-1:
Selecting the elements to automatically bookmark in the Structure Elements dialog box.

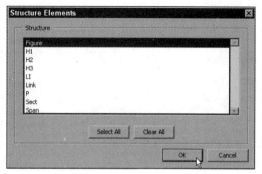

To have Acrobat generate bookmarks for particular elements in the PDF document, you then select the names of the elements for which you want the bookmarks generated (Ctrl+click on Windows or Control+click on the Mac to select multiple elements) in the Structure Elements dialog box before you click OK. Acrobat then goes through the document identifying the tags for the selected elements and generating bookmarks for each of them.

Figure 9-2 illustrates how this works. In this figure, you see a group of four automatically generated bookmarks created from the Figure tag in the original tagged PDF document. As you can see, when Acrobat generates these tags, it gives them the name of the tagged element used to create them (which in this case just happened to be Figure). These four Figure tags are automatically nested under a generic bookmark named Untitled. All that remains to do is to rename these bookmarks to something a little bit more descriptive, such as Table of Figures for Untitled, Cover for the first Figure bookmark, Title Page for the second, Half Title Page for the third, and Copyright for the fourth and last (see "Editing bookmarks," later in this chapter, for details on how to rename bookmarks).

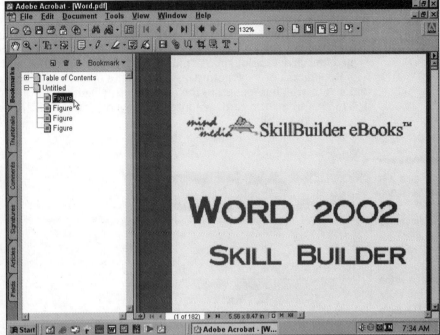

Figure 9-2:
Examining
the
bookmarks
generated
for the
Figure
element in a
tagged PDF
document.

Creating manual bookmarks

Although the automated methods are by far the fastest ways to generate bookmarks, they are by no means the only ways to add them. You can also manually add bookmarks to any PDF multipage document that you've opened in Acrobat 5. Each bookmark that you add to a PDF document has two parts: the bookmark link, which consists of a page icon followed by the name of the bookmark in the Bookmarks palette, and the bookmark destination, which is the page, page view, new document, or Web page that is displayed or the action that is executed when you click the bookmark link.

Making bookmarks to go to pages in the document

When you create a new bookmark to another page in the same PDF document, Acrobat records not only the page but also the page view and the magnification setting in effect as part of the bookmark's destination. This means that the most productive way to create manual bookmarks is to first navigate to the destination page *and* make any desired change to the page view and/or magnification settings *before* you begin creating the bookmark. Although you can designate the destination page as part of the process of creating the new bookmark, going to the page and setting things up beforehand just makes the process all the easier and more efficient.

With this tip in mind, the steps for manually creating a bookmark to a new page in the same document are as follows:

1. **Launch Acrobat and then open the PDF document to which you want to add bookmarks.**

2. **If the Navigation pane is not open in Acrobat and the Bookmarks palette is not selected, press F5. If the Navigation pane is open but the Bookmarks palette is not currently selected, click the Bookmarks tab to display its palette on top.**

3. **Using the buttons on the Navigation toolbar or navigation buttons on the Document window status bar, go to the destination page in the document for the first bookmark.**

4. **If you want the destination page to be displayed in a different page view or magnification, select the appropriate options from the View menu or click the appropriate buttons on Acrobat toolbars and the Document status bar (see Chapter 2 for details).**

5. **Click the Create New Bookmark button at the top of the Bookmarks palette, or click the Bookmarks palette menu's pop-up button and then click New Bookmark on the menu (you can also press Ctrl+B on Windows or ⌘+B on the Mac).**

   A new bookmark icon named Untitled is added (see Figure 9-3).

6. **Type a descriptive name for your new bookmark and then press the Enter key (Return on the Mac) or click the mouse pointer somewhere outside of the bookmark name to add it to the list in the Bookmarks palette.**

Making bookmarks that open other files

Instead of having your new bookmarks go to particular pages using a particular view in a PDF document, you can have them open other documents. These documents can be other PDF files that you want to view or any type of document that you have stored on your computer.

To make a bookmark that opens a new document, essentially you use the same steps as outlined in the preceding section except that because you're creating a bookmark that opens another file, you really don't care about what page is current and what view is used in the PDF document at the time you create the bookmark (so you can disregard Steps 3 and 4 in the preceding steps).

After you create the new bookmark, you need change its properties by following these steps:

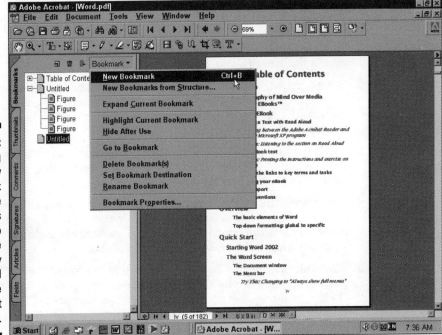

Figure 9-3:
Adding
a new
bookmark
in the
Bookmarks
palette to
the page
currently
displayed
in the
Document
window.

1. **Right-click the bookmark in the Bookmark palette (Control+click on the Mac) to open its context menu.**

2. **Click Properties on the context menu.**

   The Bookmark Properties dialog box opens.

3. **Click the drop-down button on the Type combo box (which currently reads, Go to View) and then click Open File in the pop-up menu (see Figure 9-4).**

4. **Click the Select File button (which replaces the original Edit Destination button).**

   The Select File to Open dialog box appears.

5. **Select the icon for the folder and then the file that you want to open and then click the Select button.**

6. **Click the Set Action button to close the Bookmark Properties dialog box and make the changes to the functioning of your bookmark.**

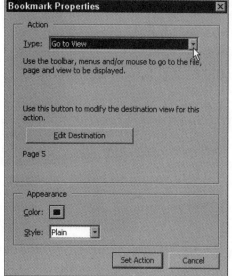

Figure 9-4:
Creating a
bookmark
that opens
a new file
in the
Bookmark
Properties
dialog box.

When you click a bookmark that opens such a document, Acrobat displays an
alert dialog box, warning you that a new program is about to be launched
from Acrobat and that this file that runs the program may contain programs,
macros, or viruses that could be potentially dangerous to your computer.
Click the Open button to ignore this warning and both launch the program
and open the specified file.

When you link a bookmark to a non-PDF document created by another application program, you must be sure that the program that created the file is
installed on your computer before you use its link. Also, be aware that you
can break the bookmark link if you delete the file that it will open or move it
to a new folder on your computer.

Making bookmarks that open Web pages

To create a bookmark that opens a Web page on the company intranet or on
the Internet, you vary the steps for creating a bookmark that opens a file on
your computer just slightly. Instead of selecting Open File as the Type in the
Bookmark Properties dialog box, you select World Wide Web Link. When you
select this option on the Type pop-up menu, the Edit Destination button
changes to Edit URL. You then click this button to open the Edit URL dialog
box. Here, you enter the URL address of the Web page in the Enter a URL for
This Link field and then click OK to close this dialog box and return to the

Bookmark Properties dialog box. Note that when entering the URL address, you must include the full address with the http, colon, double forward slash, www, periods, and all the rest as in

```
http://www.cnn.com
```

to open the CNN home page to get the latest news.

After you click the Set Action button in the Bookmark Properties dialog box, you can launch your Web browser and go to the designated page simply by clicking the bookmark. Of course, you must have Internet access available at the time you click a Web page bookmark to have the target page loaded successfully in your browser.

You can have the bookmark send an e-mail message by entering a mailto: address instead of an HTTP address in the Edit URL dialog box. For example, you could enter `mailto:gharvey@mindovermedia.com` to create a bookmark that would open a new e-mail message addressed to little old me in your e-mail program.

Making bookmarks that perform various actions

Instead of having a new bookmark go to a different page or assume a new view in the PDF file, open a new document, or visit a Web page, you can have the bookmark execute a single action. To do this, you select the particular action from the Type pop-up menu in the Bookmark Properties dialog box and then use the accompanying button to designate the file or object used in the action. The actions that you can set include:

- **Execute Menu Item** to have the bookmark select the menu item that you select from the Acrobat menus displayed in the Menu Item Selection dialog box

- **Import Form Data** to have the bookmark import data saved in a particular form data file in the fields of the current PDF form file

- **JavaScript** to have the bookmark execute the code that you enter into the JavaScript Edit dialog box

- **Movie** to have the bookmark play a movie file in the current PDF document

- **Read Article** to have the bookmark select a particular article defined in the PDF file (see Chapter 15 for details on defining articles for a PDF document)

- **Reset Form** to have the bookmark remove the data in designated fields in the current PDF form file

- **Show/Hide Field** to have the bookmark hide a field that is currently displayed and then show a field that is currently hidden

✔ **Sound** to have the bookmark play a sound file in the current PDF document

✔ **Submit Form** to have the bookmark submit all or some of the data in fields in the current PDF form file to a particular Web page in the PDF, HTML, or XML file format

✔ **None** to have the bookmark take absolutely no action when you click it!

As you can see in this list, a fair number of these action options have to do with manipulating data and fields in a form (Import Form Data, Reset Form, Show/Hide Field, Submit Form, and even JavaScript if you're creating JavaScript code for submitting the form data). Most of these form-related actions are better suited to buttons that you add to the form file rather than to bookmarks. See Chapter 14 for details on using and creating buttons to perform actions such as clearing and submitting the form data. You can also add hyperlinks to a PDF document that perform the same actions as shown in this list. See Chapter 15 for details on creating and using hyperlinks.

Editing bookmarks

If, after creating a bookmark, you discover that you need to make changes to the bookmark type or its destination, you can do this in the Bookmark Properties dialog box, which you can open by right-clicking (Control+clicking on the Mac) the name of the bookmark and then clicking Properties on its context menu. You can also edit the appearance of a bookmark in this dialog box.

To change the text color of the bookmark as it appears in the Bookmarks palette, click the Color button and then click its new color in the pop-up color palette. To change the text style of the bookmark, click the new style (Bold, Italic, or Bold & Italic) on the Style pop-up menu. To assign your new color and/or text style to the bookmark, click the Set Action button in the Bookmark Properties dialog box.

Changing the page destination for a bookmark

If you find that you've linked a bookmark that goes to the wrong page, you can easily edit just its destination by taking these few steps:

1. **Using the buttons on the Navigation toolbar or navigation buttons on the Document window status bar, go to the correct destination page in the document for the bookmark.**

2. **Right-click (Control+click on the Mac) the name of the bookmark whose destination needs editing in the Bookmarks palette of the Navigation pane and then click Set Destination on the context menu.**

3. **Click Yes in the alert dialog box that asks you if you're certain that you want to make this change.**

To test the edited destination, click the buttons on the Navigation toolbar or on the Document window status bar to move to a new page and then click the bookmark to make sure that it now takes you to the right page.

Renaming and deleting bookmarks

If you aren't happy with a name of a particular bookmark, you can rename it in a snap:

1. **Right-click (Control+click on the Mac) the name of the bookmark whose name needs changing in the Bookmarks palette and then click Rename on the context menu.**

2. **Replace the existing name by typing the new name and then pressing Enter (Return on the Mac) or by clicking the mouse pointer somewhere outside of the bookmark name.**

To delete a bookmark, right-click (Control+click on the Mac) the bookmark in the Navigation pane and then click Delete on its context menu.

Nesting bookmarks

Acrobat enables you to rearrange the bookmarks you add to a PDF document so that they are structured on different indented levels (a process referred to as *nesting*). Nesting bookmarks is important when you're dealing with a PDF document that has loads of bookmarks because you can collapse and expand nested bookmarks as needed so that you don't have to keep scrolling and scrolling in the Navigation pane in order to find the bookmark you want to use.

To nest one bookmark under another, you drag its bookmark icon and text up to the bookmark directly above it and then, when the International DON'T symbol mouse pointer (the circle with the slash in it) changes to an arrowhead pointer, release the mouse button. Acrobat responds by displaying an alert dialog box asking you if you're sure that you want to move the selected bookmark(s). Click the OK button to have Acrobat nest the bookmark by indenting it and drawing a connecting dotted line extending from it to the bookmark icon at the higher level above.

Note that you can nest a series of bookmarks at one time. Simply click the first bookmark directly beneath the one under which the entire series is to be nested and then Shift+click the last bookmark to be nested. Drag the outlines of the entire selection up to the bookmark under which they are to be nested and then click OK in the alert box asking for confirmation.

You can tighten up the bookmark list in the Navigation pane by clicking the Collapse button to temporarily hide these nested bookmarks. As soon you do this, the Collapse button changes to an Expand button (indicated by a plus sign on Windows and a triangle pointing to the right on the Mac). You can click this button to expand this portion of the bookmark list and once again display the group of nested bookmarks.

There's no set limit on the number of nested levels you can create in the Bookmarks palette. Just keep in mind as you continue nesting groups that the more levels you create, the wider you have to make the Bookmarks palette or the more horizontal scrolling you have to do to identify the bookmarks and to access their Collapse and Expand buttons.

To un-nest a group of nested bookmarks, you must select them all and then drag the bottom bookmark in the selection to the left until the International DON'T symbol mouse pointer changes to an underscore, whereupon you can drop the group and have the bookmarks returned to their original level just as soon as you click OK in the confirmation alert dialog box. Keep in mind that when dragging the group, you *must* have the mouse pointer on the last bookmark in the selected group as you drag left; otherwise, the underscore pointer never appears, so nothing happens when you release the mouse pointer!

Inserting Document Comments

In its original state, the Commenting toolbar displays the buttons for four tools — Note, Pencil, Highlight, and Digital Signature — that you can use to annotate your PDF document (the fifth button enables you to spell-check the text in the notes you add). Three of these buttons, Note, Pencil, and Highlight, contain a More Tools button that you can click to display buttons for other related tools.

When you click the More Tools button on the Note tool, it displays a pop-up menu containing the Free Text tool, the Sound Attachment tool, the Stamp tool, and the File Attachment tool. You normally use this group of tools to add different kinds of notes to comment on the contents of the PDF document you're reviewing. These notations can include editing suggestions on how to improve the content and look of the document as well as instructions on how to complete or make final editing changes to the PDF document.

When you click the More Tools button on the Pencil tool, it displays a pop-up menu containing the Square tool, Circle tool, and Line tool. The tools in this group enable you to directly mark up the text and graphics of the PDF document you're reviewing. You generally use the tools in this group to draw attention to graphics in the file that require some kind of change, be it reposi-tioning or resizing.

When you click the More Tools button on the Highlight tool, it displays a pop-up menu containing the Strikeout tool and Underline tool. You usually use this group of tools to draw attention to text in the PDF document you're reviewing that needs some type of editing (normally deletion when you use the Strikeout tool) or emphasizing (when you use the Underline tool).

Figure 9-5 shows you the Commenting toolbar with the buttons for all its tools displayed. Note that Acrobat saves all notations that you add with these tools on a distinct and invisible top layer of the PDF document, keeping them separate from the PDF document text and graphics underneath. This makes it possible for you to import comments from other reviewers and add them to the PDF document as well as to summarize all comments made in the document and export them as a separate file.

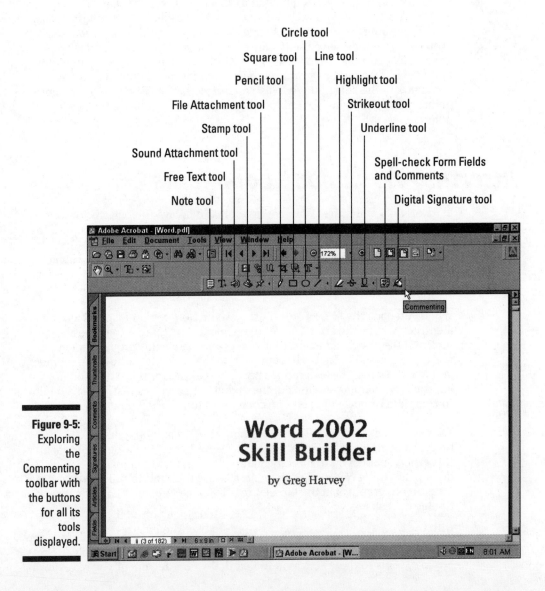

Figure 9-5: Exploring the Commenting toolbar with the buttons for all its tools displayed.

Please take Note

The notes that you can add when reviewing a PDF file run the gamut of hidden comments (identified by a note icon), simple text displayed at all times in the document, audio comments that you listen to, and predefined stamps indicating approval, confidentiality, and the like. You can even add notes that attach files to the PDF document (useful when you want to include alternate text or graphics that should be considered as possible replacements or additions).

Using the Note tool

To add a hidden comment with the Note tool, follow these steps:

1. **Click the Note tool on the Commenting toolbar or type** S.

2. **Click the Note mouse pointer at the place on the page in the PDF document where you want the Note icon to appear.**

   When you click this pointer, Acrobat opens a comment dialog box that shows your name and the current date on the title bar.

3. **Type the text of the note in the comment dialog box.**

4. **If the text of your note is short, you can resize the comment box to better suit the amount of text by positioning the mouse pointer in the sizing box in the lower-right corner and then dragging the outline of the box with the arrowhead pointer until it's the shape and size you want.**

5. **After you finish typing the text of the note, click the Close button in the upper-left corner of the comment dialog box to close it.**

After you click the Close button in the comment box, only the Note icon appears on the page (as shown in Figure 9-6). To open the note's comment box to read its text, select the Hand tool (H). Then double-click the Note icon, or right-click the icon (Control+click on the Mac) and then select Open Note on its context menu. Note that you can leave a comment box open next to its Note icon on the page by clicking outside of the box rather than clicking its Close button.

You can move notes by dragging their Note icons or their comment boxes (if they're open) with either the Hand tool or the Note tool. Simply drag the arrowhead pointer to the desired position on the page (usually off the text that you're commenting on) and then release the mouse button. To delete a hidden comment, right-click (Control+click on the Mac) its Note icon to select it and then click Delete on its context menu.

You can also change the color and icons used when you add your comments with the Note tool. This is a good feature to use when many people will be adding comments to the same PDF. By having the reviewers select individual colors and icons, you can tell at a glance which notes belong to which reviewers. To select a new color and/or icon for your notes, follow these steps:

1. Add your first note (by following the preceding steps).

2. Right-click the Note icon (Control+click on the Mac), and then choose Edit⇨Properties on the Acrobat menus or simply click the Note icon to select it and then press Ctrl+I (⌘+I on the Mac).

   The Note Properties dialog box appears, as shown in Figure 9-6.

3. To select a new Note icon, select it in the Appearance list box.

4. To select a new color for the Note icon, click the Color button and then click a new color in the pop-up palette.

5. To change the author for the note, select the name in the Author field and then replace it with a new name.

6. Click OK to put your changes into effect.

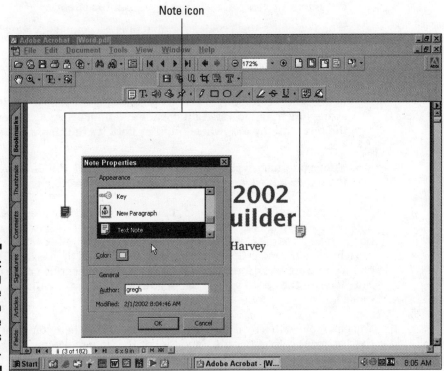

Note icon

Figure 9-6:
Changing
note
settings in
the Note
Properties
dialog box.

When you close the Note Properties dialog box by clicking OK, Acrobat changes the current comment to suit the new icon and/or color settings. All notes that you subsequently create will use the new note settings. Be aware, however, that the icons for notes previously added are unaffected by your changes to these settings (you would have to delete and then re-create them to have all your notes reflect the new color and icon settings).

Roll me over and count me up

Note that you can have Acrobat automatically open a note's comments box to display its text when you position the mouse pointer on the Note icon. You can do this by selecting the Automatically Open Pop-ups on Mouse Over check box in the Comments Preferences section of the Preferences dialog box. You can also have Acrobat automatically number the Note icons for the comments you add so that you can keep track of the sequence in which you made them by selecting the Show Comment Sequence Numbers check box.

Also keep in mind that changes you make in the Author field of the Note Properties dialog box affect only the particular note selected at that time. To have the change you make to the author setting affect all the subsequent notes that you create with the Note tool, you need to open the Preferences dialog box (Ctrl+K on Windows, ⌘+K on the Mac), click Comments in the list box, and then deselect the Always Use Identity for Author check box in the Comments Preferences area. When this check box option is selected (as it is by default), Acrobat always uses the computer owner's identity (or login if the computer is shared on a network) as the author of all notes created in Acrobat.

You can also change the font and font size for text used in the comments you create with the Note tool as well as the opacity of the comment box (by decreasing it, you can see more of the text and graphics underneath) in the Comments Preferences area of the Preferences dialog box. Note that changes you make in the Font and Font Size pop-up menus affect only new comments created with the Note tool. The same holds true for any new setting you select on the Pop-up Opacity pop-up menu.

Using the Free Text tool

You use the Free Text tool to create comments in the PDF document that are always visible. Because Free Text comments are always displayed, you need to position them in margin areas or places where they aren't obscured by document text or graphics text underneath.

To create a comment with the Free Text tool, take these steps:

1 **Click the Free Text tool on the Commenting toolbar or press Shift+S until its icon (the one with the *T* and a plus sign) is selected.**

2. **Click the I-beam mouse pointer at the place on the page in the PDF document where you want the text of the comment to appear.**

When you click this pointer, Acrobat opens a light gray bounding box (which appears dotted on some monitors) in which you type the note.

3. **Type the text of the free-text note in the note's bounding box.**

   As you type, Acrobat breaks the lines of text to fit within the width of the bounding box. If you type more lines than fit in the length of the bounding box, Acrobat scrolls the lines of text up (so some of the note text may no longer be visible).

4. **When you finish typing the text of the free-text note, click the Hand tool and then click outside of the note's bounding box.**

   Acrobat displays your free-text note in a box.

To resize the free-text note box to make all of its text visible or to eliminate excess white space around the note text, position the Hand tool somewhere on the note and then click the arrowhead pointer to display the sizing handles at the four corners of the free-text note box. Next, position the pointer on one of the sizing handles and drag the double-headed pointer diagonally until the outline of the note box is the shape and size you need. Click outside the note box to deselect the sizing handles.

To move a free-text note, click within its note box to display the sizing handles and then, with the arrowhead mouse pointer inside the box, drag the outline to a new position on the page before releasing the mouse button. To delete a free-text note from the PDF document, right-click (Control+click on the Mac) the note text or its bounding box to select it and then click Delete on its context menu.

As with comments added with the Note tool, you can change the default settings for the free-text notes you create with the Free Text tool. Click the free-text note box to select it, and then press Ctrl+I (⌘+I on the Mac) to open the FreeText Properties dialog box, shown in Figure 9-7. As you can see, the setting options in this dialog box enable you to change not only the font and font size of the note text but also its alignment in relation to the borders of its note box.

To make the border of the free-text note boxes thicker, increase the value in the Thickness field. To remove the box entirely from free-text notes, set this value down to 0. To change the color of the box border, click the Border Color button and then click a new color on the pop-up palette.

To add a background color to the free-text note box, click the Fill Color check box and then click the Fill Color button and click the background color from its color pop-up palette (for heaven's sake, don't select a background color on this palette that's so dark that you can't read the note text). When you finish making changes in the FreeText Properties dialog box, click OK to see the effects of your changes on the currently selected free-text note.

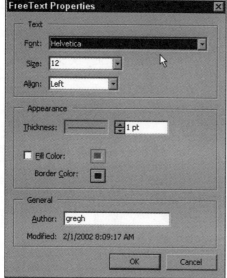

Figure 9-7:
Changing
the free-text
note
settings in
the FreeText
Properties
dialog box.

Using the Sound Attachment tool

You use the Sound Attachment tool to record a sound note or select an audio file that is played back when the user double-clicks the Sound Note icon. Note that you can't record your own sound notes and add them to your PDF document if your computer doesn't have a microphone.

To record a sound note for playback in your PDF document, follow these steps:

1. **Click the Sound Attachment tool on the Commenting toolbar or press Shift+S until its icon (the one with the speaker) is selected.**

2. **Click the Speaker mouse pointer at the place on the page in the PDF document where you want the Sound Note icon to appear.**

   When you click this pointer, Acrobat opens a Sound Recorder dialog box.

3. **Click the Record button, speak into your computer's microphone, and record the note. When you finish recording, click the Stop button (see Figure 9-8). To play the note before adding it to your document, click the Play button (which replaces the Stop button).**

4. **Click OK in the Sound Recorder dialog box.**

   The Sound Recorder dialog box closes, and the Sound Properties dialog box opens.

5. **Click the Description field and then enter a description for your sound note that identifies it when you position the mouse pointer over its Sound Note icon and then click OK.**

You can also select a prerecorded sound file to play back when the Sound Note is played. To select a prerecorded sound file, click the Choose button in the Sound Recorder dialog box to open the Choose a Sound File dialog box. Click the folder that contains the desired sound file, click the sound file icon, and then click the Select button.

To play a sound note that you've added to a PDF document, double-click its Sound Note icon with the Hand tool or right-click (Control+click on the Mac) its icon and then click Play File on the context menu.

Stop button

Record button

Figure 9-8: Recording a sound note in the Sound Recorder dialog box.

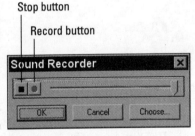

Using the Stamp tool

You can use the Stamp tool to imprint the document with a predefined graphic mark usually in the form of a stamp indicating the status of the document, such as Draft, As Is, Confidential, or Final. When you use one of these marks, you can also add a hidden comment to it just like you do when creating a comment with the Note tool. Acrobat comes with a wide variety of ready-made stamps that you can use (which are organized into different categories). You can add your own marks to these collections.

Don't confuse adding a stamp to the PDF document you're reviewing with digitally signing a PDF document. When you stamp a document, you're simply adding another, more graphic form of notation to the document. When you digitally sign a document, however, you're actually using a secure method for identifying yourself as the signatory (see Chapter 11 for details on the process involved in digitally signing a document). Use stamps when you want to call attention to the current state of the PDF document or add a very visible review comment, such as red-flagging a change with, of all things, a *red flag*. Digitally sign the PDF document when you're ready to freeze it and prevent all further changes to it.

To add a stamp to a PDF document, you take these steps:

1. **Click the Stamp tool on the Commenting toolbar or press Shift+S until its icon (the one with the hand stamp) is selected.**

2. **Click the Stamp mouse pointer at the place on the page in the PDF document where you want the stamp's imprint to appear.**

   When you click the Stamp mouse pointer, Acrobat inserts the last-used stamp at the place you click (this is the Approved mark when you first begin using this feature in Acrobat).

3. **If you want to use a different stamp, click the mark that you just added to the document to select it (you can tell it's selected because a bounding box with sizing handles at the corners appears), and then press Ctrl+I (⌘+I on the Mac).**

   The Stamp Properties dialog box opens (as shown in Figure 9-9).

4. **Select the category of the stamp in the Category pop-up menu.**

   You can choose from four built-in categories: Faces, Pointers, Standard (the default), and Words.

5. **Scroll through the list of stamps in the list box on the left until the stamp you want to use appears in the preview pane on the right.**

6. **To change the color used in the title bar of any comment box that you can add to the stamp, click the Pop-up Color button and then click the new color in the pop-up palette.**

7. **To change the author associated with the stamp, click the Author field and then edit the name.**

8. **When you finish making changes to the settings in the Stamp Properties dialog box, click OK to close the dialog box.**

When you close the Stamp Properties dialog box, an imprint of the new stamp you selected appears in the document. Note that this imprint is still selected so that you can resize it and move it to a new place on the page if you need to.

To resize the imprint, position the mouse pointer on one of the sizing handles and then drag diagonally with the double-headed pointer. To move the imprint to a new place on the page (perhaps to the side or above related text or graphic images), position the arrowhead pointer somewhere within its bounding box and then drag its outline and drop it in place. To delete a stamp from the PDF document, right-click (Control+click on the Mac) the Stamp's imprint to select it and then click Delete on its context menu.

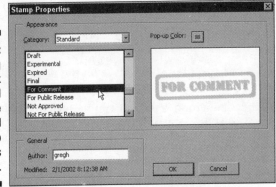

Figure 9-9:
Changing
the mark
imprinted
with the
Stamp tool
in the Stamp
Properties
dialog box.

Adding a hidden comment to a stamp imprint

If you want to add a hidden text comment to the imprint of a stamp, you can do so by following these steps:

1. **Double-click the imprint of the stamp to which you want to add the comment.**

   Acrobat responds by opening a comment box (just like the ones used to add comments with the Note tool).

2. **Type the text of your comment in the open comment box.**

3. **To resize the comment box so it better fits the text you entered, drag the sizing box in the lower-right corner diagonally until it's the right shape and size.**

Getting your hidden comments added and seen

When using stamps to annotate a PDF document, you may want to make a couple of changes to the Comments Preferences — one that will help you remember to add hidden comments and the other to let you and your reviewers know that hidden comments are attached to particular stamp imprints. To have Acrobat automatically open a blank comment box whenever you add a new stamp imprint, open the Comments Preferences section of the Preferences dialog box (by pressing Ctrl+K on Windows or ⌘+K on the Mac, and then clicking

Comments in the list box on the left) and then click the Automatically Open Other Comment Pop-ups check box. To have the program automatically display the comment boxes you add to stamp imprints whenever you position the mouse over them, click the Automatically Open Pop-ups on Mouse Over check box in this same section (note that selecting this check box option affects hidden comments added with the Notes tool as well as those added with the Stamps tool).

4. **To move the comment box so that its title bar doesn't obscure the stamp's imprint, drag the comment box by its title bar.**

5. **When you finish making changes to the comment box, click its Close button to make the box and its note disappear.**

Adding custom marks to your own stamp category

You can create your own marks in graphics programs such as Adobe Illustrator or Adobe Photoshop and then use them as stamps in Acrobat 5. To do this, you first need to convert the graphic image you want to convert to a stamp to a PDF file. You can do this directly from programs like Illustrator and Photoshop or by saving the images as PostScript files and then using the Acrobat Distiller in Acrobat 5 (as described in detail in Chapter 4).

After you have the mark saved as a PDF file, you follow these steps to make it available as a stamp in Acrobat 5:

1. **Open the PDF file with the graphic image you want to use as a stamp in Acrobat 5.**

2. **Choose Tools⇨Forms⇨Page Templates.**

   The Page Templates dialog box opens.

3. **Enter the name you want to give the stamp as the name for the new page template (something with the company name or a description of the mark) in the Name field and then click the Add button.**

4. **Click Yes in the alert dialog box that appears asking you if you want to create a new template using the current page.**

5. **Click the Close button to close the Page Templates dialog box.**

6. **Open the Document Summary dialog box by pressing Ctrl+D (⌘+D on the Mac) and then replace the filename listed in the Title field with the name of the category to which you want to assign the custom stamp.**

   You can use a new category such as Corporate or an existing one such as Standard.

7. **Click OK to close the Document Summary dialog box.**

8. **Choose File⇨Save As on the Acrobat menus and then open the Stamps folder on your hard disk and save the PDF file in it.**

   The Stamps folder is located inside the Annotations folder found within the Plug-ins folder inside the Acrobat folder. This Acrobat folder is located inside the Acrobat 5.0 folder that is located inside your Programs folder (called All Programs on Windows XP and Applications on the Macintosh) on your hard disk. After you've located and opened the Stamps folder in the Save As dialog box, click the Save button to save the new forms template file containing your mark there.

9. **Choose File⇨Close or press Ctrl+W (⌘+W) to close the PDF file with your mark that you just saved as a template in the Stamps folder.**

After you add a custom graphic as a new stamp, you can start using it in the PDF documents you're reviewing as you would any of the other built-in stamps. After clicking the Stamp tool, click its imprint to select it and then press Ctrl+I (⌘+I on the Mac) to open the Stamp Properties dialog box. In the Category pop-up menu, select the category to which you assigned the custom stamp (that is, the name you assigned in the Title field of the Document Summary dialog box in Step 6). Doing this displays the name of your custom stamp (the one you assigned as the name of the new page template in Step 3) in the list box on the left and the image of the stamp in the preview pane on the right. When you click the OK button to close the Stamp Properties dialog box, the imprint of your custom stamp appears selected in the document.

Using the File Attachment tool

You can use the File Attachment tool to attach or append another file (not necessarily saved as a PDF) to the PDF document you're reviewing. You can use this feature to attach new copy and graphics that you'd like to see replace particular text passages and images in the PDF file. You can also use this tool to attach a memo or some other text document that outlines the review steps or special instructions to the design or review team.

Don't use this feature to attach files saved in other file formats besides PDF unless you're sure that each reviewer has the software necessary to open it installed on his or her computer. Of course, the way to be sure that each and everyone concerned will be able to open and evaluate all the files you attach to a PDF document under review is to save them as PDF files before you attach them.

To attach a file to the PDF file you're reviewing, follow these steps:

1. **Click the File Attachment tool on the Commenting toolbar or press Shift+S until its icon (the one with the pushpin) is selected.**

2. **Click the Pushpin pointer at the place in the PDF document's text or graphics where you want the File Attachment icon to appear, indicating to other reviewers that a file has been attached.**

   Acrobat responds by opening the Select File to Attach dialog box.

3. **Open the folder and then select the icon for the file that you want to attach to the current PDF document and then click the Select button.**

   The File Attachment Properties dialog box opens.

4. **To select a new icon besides the pushpin, click it in the Appearance list box.**

5. **To change the color of the File Attachment icon, click the Color button and then click the new color on the pop-up color palette.**

6. **To modify the ToolTip description that appears when the user positions the mouse over the File Attachment icon, click the Description field and replace the filename.**

   Acrobat automatically displays the filename as the ToolTip if you don't modify this field.

7. **To change the author associated with this file attachment, click the Author field and edit the name that appears there.**

8. **Click the OK button to close the File Attachment Properties dialog box.**

As soon as you close the File Attachment Properties dialog box, you see the File Attachment icon (a pushpin unless you changed it) at the place you clicked in the document. To move this icon, drag it with the arrowhead pointer. To display the ToolTip with the name of the attached file (or some other description if you modified the Description field), position the arrowhead mouse pointer over the File Attachment icon.

To open the attached file, double-click its File Attachment icon, or right-click (Control+click on the Mac) the icon and then click Open File on the context menu. Acrobat responds by displaying an Open Attachment alert dialog box warning you about possible dangers in opening the file. When you click the Open button in the alert dialog box, Acrobat then goes ahead and opens the file.

If the attached file is a PDF document, Acrobat opens it and makes it the current document (you can then return to the original PDF document by selecting its name at the bottom of the Window menu). If the attached file is saved in some other file format, your computer's operating system launches the program that created the file (provided that it can be identified and that it's installed on the computer) and simultaneously opens it in a new window (you can then return to the original PDF document by clicking its program icon on the Windows taskbar or selecting its name on the Application pop-up menu in the Macintosh Finder).

To remove an attached file from the PDF document, right-click the File Attachment icon (Control+click on the Mac) and then click Delete on its context menu. To save the attached file on your hard disk before you delete it, click Save Embedded File to Disk, select the folder in which you want it saved, and click Save before you use the Delete option.

Mark it well

The graphic markup tools (Pencil, Square, Circle, and Line) enable you to mark up elements that need changing in the PDF document you're reviewing. When you use these graphic markup tools to call attention to particular passages of text and graphics, you can add hidden notes (like you can do when using the Stamps tool) that explain the type of changes you'd like to see made to the elements you've marked.

All the graphic tools work in a similar manner and share the same color and thickness settings. Which of the four tools you select varies according to the kind of document elements you want to mark up:

- **Pencil** to draw freehand shapes around text and graphics.

- **Square** to draw rectangular and square boxes around text and graphics. Hold down the Shift key to constrain the shape to a square as you draw with this tool.

- **Circle** to draw a circle or oval around text and graphics. Hold down the Shift key to constrain the shape to a perfect circle as you draw with this tool.

- **Line** to add a line to text or graphics (often referred to as *adding a rule*). Hold down the Shift key to constrain the shape to a straight line and drag left and right for a horizontal rule, up and down for a vertical rule, and diagonally for a rule on the bias at 45 degrees.

To use one of these tools to mark up a PDF document, you follow these general steps:

1. **To use the Pencil tool, click its button on the Commenting toolbar or press N. To use one of the other markup tools, press Shift+N until its icon (rectangle for the Square tool, circle for the Circle tool, and diagonal line for the Line tool) is selected.**

2. **Position the cross-hair mouse pointer near the text or graphic that you want to mark up and then drag to draw the line or shape made by the tool to call attention to it.**

   When using the Pencil tool, you can draw a freehand line or enclosing shape. When using the Square, Circle, or Line tool, remember that you can constrain the shape or line by holding down the Shift key.

3. **Release the mouse button when you finish drawing the desired line or shape with the selected tool.**

When you release the mouse button, Acrobat lays the graphic down on the page. To select the markup graphic to resize it, move it, or change its graphic settings, select the Hand tool (H) and then click the line or shape with the arrowhead pointer. If the graphic is a shape made with the Pencil, Square, or

Circle tool, Acrobat encloses it in a bounding box with sizing handles at the corners. If the graphic is a rule made with the Line tool, the program selects the line with sizing handles at either end. To move a markup graphic, drag its outline with the arrowhead pointer and then drop it in its new position. To resize it, drag one of its sizing buttons.

Remember that you can have Acrobat automatically open a comment box each time you add a markup graphic by selecting the Automatically Open Other Comment Pop-ups check box in the Comments Preferences area of the Preferences dialog box. You can also have Acrobat automatically display a hidden comment when you position the mouse on the markup graphic by selecting the Automatically Open Pop-ups on Mouse Over check box as well. See the sidebar "Getting your hidden comments added and seen," earlier in this chapter.

Hitting the Highlights

Acrobat includes three text-only markup tools: Highlight, Strikeout, and Underline:

- Use the Highlight markup tool to highlight text in a color (yellow by default just like the highlighting pens you used to mark key words and phrases to remember).

- Use the Strikeout tool to indicate words and phrases that should be deleted from the text (Acrobat puts a line through the text just like they do in voter pamphlets to show what provisions of a referendum will be removed from a statute).

- Use the Underline tool to underscore the importance of text.

Figure 9-10 shows you examples of three types of text markup: highlighting in the title, underlining in the first-paragraph text at the top of the first column, and strikeout in the title at the top of the second column.

As with the graphics markup tools, when you mark text up with the text-only tools, Acrobat automatically adds hidden comment boxes to the markups. In this case, the comment boxes contain a copy of all the text that you've marked with the text-only markup tool. You can then annotate this comment text or replace it with the corrections you'd like to see made.

The text-only tools all work the same way: After you click the desired text-only markup tool, you drag the I-beam mouse pointer through all the text you want to highlight, strikeout, or underscore. The only settings you can change for these tools are the color of the text and the author associated with it in the Comment Properties dialog box (open it by clicking the marked-up text and then pressing Ctrl+I on Windows or ⌘+I on the Macintosh).

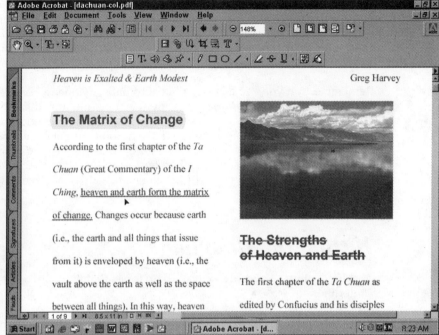

Figure 9-10:
A PDF
document
with
highlighted
text, struck-
out text, and
underlined
text thanks
to the text-
only markup
tools.

To delete the highlighting, strikeout, or underlining made to words or phrases in the PDF document, right-click (Control+click on the Mac) the marked-up text and then click Delete on its context menu.

To open the comments box attached to the words or phrases you've marked up with one of the text-only markup tools, double-click the marked-up text to open its comment box.

Remember that you can have Acrobat automatically open a comment box each time you mark up text with one of the text-only markup tools by selecting the Automatically Open Other Comment Pop-ups check box in the Comments Preferences. You can also have Acrobat automatically display a hidden comment when you position the mouse on the marked-up text by selecting the Automatically Open Pop-ups on Mouse Over check box as well. See the sidebar "Getting your hidden comments added and seen," earlier in this chapter.

Spelling it out

Acrobat includes a spell check feature that you can use to catch any and all typos you make in the comments that you add to a PDF document. You can use this feature to catch and eliminate all those embarrassing spelling errors before you send your comments out to someone else on the review team.

To spell-check the text in all comments in the document (along with all text in any form fields you've added), go to the first page of the document, click the Spell Check Form Fields and Comments button on the Commenting toolbar, or press F7, to open the Check Spelling dialog box (similar to the one shown in Figure 9-11), and then click the Start button.

Acrobat will then flag the first unknown word it encounters in either the form fields or the comments in the document, and you can then take one of the following steps:

✔ To replace the flagged word with one of the suggested corrections listed in the Suggested Corrections list box, click the correction and then click the Change button.

✔ To replace the flagged term with the selected correction in all instances in the other form fields and comments in the document, click the Change All button.

✔ To ignore the flagged word, click the Ignore button.

✔ To ignore the flagged word in all the other form fields and comments in the document, click the Ignore All button.

✔ To add the word to the dictionary, click the Add button.

When Acrobat finishes checking the spelling in the last form field or comment on the last page of the document, it automatically returns to the first page and redisplays the message, "Ready to Spell Check Forms and Comments" in the Check Spelling dialog box. You can then click the Done button to close the Check Spelling dialog box.

Figure 9-11:
Spell-
checking
the
comments
made in
a PDF
document.

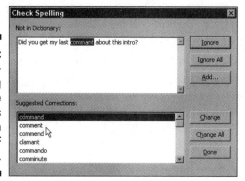

If you want to have Acrobat spell-check a passage in the document text, use the Highlight tool to highlight the text to be spell-checked, which is then automatically added to a hidden comment box. Run the spell check feature and use it to correct all the misspellings in the text's comment box. You can then use the corrected text stored in the comment box when making the corrections during the final editing phase (see Chapter 10 for details on editing).

Processing Document Comments

When you finish adding your review comments to a PDF document, then the real fun begins. Depending upon your role in the review process, you may only have to save your comments as part of the PDF document (with the normal File⇨Save command), or you may have to save only the comments in a special form data file (using a .fdf extension rather than the more familiar .pdf extension) using the File⇨Export⇨Comments command as well.

When you save only the comments, you create a much smaller data file that you can easily send as an attachment to an e-mail message to the review team leader, design team leader, or whoever's in charge of collecting and handling all the review comments. The leader can then collect the comments saved in the form data files that you and your other team members send and import them into the original PDF document. This enables him or her to assemble all the members' comments into the same PDF file where they can be evaluated together in one place. This process of assessing and compiling everyone's feedback in the same document is much easier than having to assimilate the feedback from different copies of the same document.

To save all the comments you've made in a PDF document in a separate form data file that you can e-mail, follow these steps:

1. **Choose File⇨Export⇨Comments on the Acrobat menus.**

   The Export Comments dialog box opens.

2. **Choose the folder in which you want to save the form data file.**

3. **By default, Acrobat will give the new form data file the same filename as the PDF file (with the .fdf file extension). If you want, you can rename the file or edit the filename in the File Name field.**

   I suggest appending your initials onto the original filename so that it's obvious from the filename that these are your review comments.

4. **Click the Save button to close the Export Comments dialog box and to save your comments in the new form data file.**

After exporting your document comments to a form data file, you can distribute it to coworkers by attaching the file to an e-mail message.

To keep the form data files containing your review comments small and compact for quick e-mailing, avoid attaching sound notes with the Sound Attachment tool and separate files with the File Attachment tool because both types of comments embed files that, depending upon their magnitude, can increase the size of the form data file astronomically. Sticking to the other types of text and graphical comments when working with small and easy-to-transfer form data files is very important.

Collecting all comments

After you've got the form data files with all the reviewers' comments, you're ready to bring them all together in the original PDF document. To do this, you import the individual form data files using these steps:

1. **Open the original PDF file that you sent out for review in Acrobat 5.**

2. **Choose File⇨Import⇨Comments on the Acrobat menus.**

   The Import Comments dialog box opens.

3. **Open the folder with the form data files to be imported and then click one of the file icons to select it.**

4. **Click the Select button to close the Import Comments dialog box and add the comments from the first form's data file to the PDF file open in Acrobat.**

5. **Repeat Steps 2 through 4 until all the form data files with review comments are imported.**

After all the review comments are imported, be sure to save the PDF document (if you want to keep a pristine before-comments version, choose File⇨Save As and rename the file).

Summing up

After you've assembled all the reviewers' comments in a PDF document, you can use the Summarize feature to create a summary report that lists all the different types of comments by type and page. To generate a summary report, follow these steps:

1. **Choose Tools⇨Comments⇨Summary on the Acrobat menus or press Ctrl+Shift+T (⌘+Shift+T on the Mac).**

   The Summarize Comments dialog box appears.

2. **To sort the list of comments in the summary report by some factor other than the pages of the document, select the new sorting key (Author, Date, or Type) in the Sort By pop-up menu.**

3. **To filter out particular comments from the summary report, click the Filter button to open the Filter Comments dialog box and then click the check boxes for all the types of comments you don't want included in the report (Figure 9-12 shows the options that appear in the Filter Comments dialog box). To filter out comments that have not been modified within a certain time period, select the desired period (Within the**

Last 24 Hours, Within the Last 6 Hours, Within the Last Hour, or Within the Last 30 Minutes) on the Modified pop-up menu. When you finish selecting the types of comments to filter out, click the OK button.

The Filter Comments dialog box closes, and you return to the Summarize Comments dialog box.

4. **Click the OK button to close the Summarize Comments dialog box and generate the summary report.**

Acrobat generates the summary report in a separate PDF document that it displays in the Document window using the Fit Width view. You can then save and print this summary file.

Filtering out certain types of comments

In addition to being able to filter out certain types of comments from a summary report, you can also use the settings in the Filter Comments dialog box (shown in Figure 9-12) to temporarily hide all types of comments except for exactly those that you want to work with.

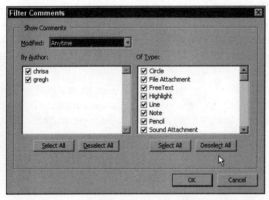

Figure 9-12:
Selecting
the types of
comments
that you
don't want
displayed in
the PDF file.

For example, to display only the Note and FreeText comments in the PDF document, you deselect all the check box options in the Of Type list except for Note and FreeText. Further, to display only these two types of comments when they've been added or modified within the last day, you select the Within the Last 24 Hours option on the Modified pop-up menu. Even further, if you only want these comments from particular reviewers, you deselect the check boxes for all the names in the By Author list except for the ones you want to see.

To open the Filter Comments dialog box, choose Tools⇨Comments⇨Filter on the Acrobat menus. Then, after you've selected the settings for just the comments you want displayed, you click the OK button.

To redisplay all the comments in the PDF document, select Anytime from the Modified pop-up menu and then click the Select All buttons beneath the By Author and Of Type lists in the Filter Comments dialog box. To temporarily hide all comments added to the PDF document, click the Deselect All buttons at the bottom of both the By Author and the Of Type lists.

Don't try to add comments of a type that you've hidden in the Filter Comments dialog box, or you'll encounter all sorts of weird problems. For example, if you add a rule with the Line tool when Line comments are hidden, the rule that you draw on the page immediately disappears (because it's part of the comments that you've hidden). If you try to attach a file with the File Attachment tool when File Attachment comments are hidden, Acrobat won't let you edit the description for the file in the Description field of the File Attachment Properties dialog box (not to mention that Acrobat will immediately hide the pushpin File Attachment icon in the document). If you experience these kinds of strange goings-on when you add comments, please open the Filter Comments dialog box to turn every type of comment back on.

Finding comments

Acrobat provides a couple of methods for locating the comments that you've added and imported into a PDF document: You can use the Comments palette in the Navigation bar to identify all the comments made on particular pages of the PDF document, or you can use the Tools⇨Comments⇨Find command on the Acrobat menu to search comments for particular words or phrases. Figure 9-13 shows the Comments palette selected in the open Navigation pane as well as the Find Comment dialog box where you enter the text to search for in the text of the comments added to the PDF document.

Locating comments in the Comments palette

To use the Comments palette to locate and select a particular comment in the document, follow these steps:

1. **Click the Comments tab or choose Window⇨Comments on the Acrobat menus to display the Comments palette (and open the Navigation pane, if it's currently closed).**

2. **By default, Acrobat sorts the comments in the Comments palette by page. To have the list sorted by comment type, author, or date last modified, select the Sort By: Type, Sort By: Author, or Sort By: Date option on the Comments pop-up menu.**

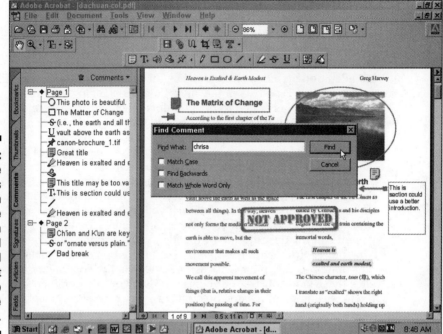

Figure 9-13:
Use the
Comments
palette in
the
Navigation
pane and
the Find
Comment
feature to
locate
comments.

3. **Click the Expand button (a plus sign on Windows and triangle pointing right on the Mac) for the page, comment type, author, or date modified (depending upon how the list in the Comments palette is sorted) that you think contains the comment or comments you want to find.**

4. **Click the icon for the comment you want selected in the expanded list of comments on that page.**

When you click a comment in the Comments palette, Acrobat displays the page and the comment in the Document pane. Because the comment you selected in the Comments palette is also selected in the PDF document, if you want to change its setting, you can then open its Properties dialog box by pressing Ctrl+I (⌘+I on the Mac). To open its comment box, however, you still have to double-click the selected text or icon.

Searching for comments

You can have Acrobat search for comments by choosing Tools⇨Comments⇨ Find on the Acrobat menus or simply by selecting Find on the Comments pop-up menu on the Comments palette (this is the easiest way if the Comments palette is currently open). Doing this opens the Find Comment dialog box (refer to Figure 9-13).

Follow these steps in using the Find Comment dialog box:

1. **In the Find What field, enter the word or phrase in the comment(s) you want to locate as the search text.**

2. **To match the capitalization of the search text, click the Match Case check box.**

3. **To prevent Acrobat from finding the search text inside of other words (as in *her* in the word *there*), click the Match Whole Word Only check box.**

4. **To have Acrobat search backwards in the document from whatever page is currently displayed, click the Find Backwards check box.**

5. **To locate and select the first comment in the PDF document that contains the search text, click the Find button.**

6. **To find the next occurrence of the search text in a comment, click the Find Again button (which replaces Find).**

7. **When you finish searching the comments in the PDF document, click the Cancel button or the Close button in the Find Comment dialog box.**

When you click the Find Again button and Acrobat can find no further occurrences of the search text, the program displays an alert dialog box informing you of this situation. When Acrobat does find a match to your search text, it displays and selects the comment's icon or markup in the Document pane. To display the matching text in its hidden comment box, you still need to double-click the selected comment to open it.

Note that you can enter the name of an author (as it appears on the title bar of the comment boxes) in the Find What field to use the Find Comment feature to locate and select comments made by a single reviewer.

Don't confuse searching for comments in a PDF document with searching for text in the document. You use the regular Edit⇨Find command to search for words or phrases in the general text of the document. You use the Tools⇨ Comments⇨Find command to search for words or phrases only within the comments that you've added or imported into the PDF document.

Removing all comments

After you've made all the required editing changes (as explained in Chapter 10), you can remove all the comments and various markings from the original PDF document by choosing Tools⇨Comments⇨Delete All from the Acrobat menus. Note that Acrobat does display an alert dialog box asking for your confirmation before removing all the comments in the current PDF document. You can, however, restore them by choosing Edit⇨Undo on the menus (Ctrl+Z on Windows or ⌘+Z on the Mac).

Before you make your edits and remove all the comments with the Tools⇨ Comments⇨Delete command, use the File⇨Save As command and rename the file to make a copy of the PDF document with all its comments. That way, you always have a copy of the original file along with all the reviewers' feedback.

Chapter 10

Editing PDF Files

In This Chapter

▶ Touching up lines of text

▶ Editing graphics on a page

▶ Editing the pages of a PDF document

▶ Renumbering pages in a PDF document

▶ Creating articles to help with online reading

▶ Editing PDF files in batches

*T*he text- and graphics-editing tools included in Acrobat 5 are designed to enable you to do last-minute touchups to your PDF document. As you will soon discover, they are simply not robust enough for heavy editing needs. If, in the course of the document review cycle (described in detail in Chapter 9), you discover that your PDF document requires major text or graphics revisions and/or changes to the document layout or structure, you may have to make these changes in the original documents with their native application programs and then re-convert them to PDF for final review in Acrobat.

In this chapter, you find out how to use the Acrobat 5 editing tools to make various kinds of editing changes and corrections to your PDF document. These changes can include correcting errors in lines of text, modifying text attributes, and repositioning graphics, as well as inserting, rearranging, deleting, cropping, and renumbering the document pages. You also find out how to edit your PDF documents by creating articles for determining the flow of text that spans columns and pages and guiding readers through their online reading experience of the document. Finally, you discover the wonderful world of batch processing that enables you to automate routine editing sequences, such as removing all file attachments or saving the text in the Rich Text Format (RTF) used by a word processor such as Microsoft Word, and perform them on several PDF documents at one time.

Touching Up the Text and Graphics

You use the TouchUp tools on the Editing toolbar to make last-minute changes to the text and graphics in your PDF document. Acrobat includes three TouchUp tools that share a single button: the TouchUp Text tool (T) that you can use to do text corrections in individual lines of text in a PDF file, the TouchUp Object tool (Shift+T) that you can use to reposition graphics, and the TouchUp Order tool (Shift+T again) that you can use to modify the reflow order of elements in tagged PDF files.

In addition to the TouchUp Text tool on the Editing toolbar, you can use any of the following items found on the Tools⇨TouchUp Text submenu in editing your text:

- **Text Attributes** to change the font, font size, alignment, or word spacing of selected text in the line.

- **Text Breaks** to display the Text Breaks window that previews how the currently selected line of text breaks when viewed with special screen-reading software on a handheld device running a special version of Acrobat Reader 5.0. You use the elements available on the Insert sub-menu (described later in this list) to force breaks at particular words or prevent them.

- **Fit Text to Selection** to have Acrobat compress or expand the text in the line to accommodate insertions or deletions that you make to the characters.

- **Insert** to insert various formatting elements into the Text Breaks window. These elements include Line Break, Soft Hyphen (that is, one that disappears when the word doesn't break across two lines), Non-Breaking Space (a space that keeps hyphenated words together on the same line at all times), and Em Dash (a longer-than-usual dash usually equal to the width of the letter *M* in the selected font that does permit line breaks across words).

- **Show Line Markers** to hide or display a bounding box around the line of text currently selected with the TouchUp Text tool. Line Markers indicate the alignment of the text by displaying diamonds on the top and bottom lines of the bounding box that reflect the kind in effect: diamonds on the left side for left alignment, in the middle for center alignment, on the right side for right alignment, and on both the left and right for justified alignment. You can increase or decrease how much the line is indented by dragging the Line Markers bounding box by these alignment diamonds.

Text editing — Acrobat style

Acrobat 5.0 not only restricts your text editing to a single line at a time, but also does not reflow any text from other lines to accommodate any insertions or deletions you might make there. This means you must keep your text edits to a minimum to things like fixing typos and punctuation errors and minor font alterations, or you'll end up with a real layout headache. Also, you're not able to edit the characters in a line of text if the text font isn't embedded in the PDF file and you don't have the font installed on your computer. This is also true if the PDF file embeds a subset of the font (that is, just the characters actually used in the document text) and you don't have the complete font installed. Instead of touch-up text editing, maybe they should call it "don't touch it" text editing.

Editing characters in a line of text

You use the TouchUp Text tool to select the line of text containing the characters you want to edit. When you click this tool on the Editing toolbar, the mouse pointer changes to an I-beam. Click the I-beam at the place in the text where you need to make your first edit. When you click, Acrobat encloses the entire line in the Line Markers bounding box, while at the same time positions the insertion point (the flashing cursor) in between the characters at the place you clicked (as shown in Figure 10-1).

To make editing changes to the surrounding characters, use one of the following techniques:

- ✔ To insert new characters at the insertion point, just type the characters.
- ✔ To delete characters to the immediate right of the insertion point, press the Delete key.
- ✔ To delete characters to the immediate left of the insertion point, press the Backspace key.
- ✔ To restore characters in error or remove ones incorrectly inserted, press Ctrl+Z (⌘+Z on the Mac), your good old trusty Undo key (keep in mind that Acrobat supports only one level of undo).

When you finish editing the characters in a line of text, click the Hand tool to ensure that you don't inadvertently select other lines of text and do unintentional editing to them. Just be aware that you can't use your good H keystroke shortcut to select the Hand tool because this only succeeds in typing the letter *h* in the line!

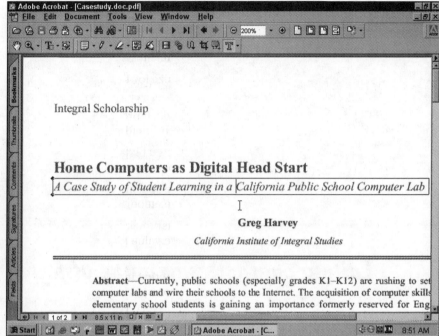

Figure 10-1:
Selecting
the place in
a line of text
to make
edits with
the TouchUp
Text tool.

Remember that some PDF files use the No Changing the Document security option to prevent anyone from making further editing changes. When this option is in effect in your document, you can't get the TouchUp Text tool to select any line of text in the PDF document no matter how hard you click.

Modifying text attributes

Provided that you have the font (or someone's been nice enough to have embedded it in the PDF document for you), you can modify the attributes of the characters that you highlight with the insertion point in the line selected with the TouchUp Text tool. Note that if your system doesn't have the font and it hasn't been embedded, Acrobat will display a nice little alert dialog box whose message says, "Warning. You cannot edit text in this font."

After highlighting the characters with the TouchUp Text tool, you open the Text Attributes dialog box (shown in Figure 10-2) by choosing Tools⇨TouchUp Text⇨Text Attributes on the Acrobat menus. This dialog box contains the following attribute options that you can change:

✔ **Font** to specify a new font for the selected text from the Font pop-up menu

✔ **Embed** to embed the font displayed in the Font combo box (see the previous bullet) in the PDF document

✔ **Font Size** to specify a new font size for the selected text in the Font Size pop-up menu

✔ **Horizontal Scale** to horizontally compress or expand the selected text by the percentage you enter in this field

✔ **Baseline Offset** to shift the selected text vertically up or down in relation to the text baseline by the number of points you specify in this field

✔ **Tracking** to uniformly adjust the spacing between more than two characters selected in the text by the amount you specify in this field

✔ **Word Spacing** to uniformly adjust the spacing between two or more words selected in the text by the value (in thousandths of an em space) you specify in this field

✔ **Indent Right** to indent the line of text in from the left edge of the paragraph by the value (in points) you specify in this field

✔ **Indent Left** to reduce the indent of the line of text in toward the left edge of the paragraph margin by the value (in points) you specify in this field

✔ **Left Align** to align the text in the current line with the left edge of the Line Markers bounding box indicated by diamonds at the top and bottom of the box's left edge

✔ **Center** to align the text in the current line with the center of the Line Markers bounding box indicated by diamonds on the top and bottom in the middle of the bounding box

✔ **Right Align** to align the text in the line with the right edge of the Line Markers bounding box indicated by diamonds on the top and bottom of the box's right edge

✔ **Justify** to align the line of current text with both the left and right edges of the Line Markers bounding box indicated by diamonds on the top and bottom of the box's left and right edges

✔ **Fill Color** to specify a new fill color (interior color) for the selected font on the Fill Color pop-up menu

✔ **Outline Color** to specify a new stroke color (outline color) for the selected font on the Outline Color pop-up menu

Depending upon the changes you make in the Text Attributes dialog box, after you finish specifying the new settings and return to the document, you may find that selected characters no longer take up the same amount of space on the line. To force them to fill the same amount of space as they did

before changing their text attributes (to ensure that the line length isn't out of place in relation to the other lines in the paragraph), choose Tools⇨Text TouchUp⇨Fit Text to Selection on the Acrobat menu.

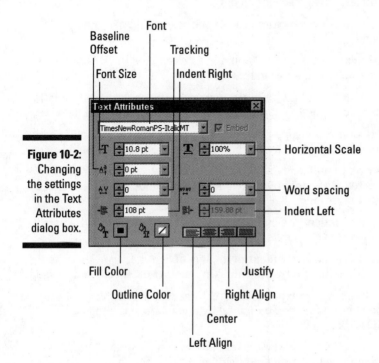

Baseline Offset

Font

Font Size

Tracking

Indent Right

Figure 10-2: Changing the settings in the Text Attributes dialog box.

Horizontal Scale

Word spacing

Indent Left

Fill Color

Outline Color

Left Align

Center

Right Align

Justify

Touching up your graphic images

You can use the TouchUp Object tool to select graphic images or other objects that have been embedded in a PDF document. This tool is the second one on the TouchUp Text button's pop-up menu, and it uses an arrowhead icon. You can select the TouchUp Object tool from the Editing toolbar by pressing Shift+T until the arrowhead icon replaces the outlined T icon used by the TouchUp Text tool.

To select a graphic with the TouchUp Object tool, you simply click it with the arrowhead pointer. After a graphic is selected (indicated by a black bounding box around the image or object — there are no sizing handles because you can't resize graphics in Acrobat), you can then reposition it by dragging its outline to the new position before you release the mouse button. You can also nudge a selected graphic image with the cursor keys: Just press the ←, →, ↑, and ↓ keys to move the graphic by small increments until it's in the desired position.

To select more than one graphic image or object on the page at the same time, Ctrl+click (Control+click on the Mac) each object. To select a group of graphic images or objects on the page, drag the TouchUp Object tool to draw a bounding box around all the graphics to select them all together.

When trying to move charts and graphs embedded on the document page (especially those originally generated in a spreadsheet program like Microsoft Excel), drag a bounding box around the entire chart to ensure that you select all of its components (such charts are actually composed of a whole bunch of individual graphic objects) before you attempt to reposition it on the document page.

Using the layout grid in repositioning graphics

Acrobat has a layout grid that you can use to help you in repositioning graphic images. To turn on the display of the layout grid in the PDF document, choose View➪Grid on the Acrobat menu or press Ctrl+U (⌘+U on the Mac).

When working with the layout grid, you can modify the default grid settings in the Layout Grid section of the Preferences dialog box by pressing Ctrl+K (⌘+K on the Mac) and then clicking Layout Grid in the list box on the left. This section contains a number of grid options that you can change:

✔ By default, Acrobat subdivides each of the major grid squares into 3 divisions across and 3 down, making a total of 9 little subdivisions. To increase the number of squares in each of the major grid squares, increase the value in the Subdivisions field.

✔ To offset the layout grid in relation to the top and left margin of the page, enter a value in the Grid Offset from Left Edge and the Grid Offset from Top Edge fields.

✔ By default, Acrobat makes each major grid square one-inch square with one inch between their vertical lines and one inch between their horizontal lines. To make the major grid squares larger so that there are fewer, farther apart, increase the values in the Width Between Lines and Height Between Lines fields. To make the grid squares smaller so that there are more, closer together, decrease the values in these fields. Note, however, that if you decrease the values in these fields too much, Acrobat is no longer able to subdivide the square using the value entered in the Subdivisions field.

✔ By default, Acrobat colors the lines in the layout grid blue. To select a new color for all grid lines, click the Grid Line Color button and then click the desired color in the pop-up color palette.

Editing graphic images from the context menu

When a graphic is selected, you can also edit it using the options available on its context menu. To open a graphic's context menu, right-click (Control+click on the Mac) the image with the TouchUp Object tool. These context menu options include:

- **Cut** to remove the selected image from the PDF document and add it to the Clipboard.
- **Copy** to copy the selected image to the Clipboard.
- **Paste** to insert a graphic object stored in the Clipboard into the selected image or onto the current document page if no image is selected.
- **Paste in Front** to insert a graphic object stored in the Clipboard on top of the selected image or on top of everything on the document page if no image is selected.
- **Paste in Back** to insert a graphic object stored in the Clipboard behind the selected image or behind everything on the document page if no image is selected.
- **Delete** to remove the selected image and place it in the Recycle Bin (Trash on the Mac).
- **Select All** to select all graphic objects on the current document page.
- **Select None** to deselect all graphic objects on the current document page.
- **Delete Clip** to remove any objects that are *clipping* the selected image (that is, cutting off part of the image in some way).
- **Edit Image** to open the selected graphic in the default image-editing program. When a graphic object is selected, this option changes to Edit Object and choosing it opens the object in the default page/object editing program. When multiple graphic objects are selected, this option becomes Edit Objects. When no graphic images are selected, this option becomes Edit Page and choosing it opens the object in the default page/object editing program as well.

When you choose the Edit Image/Object(s)/Page option, Acrobat attempts to launch the program specified as the Image Editor or the Page/Object Editor in the TouchUp section of the Preferences dialog box and open the selected image or graphic object in the application for editing with its controls. If Acrobat cannot launch the specified program, its displays an alert dialog box informing you of this fact.

To specify a new program as the default Image Editor or the Page/Object Editor, press Ctrl+K (⌘+K) to open the Preferences dialog box. Then click TouchUp in the list box on the left to display the Image Editor and Page/Object Editor sections of the Preferences dialog box. To select a new Image Editor such as Photoshop 6.0, click the Choose Image Editor button and then open the folder that contains the application and select its program icon before clicking the Open button in the Choose Image Editor dialog box. To select a new Page/Object Editor such as Illustrator 10, click the Choose Page/Object Editor button and then open the folder that contains this application and select its program icon before clicking the Open button in the Choose Page/Object Editor dialog box.

When using programs like Photoshop 6.0 and Illustrator 10 as your image editing and graphics object editing programs, respectively, you can make your changes in the programs launched from Acrobat 5 with the Edit Image or Edit Object command, and then, when you save your editing changes to the image or graphic in these programs, they are automatically updated in your PDF document.

Figure 10-3 illustrates this relationship. Here, you see the editing changes I made to the photo image of the Tibetan countryside in Photoshop 6.0 (launched by Ctrl+clicking the photo in the PDF document and then clicking Edit Image on its context menu) saved not only in Photoshop 6.0 shown in the foreground but also automatically saved in the PDF document in the background.

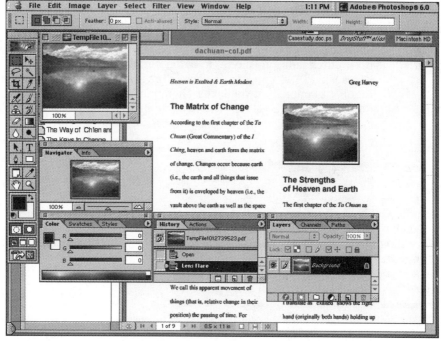

Figure 10-3:
Edits saved
to an
image in
Photoshop
6.0 are
automati-
cally
updated in
the PDF
document.

Page-Editing Practices

Acrobat makes it easy for you to perform a number of routine page edits on one or more pages of a PDF document. Possible page edits can include rotating and cropping the pages, replacing pages from another PDF document, inserting a new page, deleting pages, reordering the pages in the document, as well as assigning page numbers. To make many of these page edits, you use the Thumbnails palette in the Navigation pane, a situation underscored by the fact that most of the page-editing commands are available on the Thumbnail pop-up menu in the Thumbnails palette as well as on the Document menu on the Acrobat menu bar.

Remember when using the Thumbnails palette to navigate or edit pages that you can display more thumbnails of the pages in this palette by selecting the Small Thumbnails option at the bottom of the Thumbnails palette pop-up menu. You can also increase the number of thumbnails visible by dragging the border between the Navigation and Document panes with the double-headed arrow to the right to make the pane wider.

Rotating pages

Sometimes, you'll end up dealing with a PDF document that contains one or more sections whose pages need to be reoriented (perhaps switched from portrait to landscape mode) to better suit their text and graphics. To rotate pages in a PDF document, you select the Rotate Pages command on the Acrobat Document menu or the Thumbnails palette pop-up menu, or press Ctrl+R (⌘+R on the Mac). When you do this, Acrobat displays the Rotate Pages dialog box, which is similar to the one shown in Figure 10-4.

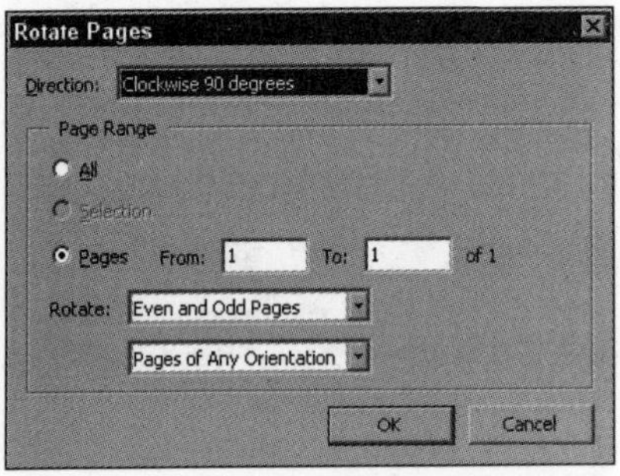

Figure 10-4: Rotating some pages in the PDF document in the Rotate Pages dialog box.

> **Rotate Pages**
>
> Direction: Clockwise 90 degrees
>
> Page Range
> ○ All
> ○ Selection
> ● Pages   From: 1   To: 1   of 1
> Rotate: Even and Odd Pages
> Pages of Any Orientation
>
> OK   Cancel

You can then select from these options in the Rotate Pages dialog box to change the orientation of the desired page or pages:

- ✔ **Direction** to specify the default Clockwise 90 Degrees, Counterclockwise 90 Degrees, or 180 Degrees

- ✔ **Page Range** to specify which pages to rotate: *All* to rotate all pages, *Selection* to rotate only the page(s) selected in the Thumbnails palette, or *Pages* to rotate the range you specify in the From and To fields

- ✔ **Rotate** to limit what type of pages in the designated page range to rotate: *Even and Odd Pages* for both even- and odd-numbered pages in the range, *Even Pages Only* for just even-numbered pages, or *Odd Pages Only* for odd-numbered pages, and *Page of Any Orientation* to rotate both portrait and landscape pages in the range, *Landscape Pages* for landscape pages only, or *Portrait Pages* for portrait pages only

Cropping pages

On occasion, you'll find that you need to crop one or more pages whose overall page dimensions conflict with the others in the PDF document. Acrobat offers two methods for doing this: You can crop pages in the Crop Pages dialog box, where you must specify the values of the crop margins, or with the Crop tool on the Editing toolbar, where you draw the crop marks right on the page.

To open the Crop Pages dialog box, select the Crop Pages command on the Acrobat Document menu or the Thumbnails palette pop-up menu, or press Ctrl+T (⌘+T on the Mac). When you do this, Acrobat displays the Crop Pages dialog box, which is similar to the one shown in Figure 10-5.

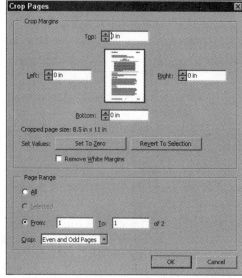

Figure 10-5: Cropping a page in the PDF document in the Crop Pages dialog box.

You can then select from the following options in the Crop Pages dialog box to resize the desired page or pages:

- **Crop Margins** to specify how much to cut off the page: *Top* to specify the top crop margin, *Left* to specify the left crop margin, *Right* to specify the right crop margin, and *Bottom* to specify the bottom crop margin. Click the *Remove White Margins* check box to have Acrobat figure out the crop margins by removing all the white space around the text and graphics on the specified pages.

- **Page Range** to specify which pages to crop: *All* to crop all pages, *Selection* to crop only the page(s) selected in the Thumbnails palette, or *Pages* to crop the range you specify in the From and To fields.

- **Crop** to limit what type of pages are cropped in the selected range: *Even and Odd Pages* to crop both even- and odd-numbered pages in the range, *Odd Pages Only* for just odd pages, or *Even Pages Only* for just even pages.

To use the Crop tool to do the cropping, follow these steps:

1. **Click the Actual Size button on the Viewing toolbar and, if necessary, the Single Page button on the status bar of the Document pane.**

2. **Click the Crop tool on the Editing toolbar.**

3. **Use the cross-hair mouse pointer to draw a bounding box that marks out the approximate cropping margins and then release the mouse button.**

   Acrobat responds by placing sizing handles at the four corners of the bounding box.

4. **If necessary, use the double-arrow mouse pointer on the edges or corners of the cropping bounding box to adjust the crop margins.**

5. **Double-click the arrowhead pointer somewhere within the bounding box.**

   The Crop Pages dialog box (similar to the one shown in Figure 10-5) opens.

6. **If necessary, adjust the values in the Top, Left, Right, and Bottom fields in the Crop Margins section of the dialog box.**

7. **If you want to crop more than just the current page in the document, specify the page range in the Page Range section of the Crop Pages dialog box.**

8. **Click OK to crop the page(s) to the specified crop margins.**

Replacing pages from other PDF files

Every now and then in editing a PDF document, you come across a situation where you need to replace just certain pages in the file. Keep in mind when replacing an original page with an updated version that only the text and graphics on the original page are replaced by those on the updated page. All interactive elements associated with the original page remain and carry over to the updated page (this could potentially cause problems if the links carried over from the original page no longer match up with buttons or linked text in the updated version).

As with cropping pages, Acrobat offers you two different ways to replace a page or pages in a PDF document. In the first method, you open just the document, select the page or pages to be replaced, and then use the Replace Pages command to specify the PDF document (which doesn't have to be open) and the page or pages in it to replace the selected pages. In the second method, you use a variation of drag-and-drop wherein you drag a thumbnail of the replacement page from its Thumbnails palette onto the page it's replacing in its Thumbnails palette (of course, to do this, you must have both documents open, tiled side by side, with both of their Thumbnails palettes selected).

Use the first method when you're sure (without looking) which pages in what PDF document to use as the replacements for the currently selected pages. Use the second method when you want to have a visual check as you make the replacements in your PDF document. The steps for using the first method with the Replace Pages command are as follows:

1. **Open the document that has the page or pages that need replacing in Acrobat 5. Make sure that all changes are saved in the file.**

   If you're not sure if the changes have been saved, choose File⇨Save on the Acrobat menus.

2. **Open the Thumbnails palette (F4) in the Navigation pane and select the thumbnail(s) of the page or pages that need replacing (Ctrl+click on Windows or Control+click on the Mac to select multiple pages).**

3. **Select Replace Pages on the Document menu or from the Thumbnails palette pop-up menu.**

   The Select File with New Pages dialog box opens.

4. **Open the folder and select the file icon of the PDF document that contains the replacement pages and then click the Select button.**

   The Replace Pages dialog box opens.

5. **Check the page numbers that appear in the Replace Pages and To fields in the Original section of the dialog box to make sure that they represent the one(s) you mean to replace.**

6. **Enter the page number of the first page of the replacement range in the With Pages field.**

   Acrobat will replace the same number of pages from the replacement PDF as are designated in the Replace Pages range.

7. **Click the OK button to display the Acrobat alert box asking you to confirm the replacements.**

8. **Click Yes to make the replacements.**

 Be aware that you can't use Undo to undo a replacement that's gone wrong. If you mess up, choose the File⇨Revert command to reopen the original PDF document with all its pages intact (and send me a thank-you for having you save the document in Step 1).

To replace pages by dragging and then dropping them in place, follow these steps instead:

1. **Open both PDF documents: the one with the pages to be replaced and the one with the replacement pages. In both documents select the Fit Width button on the Viewing toolbar and press F4 if the Thumbnails palette is not displayed in the Navigation pane.**

2. **Choose Window⇨Tile⇨Vertically on the Acrobat menus or press Ctrl+Shift+L (⌘+Shift+L on the Mac).**

3. **In the Document pane with the page or pages to be replaced, scroll the Navigation pane so that the thumbnail of the first page to be replaced is visible.**

4. **In the Document pane with the replacement page or pages, select the thumbnails of the replacement page or pages (starting with the first replacement page). Shift+click or drag a bounding box around the thumbnails to select a series of pages.**

5. **Drag the arrowhead mouse pointer from the Document pane with the selected replacement thumbnail(s) to the Document pane with the pages to be replaced.**

6. **Position the mouse pointer over the number at the bottom of the first thumbnail to be replaced and then release the mouse button.**

   You can tell when you've reached the right spot because the number and the page thumbnail become highlighted along with any subsequent pages in the palette that are to be replaced. As soon as you release the mouse button, Acrobat makes whatever page replacements are necessary to bring in all the pages you selected before dragging.

As with the first method, if you discover that you replaced the wrong pages, choose the File⇨Revert command to put the pages back where they were.

Replacing and adding PDF pages through Acrobat can result in a not-so-obvious problem involving files that have font subsets.

When you insert or replace pages containing those fonts, Acrobat automatically includes all the font subsets in the resulting file. If you do a lot of inserting and replacing, you can end up with a lot of redundant font subsets which can't be removed from the file. Mild to severe bloat can happen, depending on how may subsets are involved.

To prevent this problem Adobe recommends concatenating your PostScript files with Distiller and either the runfilex.ps or rundirex.ps files supplied on the Acrobat CD.

Inserting and deleting pages

Instead of replacing pages, you may just find that you need to insert a new page or group of pages in the PDF document. When inserting new pages, you can choose between similar methods as when replacing pages. You can insert all the pages from an unopened PDF file using the Insert Pages command, or you can use the side-by-side, drag-and-drop method to insert one or more individual pages. The big difference between these two insertion methods is that in the first dialog box method, you must insert all the pages from the incoming PDF file. In the second drag-and-drop method, you can insert a single page or a limited group of pages.

You follow these steps to insert all the pages in a single PDF file:

1. **Open the document in which you want to insert the new pages. Make sure that all your changes are saved.**

   If you're not sure if the changes have been saved, choose File⇨Save on the Acrobat menus.

2. **Choose Insert Pages on the Document menu or from the Thumbnails palette pop-up menu.**

   The Select File to Insert dialog box opens.

3. **Open the folder and select the file icon of the PDF document with the pages you want to insert and then click the Select button.**

   The Insert Pages dialog box opens.

4. **In the Page area, click one of the following radio buttons:**

   • **First** to have the pages inserted at the beginning of the PDF document either before or after the first page

   • **Last** to have the pages inserted at the end of the file either before or after the last page

   • **Page** to have the pages inserted either before or after the page number designated in the associated field

5. **By default, Acrobat inserts the pages after the page you specify in the Page portion of the Insert Pages dialog box. To have the pages inserted in front instead, select Before on the Location pop-up menu.**

6. **Click the OK button to have Acrobat insert the pages from the selected file.**

To use the drag-and-drop method for inserting one or more pages in a document, you use the same setup as described in the preceding section, "Replacing pages from other PDF files": Place the two documents in Fit Width view side by side with both their Thumbnails palettes displayed. Then select the thumbnail of the page or pages to be inserted and drag them to Thumbnails palette of the document in which copies are to be inserted.

The only difference between this method and replacing pages with drag-and-drop is that you position the mouse pointer in between the thumbnails at the place where you want the newly inserted pages to appear (and never on a thumbnail's page number). You can tell you've hit the right spot because an insertion bar (like the one shown in Figure 10-6) appears in the Thumbnails palette to let you know where the copies of the incoming pages are about to be inserted. You also notice that a plus sign appears at the arrowhead pointer indicating that copies of the pages will be inserted as soon as you release the mouse button.

Insertion bar

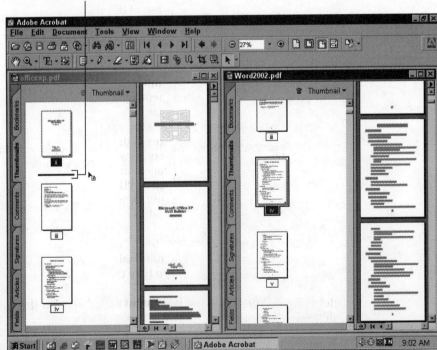

Figure 10-6: Inserting a page by dropping its thumbnail in the new document's Thumbnails palette.

Reordering the pages

You can rearrange the order of the pages in a PDF document just by relocating their page thumbnails in the Thumbnails palette. Just drag the page thumbnail to its new place in the Thumbnails palette and drop it into place when its insertion bar appears either ahead of the thumbnail of the page it is to proceed in the document or immediately after the thumbnail of the page it is to trail.

Keep in mind when reordering pages that you can move a range of pages at a time by selecting a series of thumbnails with the Shift+click method before you drag them to their new position in the Thumbnails palette.

Renumbering the thumbnail pages

You can use Acrobat's Page Numbering feature to renumber the pages in the Thumbnails palette to match the page numbers shown on the pages of the document in the Document window. You need to do this, for example, when you're dealing with a PDF document that contains front matter that uses a different numbering scheme (usually lowercase Roman numerals as in i, ii, iii, and so on) from the body of the text (usually numbered with Arabic numerals as in 1, 2, 3, and so on).

Because Acrobat automatically numbers pages in the Thumbnails palette and in the Page Number area on the status bar of the Document pane in Arabic numerals, starting at page 1, the page numbers displayed in the Thumbnails palette and on the status bar do not match those shown in the document pages themselves when they use different numbering styles. This can make it harder to find your place in the document when doing review and making touchup edits. For that reason, you should renumber the pages in the PDF document so that the page numbers in the document agree with those displayed in the Thumbnails palette and on the status bar.

Keep in mind that renumbering the pages in the Thumbnails palette has absolutely no effect on the page numbers shown on the pages in the Document pane, as these actually represent the page numbers added to header or footer of the document before it was converted to PDF. To renumber the pages of a PDF document, you need to manually edit them in Acrobat or open the source document with the original program, updating the page numbering, and then re-distill the file.

To renumber the thumbnails in the Thumbnails palette to match those shown on the pages of the PDF document, you take these steps:

1. **Select Number Pages on the Document menu or from the Thumbnails palette pop-up menu.**

   The Page Numbering dialog box opens (see Figure 10-7).

2. To renumber all the pages in the document, click the All radio button. To renumber only the pages that you've selected in the Thumbnails palette, leave the Selected radio button chosen. To renumber a specific range of pages, click the From radio button and then enter the first page number in the From field and the last page number in the To field.

3. To change the numbering style for the specified range, leave the Begin New Section radio button selected. To continue numbering when a range of pages is specified, click the Extend Numbering Used in Preceding Section to Selected Pages radio button.

4. When beginning a new numbering section, select the numbering style on the Style pop-up menu, specify any prefix to be used in the number (for example, 2- when you want the numbers to appear as 2-1, 2-2, 2-3, and so on) in the Prefix field, and enter the beginning number in the Start field if the section numbering begins at a number higher than 1.

5. Click OK to renumber the pages as specified.

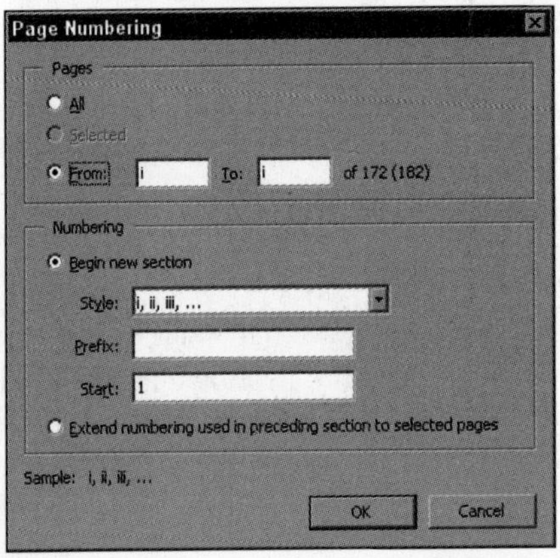

Figure 10-7: Renumbering sections of pages with the options in the Page Numbering dialog box.

Adding Articles to a PDF Document

Although Acrobat's editing features do not enable you to physically restructure the layout of the text in a PDF document in any way, its Articles feature does enable you to restructure the online reading experience. As an essential part of the Accessibility features included in Acrobat 5, articles are designed to make the reading of long disjointed sections of text, especially those set in newspaper columns that span pages, a smooth experience in Acrobat 5 or Acrobat Reader 5.

Articles accomplish this by breaking up sections of text into discrete blocks that are displayed in sequence as you click the Hand pointer, requiring no scrolling and no resetting of the page view. This eliminates the need for you to interrupt your reading experience with any type of scrolling or any other kind of page manipulation in order to get to the following section of text, a common experience in normal online reading where when you reach the end of one column, you must reset the page by scrolling back up (and often over) to continue reading at the top of the next column.

Defining articles

To add articles to a PDF document you're editing, you divide a section of text into blocks by enclosing them in a series of boxes (invisible to the user when he or she reads the article) that control the sequence in which the text blocks are displayed in the Document pane. This sequence of boxes creates a navigation path through the text formally known as an *article thread*. You use the Article tool on the Editing toolbar in Acrobat 5 to draw the succession of boxes that create the article thread and define its order.

To define a new article in a PDF document, follow these steps:

1. **Open the PDF document to which you want to add an article.**

2. **If the Navigation pane is open, press F6 to close it.**

3. **If the page view is not in Fit in Window and Continuous page mode, click the Fit in Window button on the Viewing toolbar and the Continuous button on the status bar of the Document pane.**

4. **Click the Article button (the one with a serpentine arrow icon) on the Editing toolbar, and then drag the cross-hair pointer to draw a bounding box that encloses the first block of text in the article (including all the text up to any excluded element such as a figure you don't want included or the end of the column).**

5. **After you've got the first text block outlined in the bounding box, release the mouse button to add the first article box.**

   This article box is labeled 1-1 at the top with sizing handles around the perimeter and a continuation tab (with a plus sign) at the bottom (see Figure 10-8). Note that the mouse pointer is changed from a cross-hair to the Article pointer (with a serpentine arrow).

6. **Scroll the page as required to position the Article pointer in the upper-left corner of the next block of text to be added to the article, and then drag the pointer to draw a bounding box around its text. Release the mouse button.**

   The second article box, which is labeled 1-2, is created (see Figure 10-9).

7. **Repeat Steps 4 through 6, adding as many article boxes as are required to define the reading path of the article.**

8. **To end the article, click the Hand tool (H), press the Enter key (Return on the Mac), or click the End Article button that now appears at the end of the status bar.**

   The Article Properties dialog box opens.

9. **Replace Untitled in the Title field with a descriptive name for the article.**

   This name is displayed in the Articles palette that enables users to select the articles they want to read — see Chapter 2 for details.

10. **If you want, add a brief description of the contents of the new article in the Subject field, the name of the person who authored the text in the Author field, and key terms that describe the contents separated by commas in the Keywords field (terms that you can use in searching the PDF document).**

11. **Click OK to close the Article Properties dialog box. If you pressed the Enter key (Return on the Mac) to end the article, click the Hand tool or type H to select the Hand pointer, which hides all the article boxes in the article.**

Note that as soon as you select the Hand tool after defining a new article, Acrobat adds an arrow pointing down from a crossbar to the back of the Hand icon (which looks like a tattoo to me). This form of the Hand icon appears whenever a user positions the Hand pointer over an article that you've defined in a PDF document.

Checking the flow of a new article

This Hand pointer with the arrow pointing down from a crossbar enables the reader to start reading the article at any place he or she chooses. You can use it to check the flow of your article. However, because you're currently at the end of the new article you've just defined, you need to go back to the place where you defined the first article box before you click it so that you can check the flow of the entire article from start to finish.

Before you click this pointer and start checking the flow of the article, you may want to adjust the default fit-visible zoom magnification setting that's currently in effect in Acrobat, because all articles in a PDF document apply the default fit-visible zoom magnification setting to any article that you're reading. To change this setting, press Ctrl+K (⌘+K on the Mac) to open the Preferences dialog box, click Display in the list box on the left, and enter an appropriate percentage value in the Max Fit Visible Zoom field at the bottom of the dialog box (this starts out at a whopping 800%) before clicking OK.

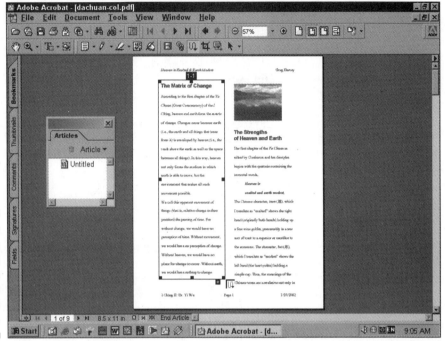

Figure 10-8:
Defining the first article box in the article with the Article tool.

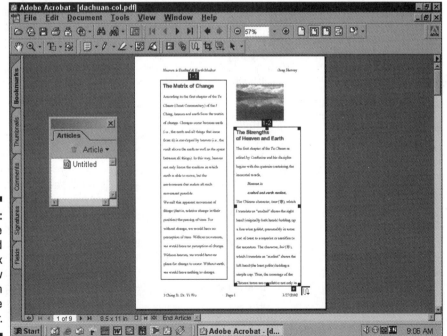

Figure 10-9:
Defining the second article box in the new article with the Article pointer.

To check the flow of the article, click the Hand pointer with the arrow pointing down from a crossbar somewhere in the text of the first article box, and
then continue to click the Hand pointer (which loses the crossbar while
retaining the downward-pointing arrow) to view in succession each portion
of every article box in the article. Acrobat lets you know when you've
reached the end of the article (the last visible portion of the last article box)
by adding a crossbar at the bottom of the downward-pointing arrow on the
Hand pointer. When you click this Hand pointer, Acrobat returns you to the
top of the article, and the page resumes the magnification setting currently
in effect in the Document window (as shown in the Magnification field on the
Viewing toolbar).

Batch Processing to the Rescue

For the final editing topic, I want to introduce you to Acrobat's batch-
processing capabilities. *Batch processing* (or *batch sequencing* as Acrobat
refers to it) automates the editing process by enabling you to perform one
or more actions on a group of PDF documents all at the same time. When
you first install Acrobat 5, it comes with a number of predefined batch
sequences. You can then edit these sequences or create your own to fit the
work you need done by Acrobat.

The key to successful batch processing is setting up an input folder in which
you've moved all the PDF documents that need processing with a particular
batch sequence and, if you're going to run a sequence that makes changes to
the PDF documents, setting up another output folder to hold all the processed
files (which you specify as part of the batch sequence).

Editing batch sequences

You can run, edit, or create new batch sequences from the Edit Batch
Sequences dialog box (shown in Figure 10-10) that you open by choosing
File⇨Batch Processing⇨Edit Batch Sequences on the Acrobat menus. To run
a batch sequence from this dialog box, click its name in the list box and then
click the Run Sequence button (you can also run a sequence by selecting its
name directly from the File⇨Batch Processing menu).

To edit an existing batch sequence, click the name of the sequence in the list
box and then click the Edit Sequence button to open the Batch Edit Sequence
dialog box (shown later in Figure 10-11). From this dialog box, you can
change the sequence of commands executed when you run the sequence

with the Select Commands button, change which files are processed by the sequence from the Run Commands On pop-up menu, and change where processed files are located in the Select Output Location pop-up menu. For details on using these options, refer to the series of steps on creating a new batch sequence in the following section (the steps for using these controls are identical for editing and creating batch sequences).

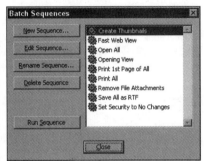

Figure 10-10: Editing a batch sequence in the Batch Sequences dialog box.

Creating new batch sequences

To create a new batch sequence, you open the Edit Batch Sequences dialog box (refer to Figure 10-10) by choosing File⇨Batch Processing⇨Edit Batch Sequences on the Acrobat menus. Then follow these steps:

1. **Click the New Sequence button in the Edit Batch Sequences dialog box.**

   The Name Sequence dialog box opens.

2. **Enter a descriptive name for the new batch sequence and then click OK.**

   The Batch Edit Sequence dialog box opens showing the name of your batch sequence in the title bar (see Figure 10-11).

3. **Click the Select Commands button.**

   This opens the Edit Sequence dialog box (shown in Figure 10-12) where you define all the commands that the batch sequence is to process in the order in which they are to be executed.

4. **Scroll through the list box on the left until you find the category (Comments, Document, JavaScript, Page, or PDF Consultant) and the name of the first command you want executed, and then click the command name to select it, followed by the Add button to add its name to the list box on the right.**

5. **Repeat Step 4, adding any additional commands to be executed as part of the batch sequence in the order in which they are to occur.**

6. **When you finish adding the commands in the sequence to the list box on the right, check them over. If you find any mistakes in the sequence, use the Move Up and Move Down buttons to rearrange the sequence, and then click OK.**

   The Edit Sequence dialog box closes, and you return to the Batch Edit Sequence dialog box.

7. **By default, all new batch sequences prompt you to specify the files for batch processing by selecting the Ask When Sequence Is Run option on the Run Commands On combo box. Here are some additional options:**

   • To have the batch sequence run on all files that you designate, select the Selected Files option on the Run Commands On pop-up menu.

   • To have all the files in a designated folder processed, select the Selected Folder option on this pop-up menu.

   • To have all the files open at the time you run the sequence processed, select the Files Open in Acrobat option.

8. **If you select the Selected Files or Selected Folder option on the Run Commands On pop-up menu, its Choose button becomes active. Click the Choose button to open the Select Files to Process or the Browse for Folder dialog box. In the case of the Select Files to Process dialog box, open the folder containing the files you want included and then select all their file icons to add their names to the File Name field and click the Select button. In the case of the Browse for Folder dialog box, select the name of the folder on your hard disk and then click OK.**

9. **If you select the Selected Folder option in Step 7, the Source File Options button becomes active. Click this button to open the Source File Options dialog box where you specify what file types in addition to PDF files to process. By default, the check boxes for all file types, BMP, CompuServe GIF, JPEG, PCX, PNG, and TIFF are selected. To eliminate a file type, click its name to remove the check mark from its check box before clicking OK.**

10. **By default, all new batch sequences put all the processed files in the same folder by selecting the Same Folder as Original(s) option on the Select Output Location combo box. Here are some additional options to choose from:**

   • To have the batch sequence prompt you for where to put the processed files at the time of the batch sequence, select the Ask When Sequence Is Run option on the Select Output Location pop-up menu.

- To have the sequence put the files in a specified folder, select the Specific Folder option on this menu.

- If you don't want changes saved in the processed files, select the Don't Save Changes option.

11. **When you select the Specific Folder option, the Output Options button becomes active. Click this button to open the Output Options dialog box (shown in Figure 10-13) where you can specify the file naming that is to be applied to the processed files and the file format in which the processed files are to be saved.**

12. **By default, Acrobat saves changes to the processed files with the same filenames in the Adobe PDF file format. To have the filenames changed in processing, click the Add to Original Base Name(s) radio button and then enter characters as a prefix to the filename in the Insert Before field and/or characters to be appended as a filename extension in the Insert After field. To prevent Acrobat from over-writing any filenames, click the Do Not Overwrite Existing Files check box.**

13. **To have Acrobat save the processed files in another file format besides Adobe PDF, select one of the supported file formats in the Save File(s) As pop-up menu. After changing all the file naming and format options that you want modified, click OK.**

    The Output Options dialog box closes, and you return to the Batch Edit Sequence dialog box.

14. **Check your command sequence along with your Run Commands On, and Select Output Location settings. If everything looks okay, click the OK button.**

    The Batch Edit Sequence dialog box closes, and you return to the Batch Sequences dialog box where the name of your new batch sequence now appears selected in the list box.

15. **To run the new batch sequence and test it out (preferably on copies of your PDF files, just in case something goes wrong), click the Run Sequence button. To close the Batch Sequences dialog box without running the new batch process, click the Close button instead.**

Whenever you create a new batch sequence, Acrobat adds its name to the File⇨Batch Processing menu. This means that you can avoid having to open the Batch Sequences dialog box to run the sequence, executing instead by clicking its name on the Batch Processing submenu.

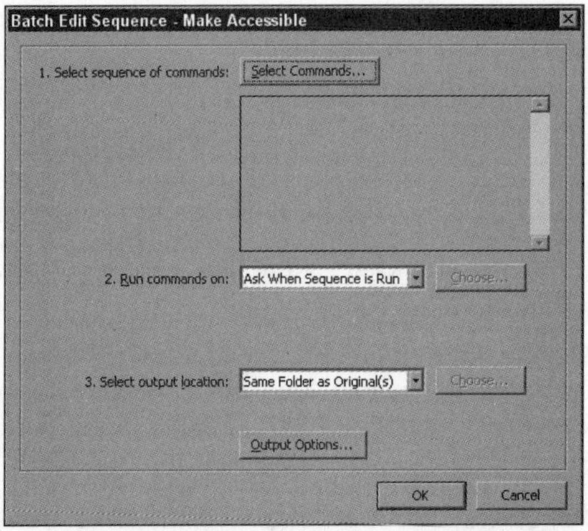

Figure 10-11:
Building a
sequence in
the Batch
Edit
Sequence
dialog box.

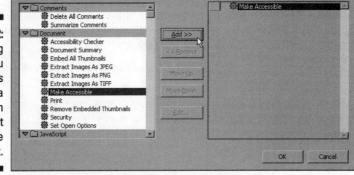

Figure 10-12:
Selecting
menu
commands
for a
sequence in
the Edit
Sequence
dialog box.

Figure 10-13:
Specifying
the file
naming and
output
format in
the Output
Options
dialog box.

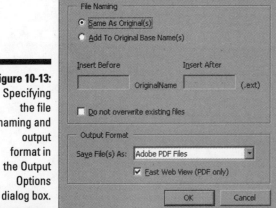

You can share the batch sequences you create for Acrobat with others who use Acrobat 5 in the office. Batch sequences that you create are saved as special sequence files using the title name you give them as the filename (with a .sequ file extension on Windows) and are stored in a folder called ENU on your hard disk. This folder is located within the Sequences folder inside the Acrobat folder. The Acrobat folder, in turn, is located in your Acrobat 5.0 folder inside your Programs folder (All Programs on Windows XP and Applications on the Macintosh).

When you send copies of your sequence files to coworkers, they must be sure to put them in this ENU folder on the hard disks of their computers. When they do, the names of the batch sequences you share appear in the list in the Batch Sequences dialog box in Acrobat 5 on their computers as though they created the batch sequences themselves.

If you use Acrobat for Windows, you might want to create a batch sequence that uses the Make Accessible plug-in to convert a bunch of regular PDF files to tagged PDF files so that they can take advantage of the Acrobat 5 and Acrobat Reader 5 Accessibility features (especially the Reflow button on the Viewing toolbar — see Chapter 2 for details).

Chapter 11

Securing PDF Files

· ·

· ·

*A*crobat 5 offers different types and different levels of security that you can apply to PDF documents. At the most basic level, you can password-protect your documents so that only associates who know the password can open the files for viewing, editing, and printing. You can further set file permissions that restrict the kind of user actions that can be performed on the PDF documents without access to a second password. You can also use the Acrobat Self-Sign Security feature to digitally sign a document and to verify the signatures and integrity of PDF files that you receive as part of your document review cycle. Finally, you can add the ultimate in security by encrypting your PDF documents using the Acrobat Self-Sign Security feature so that they can be shared only with a list of trusted associates. In this chapter, you find out all about the different ways to protect your PDF documents from unwarranted and unwanted access and editing.

Protecting PDF Files

You can password-protect the opening and editing of PDF documents at the time you first distill them (as part of their Security Settings — see Chapter 4 for details) or at anytime thereafter in Acrobat 5. When you set the security settings, you can choose between two different levels of encryption:

✔ 40-bit RC4 encryption for PDF files created when you set the Encryption level to 40-bit RC4 (Acrobat 3.*x*, 4.*x*)

✔ 128-bit RC4 when you set the Encryption level to 128-bit RC4 (Acrobat 5.0)

40-bit RC4 encryption offers a lower level of file security but is compatible with Acrobat 3 and Acrobat 4. 128-bit RC4 offers a higher level of security (it's a lot harder to hack into) but is compatible only with Acrobat 5. If you'll be sharing secured PDF documents with coworkers who haven't yet upgraded to Acrobat 5, you'll have to content yourself with the less-secure, 40-bit RC4 encryption. However, if you're dealing with really sensitive, "for-your-eyes-only" material, you may want to upgrade everybody to Acrobat 5 as soon as possible so that you can start taking advantage of the more secure 128-bit RC4 encryption.

Checking a document's security settings

You can check the security settings in effect for any PDF document you open in Acrobat 5 or Acrobat Reader 5 (of course, you can tell immediately if the file requires a user password because you must supply this password before you can open the document in Acrobat or Acrobat Reader). To check the security settings in effect, you choose File⇨Document Security or press Ctrl+Alt+S (⌘+Option+S on the Mac).

When you select this command in Acrobat, the program opens a Document Security dialog box, where you can both review and change the settings. When you select this command in Acrobat Reader, the program displays a Document Security dialog box that simply lists all the settings in effect.

The Document Security dialog box contains a Security Options combo box that shows you the type of security in effect. This box can contain one of these three options:

- ✔ **No Security** when the document uses no protection at all
- ✔ **Acrobat Standard Security** when the document uses a user password and/or master password and possibly restricts the type of edits
- ✔ **Acrobat Self-Sign Security** when the document is encrypted so that only trusted associates on a special list can open and change it

Beneath the Security Options combo box, you find a Display Settings button that you can click to display a Document Security dialog box listing all the security options in effect. Beneath the Display Settings button, you find the Change Settings button that enables you to change the security settings when either the Acrobat Standard Security or the Acrobat Self-Sign Security option is selected in the Security Options combo box above.

Securing files with 40-bit RC4 encryption

If you want to secure a PDF file that currently uses no security with the less-secure, 40-bit RC4 level of encryption (compatible with versions 3 and 4 of Acrobat and Acrobat Reader), you follow these steps in Acrobat 5:

1. **Choose File➪Document Security on the Acrobat menus, or press Ctrl+Alt+S (⌘+Option+S on the Mac).**

   The Document Security dialog box opens.

2. **Click Acrobat Standard Security on the Security Options pop-up menu.**

   The Standard Security dialog box opens, as shown in Figure 11-1.

3. **To set a user password that the user must supply in order to open the PDF document, click the Password Required to Open Document check box and then carefully enter the password in the User Password field.**

4. **To set a master password that the user must supply in order to change the user password or modify the file permissions, click the Password Required to Change Permissions and Passwords check box and then carefully enter the password in the Master Password field (this password must be different from the one you entered in the User Password field, if you followed Step 3).**

5. **Leave encryption set to 40-bit RC4 (Acrobat 3.*x*, 4.*x*) in the Encryption Level combo box and then select the check boxes for all the file permissions you wish to put into effect.**

   Your choices are No Printing; No Changing the Document; No Content Copying or Extraction, Disable Accessibility; and No Adding or Changing Comments and Form Fields.

6. **Click OK. If you set a user password, you must reenter your password in the Password dialog box that appears, asking you to confirm the password to open the document, and then click OK.**

7. **If you set a master password, reenter this password in the Password dialog box that appears next, asking you to confirm the password to change security options in the document, and then click OK.**

8. **Click the Close button in the Document Security dialog box.**

9. **Choose File➪Save to save your security settings as part of the PDF file.**

Note that if you mess up when attempting to confirm a user or master password in Steps 6 or 7, Acrobat displays an alert dialog box informing you of this fact and telling you that you have to try reentering the original password to confirm it. If you are unable to confirm the password successfully (no doubt because you didn't enter the password you had intended originally), you must revisit the User Password or the Master Password field, completely clearing out its contents and reentering the intended password from scratch.

After saving your security settings to the PDF document and closing the file, thereafter, you or whomever you send the PDF document to must be able to accurately enter the user password assigned to the file in order to open it. Further, you must be able to successfully enter the master password you assigned the file if you ever need to change the user password or modify the file permissions.

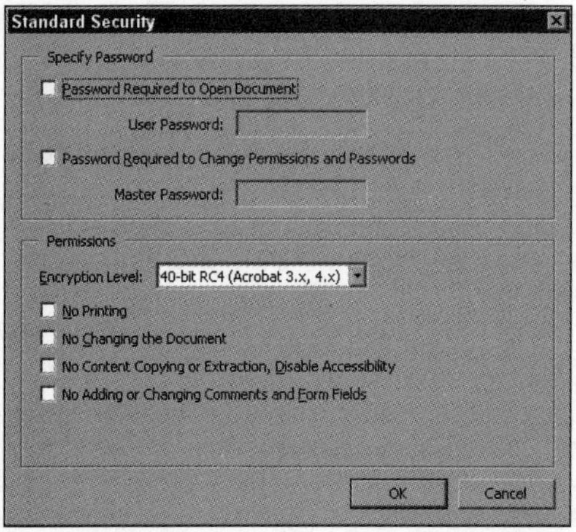

Figure 11-1:
Setting the
security
options for
40-bit RC4
encryption
in the
Standard
Security
dialog box.

Securing files with 128-bit RC4 encryption

To secure a PDF file that currently uses no security with the more secure, 128-bit RC4 level of encryption (compatible only with version 5 of Acrobat and Acrobat Reader), you follow these steps in Acrobat 5:

1. **Choose File⇨Document Security on the Acrobat menus, or press Ctrl+Alt+S (⌘+Option+S on the Mac).**

   The Document Security dialog box appears.

2. **Click Acrobat Standard Security on the Security Options pop-up menu if this field currently displays the No Security option.**

   The Standard Security dialog box appears.

3. **To set a user password that the user must supply in order to open the PDF document, click the Password Required to Open Document check box and then carefully enter the password in the User Password field.**

4. **To set a master password that the user must supply in order to change the user password or modify the file permissions, click the Password Required to Change Permissions and Passwords check box and then carefully enter the password in the Master Password field (this password must be different from the one you entered in the User Password field, if you followed Step 3).**

5. **Click the 128-bit RC4 (Acrobat 5.0) option on the Encryption Level pop-up menu.**

   When you select this higher level of encryption, the options in the Permissions area of the Standard Security dialog box change, as shown in Figure 11-2.

6. By default, the Enable Content Access for the Visually Impaired and the Allow Content Copying and Extraction check boxes are selected. In the rare event that you need to prevent the user from using the Accessibility features such as text reflow, click the Enable Content Access for the Visually Impaired check box to remove its check mark. To prevent the user from copying portions of the document or extracting graphics or text (as explained in Chapter 12), click the Allow Content Copying and Extraction check box to remove its check mark.

7. By default, the General Editing, Comment and Form Field Authoring option is selected in the Changes Allowed combo box. To restrict the changes that the user can make to the PDF document, click the None, Only Document Assembly, Only Form Fill-in option or the Signing, or Comment Authoring, Form Field Fill-in, or Signing option on the Changes Allowed pop-up menu.

8. By default, printing of the PDF document is fully allowed. To restrict the printing access, click Not Allowed or Low Resolution on the Printing pop-up menu.

9. Click the OK button. If you set a user password, you must reenter your password in the Password dialog box that now appears, asking you to confirm the password to open the document, and then click OK.

10. If you set a master password, re-enter this password in the Password dialog box that next appears, asking you to confirm the password to change security options in the document, and then click OK.

11. Click the Close button in the Document Security dialog box.

12. Choose File⇨Save to save your security settings as part of the PDF file.

Figure 11-2:
Setting the
security
options for
128-bit RC4
encryption
in the
Standard
Security
dialog box.

Signing Off Digital Style

The Acrobat Self-Sign Security option in the Security Options enables you to digitally sign a PDF document or to verify that a digital signature in a PDF document is valid. Acrobat Self-Sign Security is what is known in the trade as a *signature handler* that uses a private/public key (also known as PPK) system. In this system, each digital signature is associated with a profile that contains both a *private key* and a *public key*.

The private key in your profile is a password-protected number that enables you to digitally sign a PDF document. The public key, which is embedded within your digital signature, enables others who review the document in Acrobat to verify that your signature is valid. Because others must have access to your public key in order to verify your signature, Acrobat puts your public key in what's called a *certificate* that is shared. The Acrobat Self-Sign Security uses what is known as a *direct trust* system for sharing certificates because it doesn't use a third-party agent (like VeriSign) to do this.

Setting up your profile

The first step to be able to use Acrobat Self-Sign Security for digitally signing PDF documents is to set up your profile. Your profile contains your password along with basic information about your role. You can set up multiple profiles for yourself if you digitally sign documents in different roles.

To create a new user profile, follow these steps:

1. **Choose Tools⇨Self-Sign Security⇨Log In on the Acrobat menus.**

   The Self-Sign Security - Log In dialog box opens.

2. **Click the New User Profile button.**

   The Create New User dialog box (similar to the one shown in Figure 11-3) opens.

3. **Edit the Name, Organization Name, Organization Unit, and Country fields, if necessary (only the Name field must be filled in), in the User Attributes section of the dialog box.**

   Note the profile name that appears in the Name field is the name that appears in the Signatures palette in Acrobat 5 and is used in the naming of the Self-Sign Security profile filename.

4. **Click the Choose a Password field and enter a password of six characters or more.**

5. **Press Tab to select the Confirm Password field and then reenter the password you just entered in the Choose a Password field.**

6. **Click the OK button to open the New Acrobat Self-Sign Security Profile File dialog box. By default, Acrobat names the new profile file by combining the profile name with the `.apf` file extension in the Acrobat folder on Windows and the Acrobat 5.0 folder on the Macintosh. If you wish, edit the filename before clicking the Save button to save the new profile and open the Self-Sign Security - Alert dialog box.**

7. **Click the OK button to close the Self-Sign Security - Alert dialog box. Click the User Settings button if you want to look over or change some of the settings (see "Modifying the user settings in a profile" that follows).**

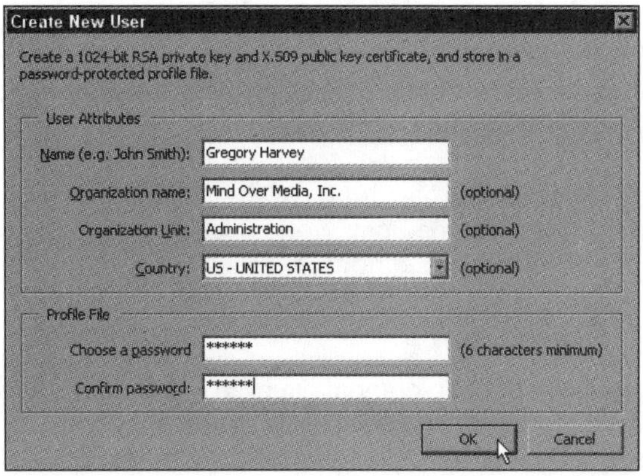

Figure 11-3:
Selecting a password in the Create New User dialog box.

Modifying the user settings in a profile

You can modify the user settings in your profile at any time. You might, for instance, want to associate a graphic with your digital signature (especially one that is actually a picture of your handwritten signature). You also might need to change the password for a profile or want to back up the profile file or change the password timeout options.

Everything you never wanted to know about Acrobat Self-Sign Security

In Acrobat Self-Sign Security, the private key encrypts a checksum that is stored with your signature when you sign a PDF document. The public key decrypts this checksum when anyone verifies the signature (by making sure that the checksum checks out). In case you're the least bit interested, Acrobat Self-Sign Security uses the RSA algorithm for generating private/public key pairs and the X.509 standard for certificates.

Before you can change any settings for your profile, you need to take these steps:

1. **Log in to your profile by choosing Tools⇨Self-Sign Security⇨Log In on the Acrobat menus.**

   The Self-Sign Security - Log In dialog box opens.

2. **Select the filename of your user profile in the User Profile File pop-up menu, enter your password in User Password field, and click the Log In button.**

3. **If the Self-Sign Security alert dialog box appears, click the User Settings button to open the Self-Sign Security - User Settings dialog box for your profile. If this alert dialog box doesn't appear (because you selected its Do Not Show This Message Again check box), choose Tools⇨Self-Sign Security⇨User Settings on the Acrobat menus to open your User Settings dialog box.**

After you're logged into your profile and have the Self-Sign Security - User Settings dialog box for your profile open, you're ready to make any of the changes outlined in the following sections.

Making a backup of your profile

You should always make a backup copy of each profile that you create so that if the original file saved in the Acrobat folder (Acrobat 5.0 on the Mac) ever becomes corrupted, you can still use it to both sign documents and verify other people's signatures. To make a backup of your profile, click the Backup button in the Self-Sign Security - User Settings dialog box for your profile. Then in the Browse for Folder dialog box that appears, click the folder in the Locate Backup Directory list box (preferably on another hard disk, if you have more than one drive on your system or are connected to a network) and click the OK button (Backup on the Mac). Acrobat then displays an alert dialog box indicating in which folder you've successfully backed up your profile file.

Changing your password settings

You can change the password you assigned to your profile, or you can change your password timeout settings (that is, how often you're prompted for a password when working with a PDF document that you've signed). Note that changing your password has no noticeable effect on your digital signature.

To change your password, follow these steps:

1. **Click Change Password in the list box on the left side of the Self-Sign Security - User Settings dialog box for your profile.**

2. **Click the Old Password field and enter your current password.**

3. Click the New Password field and enter the new password you want to set.

4. Click the Confirm Password field and reenter the new password.

5. Click the Apply button to display the alert dialog box telling you that your password has been successfully changed.

By default, Acrobat prompts you for your password each time you digitally sign a PDF document. If you don't ever want to be prompted for your password when signing off on a bunch of PDF files or you want the program to prompt again only after a certain time period (the *timeout* period) has elapsed, you can change the Password Timeout settings as follows:

1. Click Password Timeout in the list box on the left side of the Self-Sign Security - User Settings dialog box for your profile.

2. Select the new timeout setting on the Require Password Entry on Signing pop-up menu.

   The settings on this menu include Never and a fair number of timeout intervals between 30 seconds and 8 hours.

3. Enter your password in the Enter Password (Needed to Apply the Change) field.

4. Click the Apply button to display the alert dialog box telling you that your password timeout has been successfully changed.

If you change the password and password timeout settings for your profile, don't forget to replace all backed-up versions of your profile (the .apd file) with the new version that contains your updated password settings. Should you forget to do this and ever have to rely upon a backup of your profile, you'll have to be able to reproduce your old password in order to log in and sign documents with it.

Adding a graphic to your signature in a signature appearance

Although they're called digital signatures, they don't look anything like signatures you're used to seeing on documents unless you add a picture of your handwritten signature. If you have an image of your handwritten signature or you have a particular picture that you'd like to use as your identifying mark, and the image is saved as a PDF file, you can add it by creating a signature appearance as outlined in the following steps:

1. Click Signature Appearance in the list box on the left side of the Self-Sign Security - User Settings dialog box for your profile.

2. Click the New button.

   The Configure Signature Appearance dialog box, similar to the one shown in Figure 11-4, opens.

3. **Click the Title field and enter a descriptive name for the new signature appearance you're creating.**

4. **Click the Imported Graphic radio button.**

5. **Click the PDF File button.**

   The Select Picture dialog box opens.

6. **Click the Browse button to display the Open dialog box where you open the folder and then click the icon of the PDF file that contains the picture or graphic of your handwritten signature. When you're finished, click the Select button to close the Open dialog box and return to the Select Picture dialog box.**

7. **Check that you've selected the correct image in the Sample area in the Select Picture dialog box and then click the OK button.**

   The Select Picture dialog box closes, and you return to the Configure Signature Appearance dialog box.

8. **Check the preview of your digital signature in the Preview area. To remove various pieces of information from the signature display, deselect their check boxes in the Configure Text area of the dialog box.**

   Keep your eye on the Preview area as you remove individual items.

9. **When you have the digital signature looking the way you want it to appear in the PDF document, click the OK button to close the Configure Signature Appearance dialog box and then click the Close button in the Self-Sign Security - User Settings dialog box.**

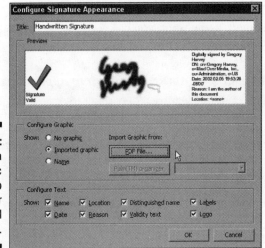

Figure 11-4: Importing a graphic image to use in your digital signature.

Palm handheld users take note

If you have a Palm handheld connected to your computer, you can use the Palm Organizer button (no longer grayed out when Acrobat detects graphic files on the device) in the Configure Signature Appearance dialog box to select a version of your handwritten signature as the graphic to be used in your digital signature in Acrobat. You can create this picture of your handwritten signature by writing with your stylus on the Palm screen and then saving the handwriting as a graphics file on your device. When you click the Palm Organizer button, you can then select the graphics file with your hand-written signature in the Palm Organizer pop-up menu, which appears to the immediate right of the button.

Signing a PDF document

After you've set up your user profile, you're ready to use it to digitally sign off on PDF documents. In digitally signing a PDF document, you add a special signature form field to the document that contains the mark and signing information that you want displayed (see Chapter 14 for more on form fields in PDF documents). The first time a document is signed by you or one of your coworkers, Acrobat saves the PDF file with the signature in a special append-only form. Every time someone digitally signs the document after that, Acrobat saves a new version of the file to which his or her editing changes and signature are appended.

Keep in mind when viewing a PDF document with multiple signatures that you're looking at the latest version of the document with all changes since the first time it was signed. If you want, you can view the original signed version of the signed document side by side with the most current version (by selecting the signatory in the Signatures palette and then clicking the View Signed Version option in the Signatures palette pop-up menu). You can also compare the changes between the original signed version and the current document (by selecting Compare Signed Version to Current Version on the same Signatures palette pop-up menu).

If you ever decide that you should manually save a PDF document that's been digitally signed, don't use the File⇨Save command to do it. Use instead the File⇨Save As command to save a copy of the PDF document under a new file-name. If you use File⇨Save to save a signed PDF document, you automatically invalidate all the signatures in it.

When signing a document, you can sign it invisibly so that no signature form field appears in the PDF document, or you can sign it so that all your signature information appears (as designated in the Configure Signature Appearance dialog box), including any graphic that you've selected.

Invisibly signing a PDF document

To sign a document invisibly so that no signature field appears in the document, you take these steps:

1. **If you're not logged in using your user profile, choose Tools⇨Self-Sign Security⇨Log In and then select the name of your profile on the User Profile File pop-up menu, enter your password in the User Password field, and click the Log In button. (Click OK if the Self-Sign Security - Alert dialog box appears, indicating that you are successfully logged in.)**

2. **Choose Tools⇨Digital Signatures⇨Invisibly Sign Document on the Acrobat menus or, if the Signatures palette is displayed, click Invisibly Sign Document on the Signatures palette pop-up menu.**

   The Self-Security - Sign Document dialog box opens.

3. **Enter your user profile password in the Confirm Password field.**

4. **If you want to add the reason for signing the document, your location, or contact information to the signature information (that can be viewed in the Signatures palette), click the Show Options button to expand the Self-Security - Sign Document dialog box so that it includes the fields shown in Figure 11-5.**

5. **To include the reason for signing the document as part of the signature information, click the reason from the list in the Reason for Signing Document pop-up menu (such as "I am approving this document" or "Document is certified").**

   Note that you can edit the reason you select by clicking the insertion point in the text and then inserting or deleting text as needed.

6. **If you wish to save your location as part of the digital signature information, click the Location field and enter your current location (as in Chicago or Corporate Headquarters).**

7. **If you wish to include contact information such as your telephone number so that coworkers can contact you if they need your certificate in order to verify your digital signature, click the Your Contact Information field and enter that information there.**

8. **Click the Save button to save your changes and signature in the document in its current location with the same filename. Click the Save As button to open the Save As dialog box where you can modify the file's location and/or save it under a new filename.**

After you click the Save button in the Self-Security - Sign Document dialog box (to save the file with the same name) or the Save button in the Save As dialog box (to save the file in a new location or with a new filename), Acrobat saves the PDF document with your invisible signature and then displays a Self-Sign Security - Alert dialog box informing you that you have successfully signed the document.

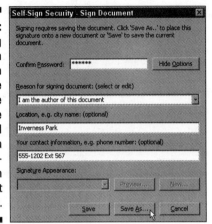

Figure 11-5:
Specifying
information
for an
invisible
signature
in the
expanded
Self-Sign
Security -
Sign
Document
dialog box.

After you click OK to close this dialog box, you can verify that you've signed the document by opening the Signatures palette (by choosing Window⇨Signatures on the Acrobat menus if the palette isn't already displayed in the Navigation pane). To display the detailed information you added to your signature (including the reason, location, and contact information), click the Expand button (the plus sign on Windows and the triangle pointing right on the Mac) to expand the signature information.

Signing a PDF document with a visible signature

If you sign a PDF document invisibly, the only way someone can tell that you've signed it is by looking for your signature in the Signatures palette on the Navigation pane. If you want your coworkers or clients to tell right away that you've signed the document, you can do so by signing the document with a visible signature field. The steps for adding a visible signature are almost identical to those for adding an invisible signature except that you position the signature field by drawing its boundary on the page and can specify what appears in the document by selecting any one of the signature appearances that you created for your signature (for details on creating a signature appearance, see "Adding a graphic to your signature in a signature appearance," earlier in this chapter).

The steps for signing a document with a visible signature field are as follows:

1. **If you're not logged in using your user profile, choose Tools⇨Self-Sign Security⇨Log In and then select the name of your profile on the User Profile File pop-up menu, enter your password in the User Password field, and click the Log In button. (Click OK if the Self-Sign Security - Alert dialog box appears, indicating that you are successfully logged in.)**

2. **Choose Tools⇨Digital Signatures⇨Sign Document on the Acrobat menus or, if the Signatures palette is displayed, click Sign Document on the Signatures palette pop-up menu.**

The Digital Signatures - Alert dialog box opens, telling you that the Digital Signatures tool has been selected for you.

3. **Click the OK button to close the Digital Signatures - Alert dialog box, and then go to the place on the page where you want your signature to appear and drag the cross-hair mouse pointer to draw a bounding box on the page that defines the boundaries of your signature field.**

When you release the mouse button, Acrobat automatically displays the Self-Sign Security - Sign Document dialog box.

4. **Enter your user profile password in the Confirm Password field.**

5. **If you want to add the reason for signing the document, your location, or contact information to the signature information or select a different signature appearance, click the Show Options button to expand the Self-Security - Sign Document dialog box so that it includes the fields shown in Figure 11-5.**

6. **To include the reason for signing the document as part of the signature information, click the reason from the list in the Reason for Signing Document pop-up menu (such as "I am approving this document" or "Document is certified").**

Note that you can edit the reason you select by clicking the insertion point in the text and then inserting or deleting text as needed.

7. **If you wish to save your location as part of the digital signature information, click the Location field and enter your current location (as in Chicago or Corporate Headquarters).**

8. **If you wish to include contact information such as your telephone number so that coworkers can contact you if they need your certificate in order to verify your digital signature, click the Your Contact Information field and enter that information there.**

9. **By default, Acrobat selects Standard Text as the Signature Appearance. To preview how this signature field will appear in the document, click the Preview button. If you wish to select a new appearance for your signature field, select its name in the Signature Appearance pop-up menu. To create a new signature appearance, click the New button. To edit the appearance you selected in the pop-up menu, click the Edit button, which replaces Preview when you select an appearance you created.**

See "Adding a graphic to your signature in a signature appearance," earlier in this chapter, for details on creating or editing signature appearances.

10. **Click the Save button to save your changes and signature in the document in its current location with the same filename. Click the Save As button to open the Save As dialog box where you can modify the file's location and/or save it under a new filename.**

As soon as you click the Save button in the Self-Security - Sign Document
dialog box or the Save button in the Save As dialog box, Acrobat saves the
PDF document with your new signature field and then displays a Self-Sign
Security - Alert dialog box informing you that you have successfully signed
the document.

After you click OK to close this alert dialog box, you can see your signature
right on the document page. Figure 11-6 shows you a PDF document with my
digital signature (using a custom signature appearance that incorporates a
facsimile of my handwritten signature). Note that the Signatures palette
shown in this figure displays a list of the detailed signature information that
also appears (much smaller) in the signature field to the right of the facsimile
of my handwritten signature.

You can always review the signatory information for a particular signature in
its Self-Sign Security - Signature Properties dialog box. You can open this
dialog box for a visible signature by right-clicking (Control+clicking on the
Mac) the signature field and then clicking Properties on the context menu.
You can also open this dialog box (for an invisible or visible signature) by
clicking the signatory's name in the Signatures palette to select it and then
clicking Properties at the bottom of the Signature pop-up menu.

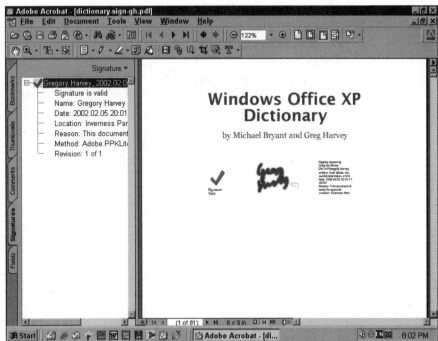

Figure 11-6:
Viewing the
PDF
document
with a new
signature
field.

Signing a PDF document using a predefined signature field

You can also digitally sign a PDF document by using a signature form field that's already been added to it (see Chapter 14 for details on how to add signature form fields to a PDF document). To sign a document in a predefined signature form field, you follow these steps:

1. **If you're not logged in using your user profile, choose Tools⇨Self-Sign Security⇨Log In and then select the name of your profile on the User Profile File pop-up menu, enter your password in the User Password field, and click the Log In button. (Click OK if the Self-Sign Security - Alert dialog box appears, indicating that you are successfully logged in.)**

2. **If the Signatures palette isn't open and selected in the Navigation pane, choose Window⇨Signatures on the Acrobat menus.**

3. **Click the name of the signature field you want to sign in the Signatures palette to highlight it and then click Sign Signature Field on the Signature pop-up menu to open the Self-Sign Security - Sign Document dialog box. If you want to see the field in the document to verify it's the one you want to sign, click the Go to Signature field on this pop-up menu first, and then after verifying the field, reopen this menu and click the Sign Signature Field option.**

4. **Enter your user profile password in the Confirm Password field and then modify the settings in the other fields (Reason for Signing, Location, Your Contact Information, and Signature Appearance) as desired.**

   Refer back to Steps 5 through 9 found in preceding section, "Signing a PDF document with a visible signature," for details.

5. **Click the Save button to save your changes and signature in the selected signature field in its current location with the same filename. Click the Save As button to open the Save As dialog box where you can modify the file's location and/or save it under a new filename.**

As with the other methods of digitally signing a PDF document, after Acrobat finishes saving the signed document, the program displays an alert dialog box informing that you have successfully signed it. As soon as you click the OK button to close the alert dialog box, you can see your signature in the signature form field. Figure 11-7 shows you a PDF document after I signed a signature form field beneath the book title and byline.

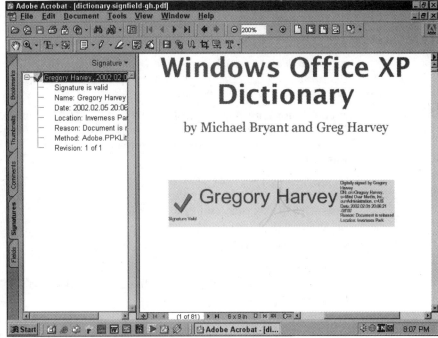

Figure 11-7:
Viewing a
PDF
document
with a
digitally
signed
signature
form field.

Verifying digital signatures

Whenever you add your own signature to a PDF document, Acrobat automatically uses your user profile information to verify your signature as valid (indicated by the green check mark and the text *Signature Valid* underneath it). When you receive a document that has been signed by other people, their signatures will not automatically be recognized as valid when you open the PDF file.

You can then verify their signatures. As part of this process, you need to get in contact with the signatory and verify that one or both of the two so-called fingerprint numbers stored in the public key attached to the signature in your PDF document match the fingerprint numbers in the signatory's public key stored as part of his or her certificate attributes on his or her hard disk. (The two fingerprints are made up of a combination of letters and numbers that make your software serial number look short; the first is called the MD5 Fingerprint, and the second is called the SHA-1 Fingerprint.)

To verify a signature in a PDF document that you have open, take the following steps:

1. **Open the Signatures palette and click the name of the unknown signatory you want to verify (indicated by a yellow question mark before the name) to highlight it, and then click Verify Signature on the Signature pop-up palette menu.**

2. **If you're not logged in, the Self-Sign Security - Validation Status dialog box appears, where you click the Log In button so that Acrobat has access to your list of trusted certificates to use in verifying the unknown signatory's identity.**

3. **In the Self-Sign Security - Log In dialog box, select your user profile in the User Profile File pop-up menu, enter your password in the User Password dialog box, and then click the Log In button.**

4. **Click OK to close the Self-Sign Security - Alert dialog box that appears indicating that you are successfully logged in.**

5. **If the unknown signatory has not been added to your list of trusted certificates, Acrobat next displays the Self-Sign Security - Validation Status dialog box.**

   This dialog box appears right after you complete Step 1 if you're already logged in and the signatory isn't in the list.

6. **Click the Verify Identity button.**

   The Verify Identity dialog box (similar to the one shown in Figure 11-8) opens.

7. **Use the contact information (if listed) to get ahold of the signatory (preferably by telephone) to verify the MD5 and/or the SHA-1 Fingerprint numbers listed at the bottom of the Verify Identity dialog box.**

   To find these numbers to read off to you, the signatory must log in to his or her user profile in Acrobat 5 and then click the User Settings button to open the User Settings dialog box. Then he or she needs to click the Details button in the Certificates section of the User Information portion of the dialog box to display the fingerprint information in a Certificates Attributes dialog box.

8. **If the fingerprint numbers on your screen match the numbers given to you over the phone, click the Add to List button to add the person to your list of trusted certificates and to validate the selected signature in the PDF document.**

You can quickly verify individual signatures for the people you've added to your Trusted Certificates list (see "Adding certificates to your Trusted

Certificates list" that follows) by simply double-clicking their signature fields. Acrobat will quickly search your list and, upon finding the person's certificate, display a Self-Sign Security - Validation Status alert dialog box informing you that the signature is valid. You can also use this technique on your own signatures in the event that they show up as unknown signatures when you reopen the PDF document even when you're still logged into your user profile. To update all the signatures in your PDF at one time, simply choose Tools⇨Digital Signatures⇨Verify All Signatures on the Acrobat menus or click the Verify All Signatures option on the Signatures palette pop-up menu.

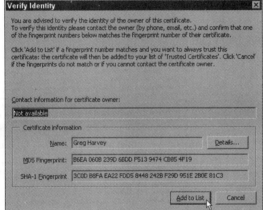

Figure 11-8:
Verifying
fingerprint
numbers in
the Verify
Identity
dialog box.

Exchanging certificates with associates

You can simplify the process of verifying signatures in the PDF files you review by having all the review team members exchange copies of their Self-Sign Security certificates. Acrobat makes this easy by adding two controls to the User Information portion of the User Settings dialog box for your user profile. The first is an Export to File button that you can use to make a copy of the certificate file that others can import into their Trusted Certificates list (for example, you can use this option if you and your coworkers are on the same network and share access to certain folders). The second is an E-Mail button that you can use to send a copy of your certificate to team members in a new e-mail message.

When you click the Export to File button, Acrobat opens an Export Certificate As dialog box where you can designate the drive and folder on which the copy of your certificate is saved (saved in a special Acrobat Self-Sign key file format that uses a .fdf file extension) when you click the Save button. When you click the E-Mail button, Acrobat opens an E-Mail Certificate dialog box similar to the one shown in Figure 11-9.

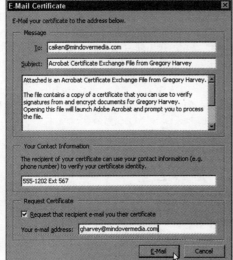

Figure 11-9:
Sending
your
certificate
via an
e-mail
message.

To send the e-mail, fill in the recipient's e-mail address in the To field and
enter your telephone number in the Your Contact Information field. If you
want to request that your recipient send you a copy of his or her Self-Sign
Security certificate, click the Request That Recipient E-Mail You Their
Certificate (sic) check box and then enter your e-mail address in the Your
E-Mail Address field below before you click the E-Mail button.

Figure 11-10 shows you the typical e-mail message that the recipient receives
when you click the E-Mail button. Note that this e-mail not only attaches a copy
of your Self-Sign Security certificate file but also instructs the recipient that
opening the attached file will automatically launch Acrobat 5 and prompt the
recipient to process the file (by verifying those lovely fingerprint numbers).

Adding certificates to your Trusted Certificates list

The way that you add the certificates that you receive to your Trusted
Certificates list depends upon how you receive them. If you receive an e-mail
message with a certificate attached, you can launch Acrobat, verify the certificate, and add the certificate to your Trusted Certificates list all by simply
opening the certificate file attached to the message in your e-mail program
(in most programs by double-clicking the file attachment icon).

When Acrobat launches, it displays the Self-Sign Security - Certificate
Exchange dialog box. To add the certificate to your list, you click the Add to
List button to open the Verify Identity dialog box (refer to Figure 11-8). You
can then get in contact with the person who sent you the certificate to match
and verify the fingerprint numbers before you add the sender's certificate to
your list.

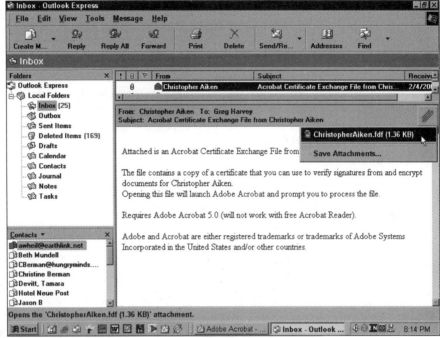

If you have access to someone's Self-Sign Security certificate file on your computer system, you can add it to your Trusted Certificates list by using the Import from File button in the Trusted Certificates portion of your User Settings dialog box. To do this, you follow these steps:

1. **If you're not logged in using your user profile, choose Tools⇨Self-Sign Security⇨Log In and then select the name of your profile on the User Profile File pop-up menu, enter your password in the User Password field, and click the Log In button.**

2. **Click the User Settings button in the Self-Sign Security - Alert dialog box that appears indicating that you're logged in.**

   The Self-Sign Security - User Settings dialog box for your user profile opens.

3. **Click Trusted Certificates in the list box on the left.**

   The list of your Trusted Certificates appears on the right.

4. **Click the Import from File button to open the Import Certificate dialog box where you open the folder and select the Self-Sign Security certificate file icon (marked with a .fdf extension on Windows) before clicking OK.**

   Doing this opens the Verify Identity dialog box showing the MD5 and SHA-1 fingerprint numbers along with the name and contact information so that you can phone the person up and match fingerprint numbers.

5. **Verify the fingerprint numbers and then click the Add to List button.**

   The Verify Identity dialog box closes, and an alert dialog box appears, indicating that the person's certificate has been successfully added to your Trusted Certificates list.

6. **Click OK to close the alert dialog box and return to your User Settings dialog box where you will now see the name of the person you just added to your Trusted Certificates list.**

7. **Click the Close button to close your User Settings dialog box.**

Comparing signed documents

As I mention earlier in the chapter, each time a person digitally signs a PDF document that already has one signature, Acrobat saves the changes and signature of each subsequent signatory in a special appended version of the file. You can then compare the various versions to note what changes, if any, each signatory made.

Acrobat notes when a PDF document that you've sent out for subsequent signatures comes back to you with changes by adding a Document Was Modified item to the Signatures palette. You can then display the details of the modifications by clicking the Expand button (with the plus sign on Windows and the triangle pointing to the right on the Mac). Note that the detailed change items shown in the expanded list are purely informational and do not perform as bookmarks.

To have Acrobat do a side-by-side comparison of the versions to let you visually compare the changes, click View Signed Version on the Signatures palette pop-up menu. Acrobat then displays the original version of the PDF file in a Document pane on the left while simultaneously displaying the most current version of the file in a Document pane on the right, tiled horizontally for a side-by-side comparison (as shown in Figure 11-11). You can then scroll through the pages visually noting the differences. When you're finished checking the changes, you close the original version on the left by clicking its document window's Close button and maximize the latest version on the right by clicking its document window's Maximize button.

If you would prefer, you can have Acrobat do a page-by-page comparison and locate all the changes between the latest signed version and the original. To do this, you click the Compare Signed Version to Current Document option on the Signatures palette pop-up menu. Acrobat then performs a page-by-page comparison and creates a second PDF document containing only the pages that have changed. These changed pages are displayed side by side.

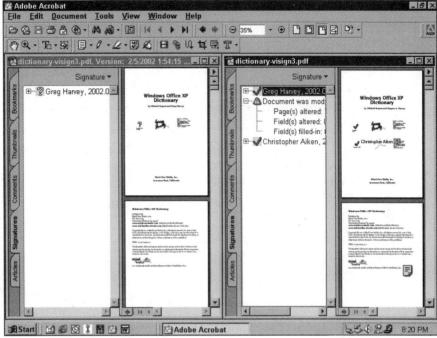

Figure 11-11:
Comparing
different
signed
versions
of the
same PDF
document.

When you have finished comparing these pages, you can close this newly created document by pressing Ctrl+W (⌘+W). You can then save it in its own PDF file by clicking the Yes button in the alert dialog box asking you if you want to save the changes before closing. If you have no further need for this comparison PDF file, you can click the No button to abandon the comparison document and just return to the most up-to-date signed version of the PDF document.

Encrypting PDF Files

The last and most secure type of security that you can add to your PDF documents employs the Acrobat Self-Sign Security system that you use to digitally sign documents along with the list of Trusted Certificates in your user profile. When you encrypt a PDF document with Acrobat Self-Sign Security, no one has access to the document other than those you specifically designate as recipients, and you can only designate as recipients those persons who are already on your Trusted Certificates list.

The steps for encrypting a PDF document with Acrobat Self-Sign Security are as follows:

1. **Choose File⇨Document Security or press Ctrl+Alt+S (⌘+Option+S on the Mac).**

   The Document Security dialog box opens.

2. **Click Acrobat Self-Sign Security on the Security Options pop-up menu.**

   The Self-Sign Security - Encryption Settings dialog box opens.

3. **In the Trusted Certificates list box on the left, click the name of the person you want to add to the Recipients list box on the right, and then click the Add button.**

4. **Click the name of the newly added recipient to highlight it in the Recipients list box.**

5. **Click the User Access button.**

   By default, Acrobat grants the recipient full access to the PDF document, whose user permissions include general editing, commenting and form field authoring privileges, the ability to print the document at any print resolution, and full copying and extraction privileges.

6. **To restrict the recipient's user permissions in some way, click the User Permissions button.**

   The User Permissions dialog box opens.

7. **Limit the permissions by deselecting the Enable Content Access for the Visually Impaired check box and/or the Allow Content Copying and Extraction check box and/or by selecting new options in the Changes Allowed and Printing pop-up menus before you click OK.**

8. **Repeat Steps 3 through 7 (as they apply) to add your other recipients from the Trusted Certificates list box and set their user permissions in the Recipients list box.**

9. **After you've added all the recipients and set their user permissions, click the OK button.**

   The Self-Sign Security - Encryption Settings dialog box closes, and you return to the Document Security dialog box.

10. **Click the Close button in the Document Security dialog box.**

11. **Save the encrypted PDF document. Choose File⇨Save to save the Acrobat Self-Sign Security encryption settings to the current document. Or choose File⇨Save As and edit the filename and/or folder location of the encrypted document before clicking the Save button.**

After you save your PDF file encrypted with Acrobat Self-Sign Security, you can distribute copies to all the people you added to the Recipients list. When someone on the list tries to open the encrypted file, Acrobat displays the Self-Sign Security - Log In dialog box, where the user selects his or her user profile and enters his or her user password. When the user clicks the Log In button to close the Self-Sign Security - Log In dialog box, followed by the OK button to close the Self-Sign Security - Alert dialog box confirming a successful logon, Acrobat checks the user's public key against the certificate information (specifically the MD 5 and SHA-1 fingerprints) in the encrypted file. When Acrobat finds they match, it then opens the PDF document. The user then has access to the opened document according to user permissions that you set. To check these permissions, the user can right-click (Control+ click on the Mac) the Document Encrypted key that now appears on the Document pane status bar, click Document Security on the context menu, and then click the Display Settings button in the Document Security dialog box.

If someone not on the Recipients list attempts to open a PDF document that's encrypted with Acrobat Self-Sign Security, upon logging in, he or she will receive the Acrobat Self-Sign Security - Alert dialog box with the message, "You do not have access rights to this encrypted document," and when the user clicks OK to clear this dialog box, the document will fail to open.

Chapter 12

Extracting Text and Graphics from PDF Files

Acrobat 5 is a great tool for distributing PDF documents for review and annotation. As you know if you read any of the sections in Chapter 10 on editing, Acrobat is not so great for making any but the most simple of editing changes, and when it comes to changes in the basic design and layout, you can just forget it. This means that you have to rely on the native applications (such as your word processing, spreadsheet, page layout, and image editing programs) for making significant edits to the content and structure of PDF documents.

This is fine so long as you have access to the original files from which the PDF document was distilled, but what about the times when you can't find or never had the original electronic documents in their native file formats? In those situations, you need to rely on Acrobat's extraction features to take out the contents and as much structure as possible from the original PDF files and save them in file formats that other more edit-friendly software programs can handle.

In this chapter, you explore the various ways in Acrobat 5 for repurposing your PDF documents by pulling out the PDF file text, specific text elements, and graphics and saving them in file formats that other popular application programs can open.

Extracting PDF Style

You can choose three basic methods when extracting content from your PDF files:

- ✔ Copying and pasting discrete sections of text and selected graphics by using the Windows or Mac OS Clipboard or dragging and dropping between open windows

- ✔ Saving the text in the entire PDF file in a completely new file format using the File⇨Save As menu command

- ✔ Exporting all the graphic images in the PDF file to separate graphics files in a new graphics file format compatible with your layout or image editing programs using the File⇨Export⇨Extract Images As menu commands

Extracting blocks of text

Before you can copy sections of text in a PDF document to the Clipboard or another open document, you need to select the text in the PDF document. To select text in a PDF document, you use one of the three different Text Select tools found on the Basic Tools menu:

- ✔ **Text Select Tool (V)** to select lines of text by dragging through them

- ✔ **Column Select Tool (Shift+V)** to select all or part of a column of text by drawing a bounding box around the text

- ✔ **Table/Formatted Text Select Tool (Shift+V)** to select a table or block of text with its formatting by drawing a bounding box around the table or text block

When you use the Text Select or Column Select tool to select lines or columns of text in a PDF document, you can then copy the selected text to the Clipboard by using the Edit⇨Copy menu command or by pressing Ctrl+C (⌘+C on the Mac). After you've copied the text to the Clipboard, you can switch to a document open in another program that's running and then paste the copied text into the file by using that program's Edit⇨Paste menu command or by pressing Ctrl+V (⌘+V on the Mac).

Using drag-and-drop to copy text

Instead of copying and pasting to and from the Clipboard, you can just drag the selected text from the PDF file open in an Acrobat window to a new document open in another program window. Figures 12-1 and 12-2 illustrate how this method works.

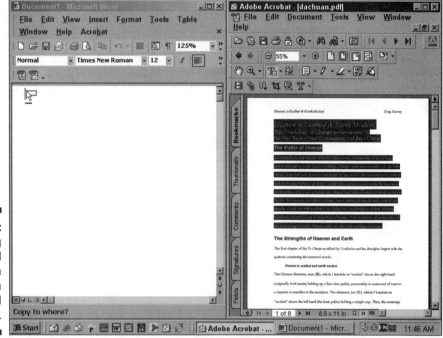

Figure 12-1:
Dragging
selected
text from a
PDF file to a
new Word
document.

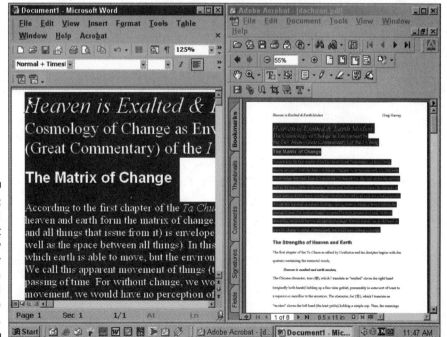

Figure 12-2:
The Word
document
window
after
dropping the
selected
text into
place.

In Figure 12-1, in the PDF document open in the Acrobat program window on the right, I dragged the Text Select tool through the lines with the title and the first paragraph of text to select it. Then I dragged this text selection to the new document window open in Microsoft Word on the left by positioning the arrowhead mouse pointer (with the outline of the text selection) at the very beginning. Figure 12-2 shows what happened when I released the mouse button to drop the text selection into place in the new Word document.

Selecting columns of text

The Column Select tool (the second one on the More Tools pop-up menu attached to the Text Select tool located on the Basic Tools toolbar) enables you to select complete columns of text without having to worry about selecting text in any adjacent columns on the page that you don't want to include. Use this tool when you need to copy all or part of columns on a single page of a PDF document that uses newspaper columns.

To select a column of text with the Column Select tool, you drag the I-beam pointer that appears in the center of a dotted rectangle to draw a bounding box around the text in the column or columns you want to copy. Figures 12-3 and 12-4 illustrate making a typical column selection with the Column Select tool.

Figure 12-3 shows a page of a PDF document set in two newspaper columns. In this figure, I have used the Column Text tool to draw a bounding box around all the text in the first column. Figure 12-4 shows what happens when I release the mouse button — all the text within the bounding box now becomes selected for copying to the Clipboard or dragging to a document in another program window.

Keep in mind that you can't use the Column Select tool to select text in columns that span different pages of a PDF document. If you need to copy columns of text in a PDF file that span more than a single page, you need to use the Text Select tool to do it. The Text Select tool enables you to drag through text that spans different pages even if the text is in different columns (you just have to be careful when doing it).

Selecting tables and formatted text

The third text tool is called the Table/Formatted Text tool, and as its name implies, you use this tool when you want to copy text set in a table or copy text along with its formatting (including font, font size, text color, alignment, line spacing, and indents when saving in an RTF — Rich Text Format — file format). To use the Table/Formatted Text tool, you use its cross-hair mouse pointer to draw a bounding box around a table or lines of text that you want to select (very much like selecting columns with the Column Select tool).

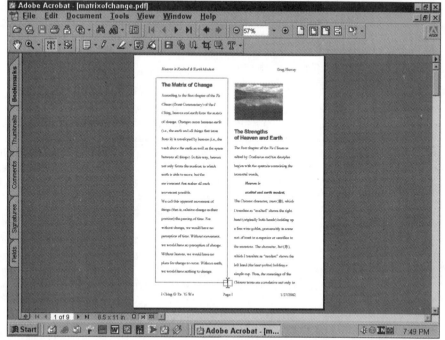

Figure 12-3:
Drawing a
bounding
box with the
Column Text
tool to
select the
text in the
first column.

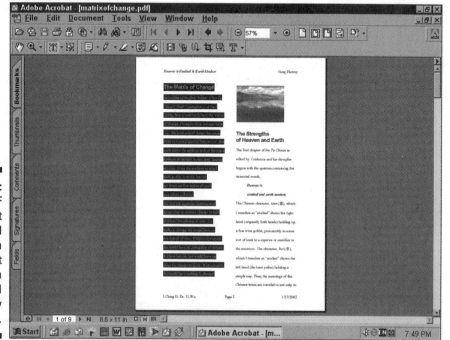

Figure 12-4:
A PDF
document
showing all
the text in
the first
column
selected
and ready
for copying.

As soon as you release the mouse button, Acrobat encloses the selected text or table in either a heavy blue outline (for tables) or green outline (for text). The program also labels the type of selection as Table, Text - Flow, or Text - Preserve. This label appears in the upper-left corner of the outline of the bounding box.

When Acrobat identifies a text selection with the Table label, it maintains the structure of the table by preserving the layout of the data in rows and columns of cells. If you then save the table data in the RTF file format for use in a word-processed document, the table maintains this layout in the new document. If you save the table data in the ANSI (American National Standards Institute) text file format, which is the default format selected by Acrobat, the program maintains the table structure by separating the data items with tabs and hard returns. This creates what is often called a *tab delimited text file* that most database and spreadsheet programs can convert easily into their own native file formats.

When Acrobat identifies a selection with the Text - Flow label, the program ignores the line breaks that appear in the PDF document, preserving the paragraph breaks in the text. When the program identifies a selection with the Text - Preserve label, Acrobat treats all the apparent line breaks in the document text as hard returns. If you save such a text selection as an RTF file, Acrobat preserves the horizontal positioning of the text in the new file with tabs.

If Acrobat ever mislabels a table or text selection that you make with the Table/Formatted Text tool (such as labeling a table as Text - Flow, or lines of text that need to wrap freely as Text - Preserve), you can change the label. Just right-click (Control+click on the Mac) within the heavy blue or green border to display the context menu. To convert Text - Flow or Text - Preserve to Table, click Table on the context menu. To convert Table or Text - Preserve to Text - Flow, choose Text⇨Flow on the context menu. To convert Table or Text - Flow to Text - Preserve, choose Text⇨Preserve Line Breaks on the context menu.

Saving table or formatted text in a new file

Unlike when selecting text with the Text Select or Column Select tool, after you highlight a table or blocks of text with the Table/Formatted Text tool, you can not only copy it to the Clipboard but also save the selection into a new file format. To do this, you right-click (Control+click on the Mac) the text or table selection and then click Save As on the context menu to open the Save As dialog box, where you specify the folder, filename, and type of file format in which to save the selection.

Select the Rich Text Format when you want to open the table or formatted text in a word processor such as Microsoft Word. Stay with the ANSI Text default file format when you're saving a table of data and you want to be able to import that data into a spreadsheet program such as Microsoft Excel or a database program such as FileMaker Pro.

Copying PDF tables into word processors and spreadsheets

The Table/Formatted Text tool makes it a joy to copy tables from PDF files into word-processed documents or spreadsheets. Figures 12-5 and 12-6 illustrate what happens when you drag a table selected with the Table/Formatted Text tool into a new Word document (Figure 12-5) and then into a blank worksheet in a new Excel workbook (Figure 12-6).

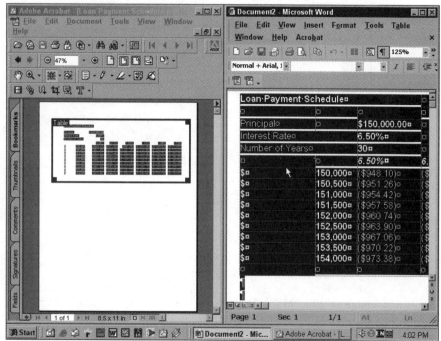

Figure 12-5: Dragging a table selected with the Table/Formatted Text Select tool to a new Word document.

As you can see in Figure 12-5, Microsoft Word automatically recognizes and preserves the table structure by creating a new Word table (indicated by the *cell indicators* — the squares with circles in them). Even more importantly, Word has maintained the number formatting as well (indicated by the dollar signs, commas, percent signs, and parentheses for the negative values).

In Figure 12-6, you see that Excel had no problem recognizing and correctly interpreting the layout and formatting of the table data as well. It immediately inserted the incoming table data into the correct worksheet cells while maintaining the correct cell formatting. (By the way, in case you aren't yet an Excel user, the #### symbols in the new worksheet merely indicate that the columns are not wide enough to display their values — these are not error indicators and are easily disposed of by widening the columns.)

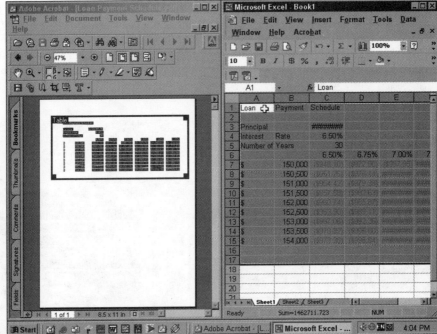

Figure 12-6:
Dragging
a table
selected
with the
Table/
Formatted
Text Select
tool into a
new Excel
workbook.

Editing the Table/Formatted preferences

If you aren't particularly fond of the dark blue for indicating and labeling
table selections and dark green for text, you can change those and a bunch of
other settings in the Table/Formatted Text Preferences dialog box. To open
this dialog box (shown in Figure 12-7), you choose Edit⇨Preferences⇨
Table/Formatted Text on the Acrobat menus.

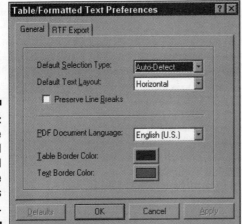

Figure 12-7:
Setting the
formatted
text and
table
preferences
in Acrobat.

As you can see in Figure 12-7, this dialog box contains two tabs: General and RTF Export. The General tab is where you change the default selection type, specify the language of the PDF document, and specify the colors to be used for table and text selection borders and labels.

By default, Acrobat uses Auto-Detect to attempt to automatically identify the correct selection (something it doesn't always do successfully). If you want to make text or table the new default, you can do so by selecting Text or Table on the Default Selection Type pop-up menu. If you select Text as the new default, and you want Acrobat to always maintain the line breaks as they appear in the document, click the Preserve Line Breaks check box as well.

To select a new language for the PDF document, click the language in the PDF Document Language pop-up menu. To select a new text border or table border color, click the Table Border Color button or the Text Border Color button and then click the new color on the Color pop-up palette that appears before clicking OK.

The RTF Export tab contains a bunch of check box options (all of which are selected) that determine which kinds of character formatting (Font Name, Font Style, Font Size, Text Color, and Superscripts) and which kinds of paragraph formatting (Alignment, Line Spacing, Space Before/After, and Indentation) to preserve when you save the selected text or table in an RTF file. You will rarely, if ever, need to deselect any of these options because they are all important to some extent in preserving the layout and formatting in the new RTF document.

Selecting and copying graphic images

You use the Graphics Select tool located at the tail end of the Basic Tools toolbar to select individual graphic images for copying. When you select the Graphics Select tool, the mouse pointer becomes a cross-hair that you use to draw a bounding box around the graphic. After you've enclosed the entire graphic (and you don't have to worry if your marquee is a little larger than the image borders), you can copy the graphic to a new document open in another program either by copying it to the Clipboard (Edit⇨Copy) or by dragging it to a new document window.

Keep in mind when you copy images to the Clipboard that Acrobat uses the graphics resolution of your monitor and that set for the Clipboard by your computer's operating system rather than the resolution of the images as saved in the PDF document (which could well be a lot higher than either of the two). Also, be aware that all images you copy into the Clipboard are automatically converted onto the Clipboard as pixels even if they are saved as vector (or line) graphics in the PDF file.

Saving entire PDF files in a new file format

Copying and pasting and dragging and dropping are fine as long as you only need to work with portions of text in the PDF document. In those situations where you need to repurpose all the text in a PDF file, you simply use the File⇨Save As command. In the Save As dialog box that appears, select the appropriate file format in the Save as Type pop-up menu and then click the Save button.

Saving PDF files as text files

When saving PDF files as text files for use with text editors and word processing software, you have a choice between saving the PDF document in a Plain Text or an RTF. Select Plain Text when your only concern is getting the raw text into a more editable format. Select the RTF format whenever you want to preserve not only the document text but also as much formatting as possible. Always select the RTF file type when saving the text of PDF documents that you intend to edit with Microsoft Word.

Keep in mind that although RTF attempts to preserve much formatting from the PDF document, it is far from flawless, and in most cases you will end up having to do extensive reformatting in the resulting Word document. On those occasions, perhaps you can content yourself with the fact that you didn't have to retype any of the text.

Saving PDF files as HTML files

Acrobat 5 now supports a new Adobe plug-in that enables you to save your PDF files in the HTML (Hypertext Markup Language) file format, in essence turning them into Web pages. To download and install this Save as XML plug-in, visit the following Web page on the Adobe Web site:

```
www.adobe.com/products/acrobat/main.html
```

After you have the Save as XML plug-in installed, Acrobat lets you choose between saving your PDF document in various versions of the HTML file format and in the newer XML (Extensible Markup Language) file format, which is used by many Web sites to improve Web page layout and interactivity.

Exporting images in various graphics formats

Just as you use the File⇨Save As menu command to save all the text in new text or HTML format, you can use the File⇨Export⇨Export Images As command to save all the graphic images in the current PDF document in one of three different file formats that you select from the Export Images As submenu:

- ✔ **JPEG (Joint Photographic Experts Group) Files** for true color compressed images

- ✔ **PNG (Portable Network Graphics) Files** for compressed bitmap images

- ✔ **TIFF (Tagged Image File Format)** for compressed bitmap images using both text and graphics (TIFF is usually the format used to store the paper pages you scan)

After you select a graphics file format from the Export Images As submenu, Acrobat then displays the Extract Images and Save As dialog box where you select the drive and folder where you want the images saved. As soon as you click the Save button, the program goes through the current document and saves all the images in separate graphics files in the selected folder in the designated graphics file format.

Acrobat names these new graphics files by adding sequential numbers (starting with 0001) to the filename of the original PDF document (and tacking on the filename extensions `.jpg` for JPEG, `.png` for PNG, and `.tif` for TIFF files on Windows). You can rename these numerical files with descriptive, more meaningful filenames either in Windows or the Mac OS or after opening them in an image editing program such Adobe Photoshop 6.0.

Chapter 13

Cataloging and Distributing PDF Files

● ●

In This Chapter

▶ Preparing your PDF document collection

▶ Modifying the Catalog Preferences

▶ Creating the indexes for a PDF document collection

▶ Searching the PDF files in a document collection

▶ Circulating your PDF document collections

● ●

As you continue on your journey toward the goal of a truly paperless office, your collections of PDF files will undoubtedly grow exponentially. To keep on top of this burgeoning mountain of electronic information, you can start cataloging your PDF documents by organizing them into discrete collections and then creating indexes that make the collection fast and easy to search. Catalogs provide a perfect way to archive the PDF files that are no longer in current use but contain valuable information that you may need to find and reuse at anytime in the future.

In this chapter, you discover the ins and outs of creating, maintaining, and searching PDF document collections. In addition, you pick up some pointers on how to package and distribute your collections for archiving or for general use on your network.

Cataloging 101

Cataloging your PDF files entails two basic steps: organizing your PDF files into a document collection ready for indexing and then building the index. The indexes that you build for your collection are what make it possible to search for information across all the PDF files it contains and are also responsible for speeding up the search significantly.

Creating the PDF document collection

The keys to creating a successful PDF document collection are organizing the files and preparing them for indexing. To organize the files, you copy or move them all into a single folder (you can organize files into subfolders within this folder, if necessary). Before copying or moving the files into the collection folder, make sure you're using only final versions of the PDF documents, which contain all necessary bookmarks, links, and form fields, and for which you've completed editorial review and made the final touch-up edits as well.

In preparing the files for indexing, you should make sure that you've added the title, subject, author, and keywords metadata for each PDF document, and in the case of documents that require a user password to open, you must remove the password because Acrobat 5 cannot catalog PDF files that are password-protected.

Checking and editing the metadata

To check a PDF document's metadata and, if necessary, add this information, you take these steps:

1. **Launch Acrobat 5 and then open the PDF file whose metadata you want to check.**

2. **Choose File⇨Document Properties⇨Summary on the Acrobat menus or press Ctrl+D (⌘+D on the Mac).**

   The Document Summary dialog box for the file (similar to the one shown in Figure 13-1) opens.

3. **Add to or edit the Title, Subject, Author, and Keywords fields as needed to make it easier to identify and find the document later.**

4. **Click OK to close the Document Summary dialog box.**

5. **Choose File⇨Save on the Acrobat menus to save any changes you made to the document's metadata.**

Optimizing PDF files for indexing

When creating a collection you want to make searchable across a network, especially in a cross-platform environment (that is, one that networks both Windows and Mac machines), you should consider renaming the files using the so-called eight-dot-three file naming convention (no more than eight characters for the main filename with no spaces and a three-character filename extension separated by a period). Also, make sure that all PDF files in the collection use the .pdf filename extension (necessary on the Windows platform). Finally, you can optimize indexing and speed up searches by splitting long documents up into smaller files, each of which contains a chapter or major section.

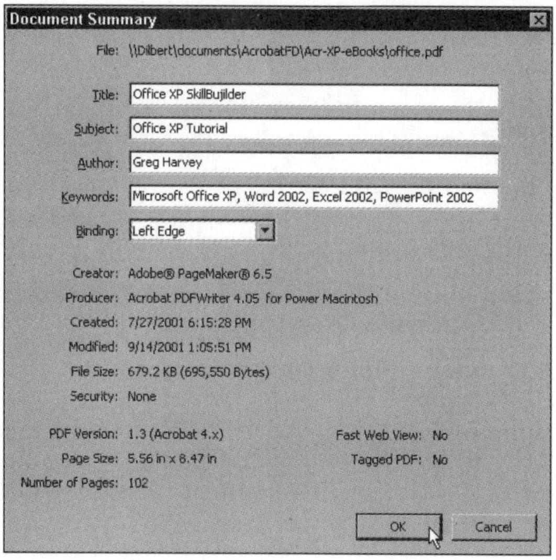

Figure 13-1:
Entering the
title,
subject,
author, and
keywords
metadata
for a PDF
document.

Removing password protection and checking the extraction file permission

Because Acrobat can't search password-protected files, you must remove the user passwords from all files in the collection. Also, you need to make a change to the Options section of the General Preferences if some of the file permissions in any of the documents prevent the user from doing content copying or extraction.

To be able to remove a user password from a PDF document, you not only have to have access to the user password (or you can't open it) but also have access to the master password (or you can't get rid of the user password). Assuming that you're armed with both, you follow these steps to clear the user password:

1. **Launch Acrobat and open the PDF document whose password you want to remove.**

   Acrobat responds by displaying the Password dialog box in which you must successfully enter the user password.

2. **Enter the user password when prompted in the Password dialog box and then click OK to open the document.**

3. **Choose File⇨Document Security or press Ctrl+Alt+S (⌘+Option+S on the Mac).**

   The Document Security dialog box opens.

4. **Click the Change Settings button.**

   Acrobat responds by displaying another Password dialog box where you must successfully enter the master password.

5. **Enter the master password in the Password dialog box and click OK.**

   The Standard Security dialog box appears.

6. **Click the Password Required to Open Document check box to remove the check mark and simultaneously clear the User Password field.**

7. **Check to see if the No Content Copying or Extraction, Disable Accessibility check box is selected because if it is, you'll need to make a further change to the General preference settings.**

8. **Click the OK button to close the Standard Security dialog box and then click the Close button to close the Document Security dialog box.**

9. **Choose File⇨Save to save your security changes to the PDF document.**

If any of the PDF files in your collection use the No Content Copying or Extraction, Disable Accessibility security option, you must also make a change to the Options section of the General Preferences to select the Certified Plug-ins Only check box as follows:

1. **Choose Edit⇨Preferences⇨General or press Ctrl+K (⌘+K on the Mac) to open the Preferences dialog box.**

2. **Click Options in the list box on the left.**

3. **Click the Certified Plug-ins Only check box.**

4. **Click the OK button to close the Preferences dialog box.**

Building an index for your collection

After you've prepared your document collection, you're ready to build the index for it. When you create the index, you specify the folder that contains the PDF document collection (this is also the folder in which the index file and its support folder must reside). You also can specify up to a maximum of 500 words that you want excluded from the index (such as *a, an, the, and, or,* and the like) and have numbers excluded from the index to speed up your searches. Words that you exclude from an index are called *stop words.* Keep in mind that while specifying stop words does give you a smaller and more efficient index (estimated at between 10 and 15 percent smaller), it also prevents you and other users from searching the collection for phrases that include these stop words (as in "in the matter of Smith and James").

When specifying search options for the new index, you can also enable or disable any of the following three word search options:

✔ **Case Sensitive** to limit matches in a search to the words in the document collection that exhibit a strict upper- and lowercase correspondence to the ones for which you're searching

✔ **Sounds Like** to expand matches in a search to proper names in the document collection that sound like the ones for which you're searching (this enables you to search for a name without knowing the exact spelling)

✔ **Word Stemming** to enable the Word Assistant preview (that you can use to refine searches — see "Refining your search" that follows) and expand matches in a search to words in the document collection that use the same word stem (so that occurrences of *foremost*, *foreman*, and *foresee* in the collection all match when you specify *fore* as the search term).

Note that all these word search options are automatically selected when you build a new index. Keep in mind, however, that even when you build an index that uses all of them, you still have to individually select them to use them when you do a search. By disabling these options at the time you build an index, you make them unavailable in all searches that you perform with that index.

To build a new index, you follow these steps:

1. **Launch Acrobat and then choose Tools⇨Catalog from the menus (you don't have to have any of the files in the PDF document collection open at the time you do this).**

   The Adobe Catalog dialog box (shown later in Figure 13-4) opens.

2. **Click the New Index button in the Adobe Catalog dialog box.**

   The New Index Definition dialog box (similar to the one shown in Figure 13-2) opens.

3. **Enter a descriptive title that clearly and concisely identifies the new index in the Index Title field.**

4. **Click the Index Description field and enter a complete description of the index.**

   This description can include the stop words, search options supported, and the kinds of documents indexed.

5. **Click the Add button to the right of the Include These Directories list box and then select the folder that contains your PDF document collection in the Browse for Folder dialog box and click OK.**

6. **To specifically exclude any folders that reside within the folder that contains your PDF document collection (the one whose directory path is now listed in the Include These Directories list box), click the Add**

button to the right of the Exclude These Subdirectories list box, and then select the subfolders of the folder you selected in Step 5 and click OK. Repeat this step for any other subfolders that need to be excluded (actually, you should be able to skip this step entirely because the folder that contains your PDF document collection really shouldn't have any other folders in it).

7. **To specify stop words for the index or to disable any of the word search options, click the Options button.**

   The Options dialog box (shown in Figure 13-3) opens.

8. **To specify a stop word that is not included in the index, enter a term in the Word field and click the Add button. Repeat this step until you've added all the stop words you don't want indexed.**

9. **Click the Do Not Include Numbers check box to exclude numbers from the index.**

10. **Click any of the three Word options (Case Sensitive, Sounds Like, and Word Stemming) to disable them.**

11. **Click the Optimize for CD-ROM check box if you plan to back up the PDF document collection onto a CD-ROM.**

12. **In the rare event that your PDF document collection contains PDF files saved in the original Acrobat 1.0 file format, click the Add IDs to Acrobat 1.0 PDF Files check box.**

13. **Click OK to close the Options dialog box and return to the New Index Definition dialog box.**

14. **Check over the fields in the New Index Definition dialog box and, if everything looks okay, click the Build button.**

    The Save Index File dialog box opens.

15. **If you want, replace the generic filename index.pdx in the File Name (Name on the Mac) field with a more descriptive filename and then click the Save button. When editing the filename, be sure that you don't select a new folder in which to save the file (it must be in the same folder as your PDF document collection) and, on Windows, don't remove the .pdx (for Portable Document Index) that identifies it as a special Acrobat index file.**

Acrobat responds by displaying the Adobe Catalog dialog box that keeps you informed of its progress as it builds the new index. When the Progress field reaches 100% and the program finishes building the index, you can then click the Close button to close the Adobe Catalog dialog box and return to the Acrobat program, where you can start using the index in searching the files in the PDF document collection. Note that when Acrobat builds an index, it not only creates a new index file (with the .pdx filename extension on Windows) but also creates a new support folder using the same filename as the index file.

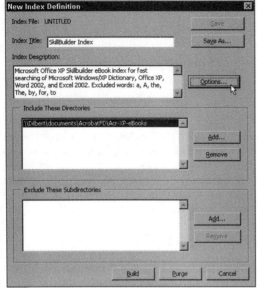

Figure 13-2:
Specifying
what folder
to include
in a new
index in the
New Index
Definition
dialog box.

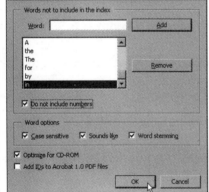

Figure 13-3:
Specifying
stop words
and word
search
options in
the Options
dialog box.

Rebuilding an index

If you modify a PDF document collection for which you've created an index
by removing or adding files to the collection, you must rebuild the index in
order to have Acrobat search its entire contents. Before you rebuild an index
for a collection from which you have removed some PDF files, you need to
purge the index. When you do this, Acrobat actually removes the files no
longer part of the collection from the index rather than just marking them as
invalid. Purging them from the index streamlines it considerably and makes
searching it as fast as possible.

There is, however, one hitch to purging an index. Acrobat delays purging an index for a period of 905 seconds (that's 15 minutes to you and me) from the time you click the Purge button. The program uses this long delay time to give everybody on the network who might be using the index you're about to purge time to finish their searches with it. If your computer is not part of a network, or you have quicker ways of informing everyone not to use the index until you've finished purging and rebuilding it and give them the go ahead, you can significantly reduce this purge delay time.

To do this, open the Adobe Catalog dialog box by choosing Tools⇨Catalog on the Acrobat menus, and then click the Preferences button to open the Catalog Preferences dialog box with the General options displayed. Click the Delay Before Purge (Seconds) field and replace 904 with a new, smaller number of seconds (30 being the minimum value you can enter in this field) before you click OK.

To purge and then rebuild an index, you follow these steps:

1. **In the Adobe Catalog dialog box (Tools⇨Catalog), click the Open Index button.**

   The Select Index File dialog box opens.

2. **Select the folder that contains the PDF document collection and the index file and support folder, and then click the index file icon (the one with the** .pdx **file extension on Windows) before you click the Open button.**

   The Select Index File dialog box closes, and you return to the Adobe Catalog dialog box.

3. **Click the Purge button at the bottom of the Adobe Catalog dialog box.**

   Acrobat responds by displaying an alert dialog box warning you of the purge delay time.

4. **Click the OK button in the alert dialog box to begin the delay time and the ensuing purge of the index.**

   When Acrobat finishes purging the index, the program displays another alert dialog box indicating the index has been purged and possibly indicating that some files will be deleted when the index is rebuilt.

5. **Click OK to close the second alert dialog box and to return to the Adobe Catalog dialog box.**

6. **To rebuild the purged index, click the Open Index button again and then click the index file icon followed by the Open button to once again close the Select Index File dialog box and return to the Adobe Catalog dialog box.**

7. **Click the Build button to rebuild the index using only the PDF files left after the purge.**

8. **After Acrobat finishes rebuilding the index, click OK to close the Adobe Catalog dialog box.**

After you've finished purging and rebuilding an index, you can then immediately start using it in the searches you perform on the PDF document collection. Although not specifically noted in the preceding steps, keep in mind that prior to clicking the Build button, you can use the Options button to modify stop words or change the other number and word search options as discussed earlier in this chapter in the section "Building an index for your collection."

If you only use one particular index that you built when searching a particular PDF document, you can associate the index file with the PDF file. That way, Acrobat automatically mounts the index so you're ready to search the document with it every time you open the PDF document in Acrobat. To do this, choose File⇨Document Properties⇨Associated Index from the Acrobat menus to open the Document Associated Index dialog box. Then in the Index to Mount When the Document is Opened field, select the index file that is to be used in searching the document before you click OK.

Searching a Collection

After you've created the indexes you need to search your PDF document collections, you can use the Search feature in Acrobat 5 or Acrobat Reader 5 to quickly locate key terms and phrases. Keep in mind that when you use the Search feature, Acrobat is searching for the occurrence of your terms in any of the indexed documents included in the PDF document collection. Therefore, along with specifying the search terms, you need to specify which index should be used in doing the search.

In order to be able to search collections in Acrobat Reader 5 (as opposed to Acrobat 5), you must include the option for searching PDF files and accessibility support at the time you download a version of Acrobat Reader. To do this, you must select the Include Option for Searching PDF Files and Accessibility Support check box at the bottom of Step 1 on the download instructions on the Adobe Web site. If you don't select this check box option, Adobe downloads a smaller version that lacks the Search feature.

When specifying the search terms, you can use wildcard characters: * (asterisk for any number of missing characters) and ? (question mark for single missing characters). You can also use the so-called Boolean operators:

✔ **NOT** to exclude documents in the collection that contain a certain word or phrase such as NOT "Chicago". You can also use the NOT operator by entering the ! (exclamation point) in front of the term to be excluded.

✔ **AND** to narrow the search to documents that contain both terms such as "Chicago" AND "New York". When you use the AND operator, Acrobat matches a document only when it contains both terms.

✔ **OR** to expand the search to include documents that include either search term such as "Chicago" OR "St. Louis". When you use the OR operator, Acrobat matches any document that contains one or the other term.

When specifying a search term, you can also include any of the following word search options:

✔ **Word Stemming** to match words that contain part of the search term (such as matching *totally*, *totaling*, and *totals* when total is your search term)

✔ **Sounds Like** to find words that sound like the search term

✔ **Match Case** to match the exact spelling in the search term

✔ **Thesaurus** option to have Acrobat search for synonyms for your search term as well as the search term itself (so that if you look for the term settlement in the PDF document collection, Acrobat will also look for the synonyms *compromise* and *give-and-take*)

✔ **Proximity** option to have Acrobat ignore any matches unless one instance of the search term occurs within three pages of another instance of it in the documents included in the PDF document collection. For example, if you search for the phrase custom satisfaction guaranteed, Acrobat will show matches only when this phrase occurs more than once in the document within three pages of each other.

Remember that you can't use the Word Stemming, Sounds Like, or the Match Case word search options if you disable the Word Stemming, Sounds Like, or Case Sensitive options when building the index (see "Building an index for your collection," earlier in this chapter, for details).

The steps for finding terms or phrases in a PDF document collection with the Search feature are as follows:

1. **Choose Edit⇨Search⇨Query on the Acrobat menus, click the Search button on the File toolbar (the one with a pair of binoculars in front of a page), or press Ctrl+Shift+F (⌘+Shift+F on the Mac).**

    The Adobe Acrobat Search dialog box (similar to the one shown in Figure 13-4) opens.

2. **Click the Indexes button.**

   The Index Selection dialog box (like the one shown in Figure 13-5) opens.

3. **If the index you want to use is not listed in the Available Indexes list box, click the Add button, and then open the folder with the PDF document collection you want to search, click the index file icon, and then click the Open button.**

   The Select Index dialog box closes, and you return to the Index Selection dialog box.

4. **If an index you want to use in the search is not selected (indicated by an empty check box), click its check box to select it. If an index you don't need to use is selected (indicated by a check mark in its check box), click its check box to remove the check mark from it (for example, you don't need to include the Acrobat 5.0 Online Guides index that's selected by default). After you have selected only the index or indexes you want to use in the search, click OK.**

   The Index Selection dialog box closes, and you return to the Adobe Acrobat Search dialog box.

5. **Enter the search term(s) or phrase in the Find Results Containing Text list box.**

   Remember that you can use wildcard characters for characters of which you're uncertain in the search term or phrase.

6. **Select any of the search options (Word Stemming, Thesaurus, Sounds Like, Match Case, and Proximity) that you want to apply.**

7. **Click the Search button to have Acrobat search the designated index or indexes.**

   The results are displayed in the Search Results dialog box (similar to the one shown in Figure 13-6).

Figure 13-4:
Specifying the search terms in the Adobe Acrobat Search dialog box.

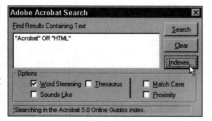

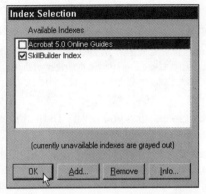

Figure 13-5:
Specifying
the index to
use in the
Index
Selection
dialog box.

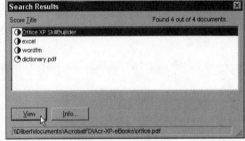

Figure 13-6:
Checking
over the
PDF
documents
ranked by
matches in
the Search
Results
dialog box.

Search versus Find in Acrobat

Don't confuse the Find and Search features in Acrobat and Acrobat Reader. The Find feature (Edit⇨Find) enables you to search for terms in any PDF document that you have open. The Search feature (Edit⇨Search⇨Query) enables you to search for terms in any PDF document that has been included in the index. To search with the Find feature, you must have the PDF document that you're searching open and current in Acrobat or Acrobat Reader. To search with the Search feature, you don't have to have any PDF document open in Acrobat or Acrobat Reader because the program automatically opens and highlights matches as needed in the indexed files in the PDF document collection.

Viewing the search results

When Acrobat finishes doing the search (which it completes very quickly except in the cases of huge document collections), it displays all matching files and ranks them in order of relevance in the Search Results dialog box (refer to Figure 13-6). The Search Results dialog box indicates the predominance of a search term in a document by the degree of blackness in the circle in front of the PDF document's filename. The blacker the circle, the greater the number of matches in the file. The whiter the circle, the fewer the number of matches.

To have Acrobat open a document in the Search Results list and show you the first occurrence of the search term, click the filename in the Score Title list box, and then click the View button to open the document and display the first match to the search term highlighted in the document text. To view the next match in the document, click the More Tools button to the right of the Search button and then click Next Highlight on the pop-up menu. To view the matches in another document in the Score Title list, click the Search Results dialog box to activate it and then click the document's filename before you click the View button.

You can close the Search Results dialog box so that it doesn't obscure any of the matches highlighted in the selected document. To redisplay the Search Results dialog box so that you can view matches in a different document in the Score Title list box, press Ctrl+Shift+G (⌘+Shift+G on the Mac).

Refining your search

Sometimes, your first search for a particular term results in too many matching files pulled from the PDF document collection, and you find that you need to further narrow your search results by refining the search. To do this, follow these steps:

1. **Click the Close button on the Search Results dialog box to close it.**

2. **Redisplay the Adobe Acrobat Search dialog box with your original search term by choosing Edit⇨Search⇨Query on the Acrobat menus or by pressing Ctrl+Shift+F (ZZZZZ+Shift+F on the Mac).**

3. **Replace or further refine the search term in the Find Results Containing Text list box and/or by selecting different word search options in the Options section.**

4. **Hold down the Ctrl key (Option key on the Mac) and notice that the Search button changes to Refine; then click the Refine button (don't release the Ctrl/Option key until after you've clicked the Refine button).**

Acrobat includes a great little utility called Word Assistant that can help you find alternate terms to use in refining your search. To open Word Assistant, choose Edit⇔Search⇔Word Assistant or press Ctrl+Shift+W (⌘+Shift+W on the Mac). You can then look up synonyms, sound-alike terms, and even word stems by entering the term in the Word field; clicking Thesaurus, Sounds Like, or Stemming in the Assist pop-up menu; and then clicking the Lookup button.

Adding document information (metadata) and date filtering to your searches

Earlier in the section on creating a PDF document collection, I go through a big thing about recording your metadata in the Document Summary dialog box in the Title, Subject, Author, and Keywords fields. However, in the section on how to conduct a search, you may have noticed that I never once make mention of how to use any of this metadata in your search. And the reason for this is that Acrobat doesn't automatically include document information (otherwise known as *metadata*) as part of the search. Nor does it include an equally powerful search feature called date filtering (which enables you to match documents in a collection that were created or modified within a range of dates).

To add these more useful and powerful searching features, you follow these steps:

1. **On Windows, choose Edit⇔Preferences⇔General on the Acrobat menus or press Ctrl+K, and then click Search in the list box on the left of the Preferences dialog box. On the Macintosh, choose Edit⇔Preferences⇔ Search on the Acrobat menus to open the Acrobat Search Preferences dialog box.**

2. **Click the Document Information check box in the Include in Query area to add the ability to search the metadata in your PDF document collection.**

3. **Click the Date Filtering check box in the Include in Query area to add the ability to search for documents created or modified within a certain range of dates.**

4. **Click the OK button to close the Preferences (Acrobat Search Preferences on the Mac) dialog box.**

Figure 13-7 shows you what happens to the Adobe Acrobat Search dialog box after you turn on these search features. As you can see, you can now search for the metadata that you so assiduously entered for each PDF document in the collection (at my gentle insistence). Simply enter the words or names to search for in the appropriate fields (Title, Subject, Author, and Keywords) in the new With Document Info section of the Search dialog box.

By adding the date filtering fields (Created After and Before and Modified After and Before) in the new With Date Info section, you can also refine a search by the approximate date particular PDF files in the collection were originally created and/or modified. This makes it possible to find a document that shares essentially the same metadata as others in the collection but was created or last modified on a particular date.

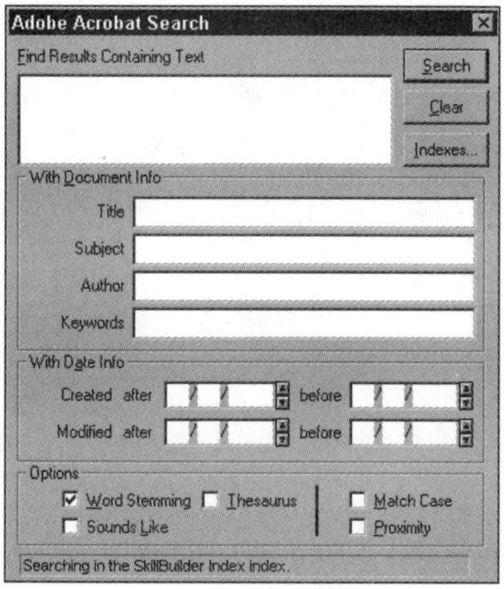

Figure 13-7:
The Adobe
Acrobat
Search
dialog
box after
turning on
Document
Information
and Date
Filtering.

Distributing PDF Document Collections

After you've established your PDF document collections, you can make them available to your coworkers in a couple of ways. One of the most popular methods is to back up one or more of the collections (depending upon the number of PDF files they contain) on CD-ROMs that you can send out or make available for use from a central archive. Another method available to users whose computers are part of a company-wide network is to copy the PDF document collections onto a volume on the network server and share that volume with all the users who need to access its information.

The biggest potential problem with making PDF document collections available on a network is that together they can eat up a lot of disk space, depending upon how many PDF files they contain. Of course, this isn't a problem when you distribute collections on individual CD-ROMs, although it does mean that you have to be smart about how you classify and categorize the collections on each CD-ROM because they can only be mounted and searched individually. This means that you can't peruse the various collection folders at one time as you can when they're all located together on a shared volume of a network.

You may wonder about making PDF document collections available from a corporate intranet or Internet Web site. Unfortunately, as of now, the only way to make PDF document collections searchable on Web servers is with the Adobe PDF iFilter, a free downloadable DLL (Dynamic Link Library) that enables searching PDF files using Microsoft's specifications for filtering text. Of course, this is no solution if your company doesn't happen to use a version of the Microsoft Internet Information Server and Microsoft Index Server (both of which have to be in place for the PDF iFilter to work). For more information on the Adobe iFilter and to download it, go to the following Web address:

```
www.adobe.com/support/downloads/
```

Part IV
PDFs as Electronic Documents

The 5th Wave   By Rich Tennant

"...and I'd also like to thank Doug Gretzel here for all his work in helping us develop our interactive, multimedia stapling division."

In this part . . .

*P*art of the allure of Adobe's Portable Document
Format is its promise to reduce the amount of paper
documents in the office by replacing them with fully functional electronic counterparts. This part of the book covers
the major electronic forms of PDF files, interactive forms,
eBooks, and online presentations you will encounter more
and more in your work.

In Chapter 14, you find out all about creating and using
electronic PDF forms, including collecting their data from
Web sites on the company's intranet and the Internet. In
Chapter 15, you are introduced to the world of Acrobat
eBooks using PDF documents designed specifically and,
sometimes, exclusively for online reading. Finally, in
Chapter 16, you find out how you can turn PDF files into
multimedia presentations by adding audio and video elements to be viewed in Acrobat 5 and Acrobat Reader 5.

Chapter 14

Creating Interactive Forms

• •

• •

*F*illing out forms is a way of life in the Information Age. These everyday documents come in all shapes and sizes and are perfect candidates for conversion in Acrobat 5, where they take advantage of the fixed layout, portability, editing, and import/export features of Adobe PDF. The results are interactive electronic forms that are cross-platform and easily distributed over a computer network. The ability to create and modify electronic forms with Acrobat 5 is arguably the greatest thing since sliced bread, especially for those who rely on a company intranet or the World Wide Web to gather and distribute crucial information.

This chapter introduces you to *form fields*, the main components used to create an interactive PDF form. In the process, you find out about the various types of form fields and the way they define and add interactivity to a form. You also discover how to format and modify fields, use them to build a form from scratch, and create forms that automatically calculate entered data. Finally, you find out how to use Acrobat 5's import/export feature and submit your form online so that it can be distributed and used to gather data.

Introducing Form Fields

The term *electronic form* is used to describe forms that can be distributed over a computer network (including a company intranet or the Internet). In the old days (before PDF), to create an electronic form you either scanned an existing paper form into a graphics-editing program or built one from scratch using a word processor or page layout program. Recipients could only view these electronic forms if they had the proper software and the forms were not "interactive," meaning that you still had to print one and fill it out with a pen or pencil. At that point, your form wasn't electronic anymore either.

What makes Acrobat 5 so fantastic is that, in addition to creating PDF forms by scanning existing forms or developing them right in the program, it also lets you produce truly interactive and portable forms that can be filled out on a computer screen and submitted over a computer network. This amazing feat is accomplished through the magic of form fields.

Although some of you might think of fields as those places that keep disappearing to accommodate urban sprawl, for the purpose of PDF forms they are containers for specific types of information and interactive elements. For example, the Name box on a form, where you put — you guessed it — your name, is a *text field*. An example of an interactive element field is a *check box* or *list box* that makes it easier for a user to fill out a form by selecting rather than entering data. (To find out all about the different types of form fields, see the "Getting Acquainted with Field Types" section in this chapter.) Adding different types of fields to a PDF document enables you to distribute it online, and users can fill it out in the comfort of their own computer desktop.

Adding Fields to Forms

Although creating a simple interactive form from scratch in Acrobat 5 is certainly possible (see "Creating form field tables," later in this chapter), most people find that what they really want is to add interactivity to a form that is already set up. For example, say that in the past you've paid big bucks to a graphic designer for a logo and spent even more to print reams of forms with your new logo on them. However, now you want people to fill out your forms online to save trees (and money). To do so, you just need to convert your form to PDF and then add the necessary form fields. See Chapter 15 for details on creating PDF files from a variety of popular Windows and Macintosh graphics and page layout programs.

Figure 14-1 shows an order form I created in Microsoft Excel and then converted to PDF (see Chapter 5 for details on converting MS Office documents to Acrobat files). Like most forms, this example uses numerous cells (such as the Name and Data cells) for writing information in. You need to add fields to these areas so that users can enter data on-screen in the finished product.

Form tool

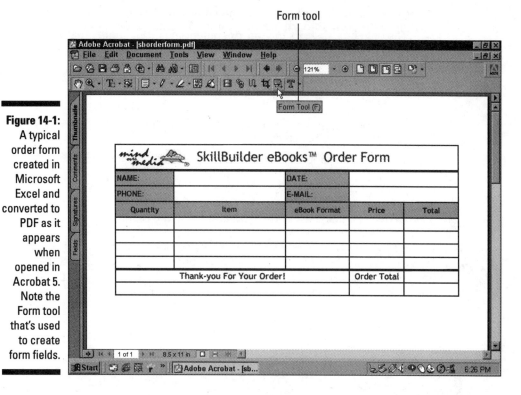

Figure 14-1:
A typical
order form
created in
Microsoft
Excel and
converted to
PDF as it
appears
when
opened in
Acrobat 5.
Note the
Form tool
that's used
to create
form fields.

After you convert your form to PDF and open it in Acrobat 5, use the follow-ing steps to add form fields:

1. **Click the Form Tool button on the Editing toolbar or press (F) to select the Form Tool.**

    The cursor turns into a cross-hair pointer, which you use to draw square or rectangular shapes for your fields.

2. **Drag the Form tool pointer to draw a box in the desired field area of your PDF form and then release the mouse button.**

    The Field Properties dialog box (shown in Figure 14-2) opens.

3. **Type a name for the field in the Name text box, and select a field type on the Type drop-down list. You can type further descriptions or notes about the field in the Short Description text box. Your entries are dis-played there for future reference when editing the field.**

4. **Choose options for the selected field type from the tabs provided.**

    Field options are covered in detail in the section "Selecting Form Field Options," later in the chapter.

5. Click OK to close the Field Properties dialog box.

The field box appears in your document in editing mode, that is, out-lined in bold red with its name in the middle of the box.

Presto, you've added a form field to your PDF document! Here are some important characteristics of your new form field:

- Unselected fields are colored black but then turn bright red when you click the mouse to select them.
- Sizing handles appear on a selected field box to facilitate resizing.
- To edit a field's name or change options, double-click the field to open the Field Properties dialog box.
- To delete a field, select the field and press the Delete key.

When drawing a text field box with the Form tool's cross-hair pointer, make sure to keep the lines of the box inside the boundaries of the cell or line you've chosen in your PDF form. This ensures that when a person is filling out the form, his or her data won't overflow those boundaries.

Form field

Figure 14-2:
The Field
Properties
dialog box
appears
when you
draw a field
in your PDF.
Note the
new field as
it appears
before
selecting
options and
closing the
dialog box.

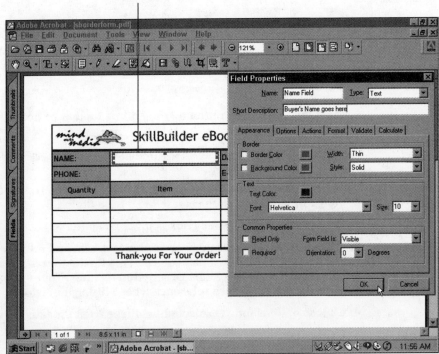

Move those fields!

You can move, resize, and align form fields numerous ways after you add a few to your form. Here are the basic techniques that you can apply to one or more fields:

- ✔ **To move:** Click a field and drag it to a new location. To make more precise movements, select a field and nudge it with the arrow keys. You can apply these same techniques to multiple field selections. Select multiple fields by holding down the Shift key while making your selections. The first selected field turns red, and subsequent selections are outlined in blue. Note that multiple field selections can be non-contiguous. After you've made your selections, release the Shift key and drag the selections to another location or nudge them with the arrow keys.

  When using the mouse to move multiple fields, you can constrain field movement to a horizontal or vertical direction by pressing the Shift key after you've started to drag the selected group of fields. To center single and multiple field selections on a page, choose Tools⇨Forms⇨Fields⇨ Center and select Vertically, Horizontally, or Both on the Center continuation menu.

- ✔ **To resize:** Position the mouse pointer on any of the sizing handles that appear on a selected field. When the mouse pointer turns to a double-headed arrow, drag in the direction of the arrows to change the size of a form field. To resize a single field or multiple field selections in smaller increments, hold down the Shift key while pressing the arrow keys. You can also resize multiple fields by choosing Tools⇨Forms⇨Fields⇨Size and selecting Height, Width, or Both on the Size continuation menu. These commands resize all selected fields to the respective Height, Width, or Both of the first selected field.

- ✔ **To align:** Select the field that you want other form fields to align with first and then select the fields you want to align. To align all selected fields with the respective border of the first field selected, choose Tools⇨ Forms⇨Fields⇨Align and select Left, Right, Top, or Bottom on the Align continuation menu. Choosing Vertical or Horizontal from this menu aligns the selected fields along the vertical or horizontal axis of the first selected field. See "Looking at the Layout Grid," later in this chapter to find out about Acrobat 5's best feature for keeping fields straight.

Duplicating form fields

At some point, you may need to create a whole bunch of fields that have the same attributes or properties — such as a group of check boxes or radio buttons. You can streamline this process by duplicating fields. After you've configured the size and properties of the field you want to duplicate, select it, hold down the Ctrl key (the Option key on the Mac), and drag the field to a new location using the marquee lines that appear as a guide. Repeat this process until you've created the desired number of fields. If you have mega-amounts of fields to duplicate, you can use the same method on multiple field selections, which doubles the number of selected fields. Note that all fields created in this manner have the same name, which is perfect for radio buttons (see "Understanding the Options tab," later in this chapter).

You can edit properties of individual fields you've duplicated, but be aware that if you want to change a duplicated field's type, you also have to change its name in the Field Properties dialog box because different field types must have different names.

To copy and paste fields using key commands, select a desired field for duplication and press Ctrl+C (⌘+C on the Mac) to copy the field to the Clipboard. Then press Ctrl+V (⌘+V on the Mac) to paste the field into your PDF. Note that you can copy and paste multiple field selections in this manner and that pasted items will appear centered on the PDF page.

Be careful when deleting duplicated form fields. If you select a duplicated field and press the Delete key, a warning box appears saying "This field exists at more than one location or page in the document. Do you wish to delete all fields with the same name?" Clicking Yes will delete all the duplicated fields you've created, which will come as quite a surprise if that wasn't your intention. To delete just the selected field, click No. To close the warning box and rethink the whole maneuver, click Cancel.

Getting Acquainted with Field Types

You choose field types on the Type drop-down list in the Field Properties dialog box, shown in Figure 14-3. Each field type has its own associated options that appear on tabs in the dialog box when that field type is selected. These options are described in detail in the next section "Selecting Form Field Options."

Acrobat 5 provides you with the following seven field types that define the type of information you want to collect and add interactivity to your form:

✔ **Button:** To perform an action in a form, such as a Reset button that erases previously entered information so you can start over, or a Submit button that sends the form information to a network server. In addition, buttons can play sounds and movies, open files, or download Web pages from the

Internet. Acrobat 5 also lets you automatically create JavaScript button rollovers. These types of buttons change appearance when the mouse is hovered or *rolled over* the button.

✔ **Check Box:** To make multiple selections from a list of items. Check boxes were used extensively in old-fashioned paper forms and usually followed the instruction "check all that apply."

✔ **Combo Box:** Enables the user to pick an item from a list, with the added advantage of saving space on a form by presenting the items in a drop-down list.

✔ **List Box:** For a long list of items to present in your form, a list box is a good solution because it has scroll bars that allow the user to scroll through the list to select an item.

✔ **Radio Button:** When only one item from a list can be selected. For example, you can use a radio button to have users indicate whether they're male or female or to specify which credit card they want to use to pay for an online transaction.

✔ **Signature:** To enable the user to digitally sign a document. Like hand-written signatures, digital signatures represent the user's identity and his or her approval or acceptance of a document. They have the added advantage of storing information about the signer and the exact state of the PDF form when it was signed.

✔ **Text:** For entering text and numbers, such as a person's e-mail address or birth date. You can set up text fields to format and limit the type of information entered in them as well as to perform calculations. You can also attach JavaScript actions and data validation to text fields.

Figure 14-3:
Selecting a field type in the Field Properties dialog box. Note the selected field box as it appears in editing mode after being drawn in a PDF form.

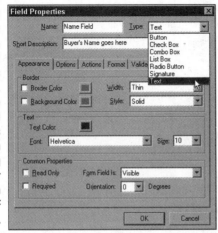

Selecting Form Field Options

The Field Properties dialog box displays up to six different tabs of options, depending on which field type you choose when you're adding a field to your PDF form. Field options govern characteristics such as the way a field appears in a form, the format and type of data that can be entered in the field, actions that you attach to a field (such as playing a sound or movie), and also the types of calculations performed on data entered in a field.

To edit field options, double-click the field to open the Field Properties dialog box and then click the desired tab. The separate tabs and options (in all their copiousness) are described in the following sections.

Applying Appearance tab options

The options on the Appearance tab (shown in Figure 14-4) are applicable to every field type and are used to specify the way a field is displayed in a PDF form. Note that after selecting appearance options (or any other field option for that matter), you must click OK to close the Field Properties dialog box and then click the Hand tool on the Basic Tools toolbar or press (H) in order to view your changes.

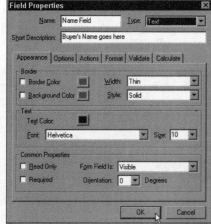

Figure 14-4:
The options
on the
Appearance
tab of the
Field
Properties
dialog box.

The following list describes the options found in the labeled areas of the Appearance tab that you can use to change the way a form field is displayed in a PDF form:

✔ **Border:** Provides options for setting the border and background of a field. Click the Border Color or the Background Color check box and then click its associated color box to select from the color palette (Windows) or the color picker dialog box (Mac OS) that appears. Click the Width drop-down list to select Thin, Medium, or Thick border lines and the Style drop-down list to select Solid, Dashed, Beveled, Inset, or Underlined border line styles.

✔ **Text:** Provides options for setting the color, font, and font size of text as it appears when either typed in a text or signature field or displayed in a button label, combo box, or list box. The option is not available for check boxes and radio buttons. Click the Text Color box to select from the color palette (Windows) or the color picker dialog box (Mac OS) that appears. Click the Font or Size drop-down list to make font selections.

✔ **Common Properties:** Provides miscellaneous options that apply to all field types. Clicking the Read Only check box specifies text fields that cannot be modified by a user. Clicking the Required check box specifies that a field must be filled in before form data can be submitted. Use the Form Field Is drop-down list to select whether a field is Visible, Hidden, Visible but Doesn't Print, or Hidden but Printable. The Orientation drop-down list lets you choose the text orientation in 90-degree increments for text that is either entered in a text field, selected in a combo or list box, or used as a button label.

You can apply appearance changes to multiple form fields even if they are different field types. Hold down the Shift key and click to select multiple fields and then double-click one of the selected fields to open the Field Properties dialog box. The Appearance tab is always displayed, and on occasion, the Option tab appears as well. Sometimes a particular field property differs among the selected fields. In these instances, the option either appears blank, in which case you can't select the option, or contains a grayed-out check or question mark, which allows you to apply the setting to all selected form fields or keep their existing properties so they can be edited separately.

Understanding the Options tab

In general, these field options set the degree or appearance of interactive features for a given field type. For example, you can use them to define a list in a combo box or set the shape of the check mark when the user selects a check box field. Commands that appear on the Options tab differ depending on which field type is selected in the Type drop-down list. The one exception is the Signature field type, which does not display the Options tab when selected.

Because field options are contextual, the following list describes the commands that appear on the Options tab when you select a specific field type:

- **Button field options:** These field type options, shown in Figure 14-5, add visual enhancements to a button field by creating actions associated with mouse movement. Note that these actions affect only the button's appearance as opposed to the more advanced special effects actions discussed in the "Interacting with the Actions tab" section, later in this chapter. Here's a rundown of the options:

  - **Highlight drop-down list:** Lets you choose how a button reacts when you click it with the mouse. Choose Invert to invert the colors in the button, None to cause no change in a button's appearance, Outline to highlight the button field border, and Push to use the elements defined in the Button Face When list box that displays mouse actions. The standard mouse behaviors for button actions are Rollover (when the user hovers the mouse pointer over an object), Down (when the user clicks the mouse button), and Up (when the user releases the mouse button). See Chapter 17 to find out how to apply this feature.

  - **Layout drop-down list:** Lets you choose whether a button will display the text entered in the Button Face Attributes area text box (Text Only), or a graphic (Icon Only). To select a button graphic, click the Select Icon button to open the Select Appearance dialog box and then click the Browse button to locate a suitable graphic on your hard drive in the Open dialog box that appears. You can also use the Layout option to select various mixtures of Icon and Text (Icon Top, Text Bottom or Text Top, Icon Bottom and so on).

Figure 14-5:
The Options tab of the Field Properties dialog box when Button is selected as the field type.

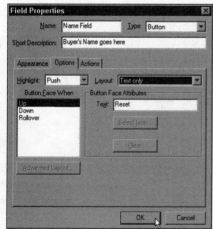

✔ **Check box and radio button field options:** The commands that appear on the Options tab when you select the Check Box or Radio Button field types are identical. Here's a rundown:

- **Check Style drop-down list:** Choose from a list of six different check mark styles that include the traditional Check, as well as Circle, Cross, Diamond, Square, and Star. The selected check style appears when the user clicks a check box in your form.

- **Radio Style drop-down list:** When you select the Radio Button field type, the same options appear that are described in the preceding bullet.

- **Default Is Checked check box:** Specify that the radio button or check box will appear selected by default in your PDF form.

- **Export Value text box:** Enter a value that will be exported to a CGI application in order to identify that the check box or radio button has been selected in a form. See the "Exporting CGI values" sidebar in this chapter.

✔ **Combo box and list box field options:** The commands that appear on the Options tab when you select the Combo Box or List Box field types are nearly identical. These options are used to define and configure the lists you want to appear in a combo or list box field:

- **Item text box:** Type an item for your list in this text box and then click the Add button to display it in the Selected Item Is Default list box (described next).

- **Selected Item Is Default list box:** Use this list box to arrange the order of items in a combo or list box. You can delete an item in the list by selecting it and clicking the Delete button. To change the order of an item, select it and click the Up or Down button to move the item up or down the list. To sort the list first numerically, if numbered items are present, and then alphabetically, click the Sort Items check box. As the name Selected Item Is Default suggests (it's more of a direction than a name, isn't it?), click an item in the list to have it appear by default in a form.

- **Editable check box:** The Combo Box field type provides an option that allows a user to edit and spell-check its list. Click the Editable check box to activate this feature.

- **Do Not Spell check box:** You can prohibit spell-checking by clicking this check box.

- **Multiple Selection check box:** The List Box field type provides an option that allows a user to select multiple items in its list. Click the Multiple Selection check box to activate this feature.

- **Export Value text box:** Enter a value that will be exported to a CGI application in order to identify a user's selection in a combo or list box. See "Exporting CGI values," later in this chapter.

✔ **Text field options:** Commands that appear on the Options tab when you select the Text field type let you configure the text that a user enters in a form text field. Here are your options:

  - **Default field:** Enter text in this field when you want to display a suggested default value in a text field.

  - **Alignment drop-down list:** Choose Left, Center, or Right to specify the alignment of the text entered by a user.

  - **Multi-line check box:** Click to create a text box with more than one line.

  - **Do Not Scroll check box:** Click if you want to limit data entry in a multiline text field to the amount of text that can be displayed within the text field borders.

  - **Limit Of check box:** To limit the number of characters that can be entered in the field, click this check box and enter a number from 1 to 32,000 in the Characters field.

  - **Do Not Spell check box:** Click to have the spell checker bypass the text field. Clicking this check box also allows you to use the Password and Field Is Used for File Selection options that are grayed out by default.

  - **Password check box:** Click to specify that text entered in the field will be displayed as a series of asterisks so it can't be read.

  - **Field Is Used for File Selection check box:** Click to have a file submitted along with the form by entering a file path as the field's value. This feature requires a JavaScript, which is covered in the next section.

Interacting with the Actions tab

You can apply the commands on the Actions tab to every field type. They allow you to choose from a list of different mouse behaviors and then associate those behaviors with a variety of actions that are built into Acrobat 5. You might, for example, attach a Sound action to the Mouse Up behavior so that a sound plays when the user clicks a field item in a form.

Figure 14-6 shows the Actions tab of the Field Properties dialog box. The following list defines the mouse behaviors you encounter in the When This Happens list box:

✔ **Mouse Up:** When the mouse button is released

✔ **Mouse Down:** When the mouse button is clicked

✔ **Mouse Enter:** When the mouse pointer moves into the field boundaries

✔ **Mouse Exit:** When the mouse pointer moves out of the field boundaries

✔ **On Focus:** Using either the mouse pointer or key tabbing to move into the field boundaries

✔ **On Blur:** Using either the mouse pointer or key tabbing to move out of the field boundaries

Figure 14-6: The options on the Actions tab of the Field Properties dialog box.

Attaching an action to a form field

Use the following steps to attach an action to a selected form field:

1. **Choose a mouse behavior in the When This Happens list box.**

2. **Click the Add button.**

   The Add an Action dialog box opens, as shown in Figure 14-7.

3. **Select an action in the Type drop-down list.**

   Each selected action displays a specific editing button that, when clicked, opens an editing dialog box. These actions and corresponding editing features are described in detail in the section "Taking in the Action" below.

4. **Click the editing button and choose options for your selected action, click OK to close the editing box, and then click the Set Action button to close the Add an Action dialog box.**

   The selected action appears in the Do the Following list box on the Actions tab of the Field Properties dialog box.

5. **Repeat Steps 1 through 4 to add more actions to this list.**

6. **If you need to rearrange the order of the actions, select an action in the Do the Following list box and click the Up or Down buttons.**

   Note: Actions in this list are executed from top to bottom.

7. **To edit or replace an action that you've added to the list, select the action and click the Edit button.**

   The Edit an Action dialog box opens.

8. **To delete an action from the list, select the action and click the Delete button.**

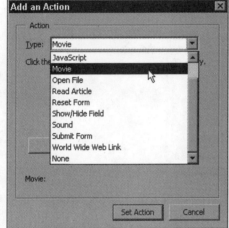

Figure 14-7:
The Add an
Action
dialog box,
where
Acrobat 5's
built-in
actions are
displayed.

Taking in the Action

The following list describes the actions and corresponding editing options that appear in the Add an Action dialog box:

✔ **Execute Menu Item:** To select a specified menu command when the associated mouse behavior occurs in a field. Click the Edit Menu Item button and select a menu command in the Menu Item Selection dialog box.

✔ **Import Form Data:** To import form data stored on a server. This action is typically used to fill in forms with often-used data, such as the address of a company. If you're familiar with JavaScript, click the Edit button to open the JavaScript Edit dialog box, which is a basic script editor for writing a JavaScript. See "Importing/exporting form data," later in this chapter.

✔ **JavaScript:** To run a custom JavaScript when the associated mouse behavior occurs in a field. You write scripts in the JavaScript Edit window, which is a basic JavaScripting tool. The Go To button lets you jump to a specific line in the written code for editing purposes.

✔ **Movie:** To play a QuickTime or AVI movie that has been linked to the PDF document. (See Chapter 16 for the lowdown on adding movies to a PDF file.) After movies are linked to a PDF, click the Select Movie button to open the Movie Action dialog box, and then select a linked movie from the Select Movie drop-down list. The selected movie will play when the associated mouse behavior occurs in a field.

✔ **Open File:** To open a file when the associated mouse behavior occurs in a field. Note that if the file is not a PDF (which will open automatically in the user's PDF reader), the file's native program must be installed on the user's desktop in order for the file to open. Click the Select File button in the Add an Action dialog box, locate the file in the Select File to Open dialog box, and then click Select (Open on the Mac).

✔ **Read Article:** To follow an article thread in the current document when the associated mouse behavior occurs in a field. (See Chapter 10 to find out about creating articles in a PDF file.) To read an article, click the Select Article button and choose from the list of articles residing in the current document before clicking OK to close the Select Article dialog box.

✔ **Reset Form:** To clear previously entered data from form fields. You can choose which fields are reset in a form by clicking the Select Fields button to open the Field Selection dialog box. You are presented with three radio button choices: All Fields, All Except, and Only These. If you choose the All Except or Only These radio buttons, you can choose which fields to include or exclude when the form is reset. Just click the Select Fields button and then click either the Add button to move a field to the Include Fields window, or the Remove button to move a field to the Exclude Fields window. When you're finished selecting fields, click OK.

✔ **Show/Hide Field:** To show or hide a field when the associated mouse behavior occurs in a field. Click the Edit button and choose either the Show or Hide radio button in the Show/Hide Field dialog box. Note that to toggle between showing and hiding a field, you must associate one or the other state with the Mouse Up and Mouse Down behaviors in the When This Happens list box.

✔ **Sound:** To play a specified sound file when the associated mouse behavior occurs in a field. Click the Select Sound button to locate a sound file in the Open dialog box and then click the Open button. Acrobat 5 embeds the sound in a cross-platform format that will play in Windows and Mac OS. In Mac OS, you can add QuickTime, System 7, AIFF, Sound Mover (FSSD), or WAV format sound files. In Windows, you can add AIF or WAV files. Note that selected sound files must be uncompressed in order for Acrobat to embed them in a PDF form.

✔ **Submit Form:** To send all form field data to a specified URL for collection. See the next section, "Adding Submit and Reset buttons."

✔ **World Wide Web Link:** To download a Web page from the Internet. Click the Edit URL button to type in a World Wide Web destination. Note that besides the http network protocol used for Web pages, you can also use the ftp and mailto protocols when defining this action link. See Chapter 7 for more on capturing Web pages.

✔ **None:** To specify that no action occurs when the associated mouse behavior occurs in a field. This feature is often used to create bookmark section headings and is not useful as a form field action. See Chapter 9 for the lowdown on creating bookmarks in a PDF document.

You can greatly enhance form field interactivity by using custom JavaScript actions. You can find out a great deal about writing your own scripts in the "Acrobat JavaScript Object Specification" PDF provided with the Acrobat 5 online help. You'll also find numerous ready-made JavaScripts that perform a wide variety of actions there. Choose Help⇨Acrobat JavaScript Guide on the menu bar to open this PDF.

Exporting CGI values

When a form is submitted to a server on the World Wide Web, it is processed by a CGI, or Common Gateway Interface. This method requires a script that tells the server to process the form by handing it off to a separate program, in this case a database, which stores the form data and makes it available for redistribution over the network.

You can define CGI export values for Check Box, List Box, Combo Box, and Radio Button field types. Note that you need to define an export value in the Options tab of the Field Properties dialog box only if both of the following are true: The form data will be collected on a network or Web server and the data is different from the item designated by the form field, or the form field is a radio button.

Here's how these rules apply to form field types that can export CGI values:

✔ **Check Box:** Use the default export value *Yes,* which tells the CGI application that the check box has been checked.

✔ **List and Combo Box:** The item selected in a combo or list box is usually used as the export value. Enter a value in the Options tab of the Field Properties dialog box only if you want the value to be different from the item listed. For example, you might ask a user to choose from a list of abbreviated state names like *AZ* but need to export the value *Arizona* to match that field in a database on the server.

✔ **Radio Button:** A radio button by itself can use the default export value *Yes* to indicate it has been selected. If the radio buttons are related — for example, you've presented users with a series of radio buttons to indicate their yearly income among several ranges — the radio buttons must have the same field name but different export values so that the correct values will be collected in the database.

As a rule, note you should attach JavaScripts that execute special-effect actions or major changes, such as playing a sound or movie, submitting the form, or downloading a page from the World Wide Web, to the Mouse Up behavior. This allows users a last chance to change their minds about executing an action by moving the mouse away from a form field before releasing the mouse button. If the action is attached to the Mouse Down behavior, the action will execute the moment the mouse is clicked.

Adding Submit and Reset buttons

Reset and Submit buttons on a form perform two basic form field actions that are important features to use when setting up an interactive form that will be submitted over a network. The following steps show you how to add these components to a form.

To add a Reset button, follow these steps:

1. **Add a form field to your PDF form document in the area you want your Reset button to appear and choose the Button field type.**

   See "Adding Fields to Forms," earlier in this chapter, for details.

2. **In the Field Properties dialog box, click the Actions tab, select the Mouse Up behavior in the When This Happens list, and then click the Add button.**

   The Add an Action dialog box opens.

3. **Choose Reset Form from the Type drop-down list and then click the Select Fields button.**

   The Field Selection dialog box, shown in Figure 14-8, appears.

4. **Choose All Fields in the Field Selection dialog box.**

   Note that you specify the fields you want to have reset as opposed to accepting the default All Fields.

5. **Click OK to accept your choices and close the Field Selection dialog box.**

6. **Click Set Action to close the Add an Action dialog box and finally click OK to close the Field Properties dialog box.**

To view and test your Reset button, click the Hand tool on the Basic Tools toolbar or press (H) then enter data in the various fields of the form before you click the Reset button.

Follow these steps to add a Submit button:

1. **Add a form field to your PDF form document in the area you want your submit button to appear and choose the Button field type.**

   See "Adding Fields to Forms," earlier in this chapter, for details.

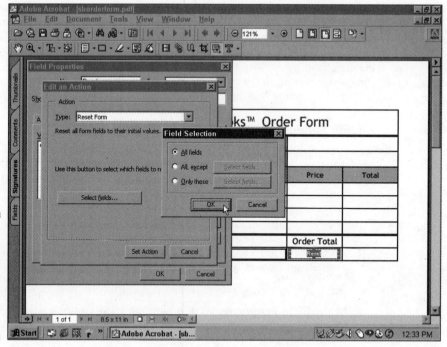

Figure 14-8:
Editing the
Reset Form
action type
in the Field
Selection
dialog box.

2. **In the Field Properties dialog box, click the Actions tab, select the Mouse Up behavior in the When This Happens list, and then click the Add button.**

   The Add an Action dialog box opens.

3. **Choose Submit Form from the Type drop-down list and then click the Select URL button.**

   The Submit Form Selections dialog box opens, as shown in Figure 14-9.

4. **Type a URL for the destination server in the Enter a URL for This Link text field.**

5. **Click one of the four radio buttons and select options in the Export Format area. Form data can be exported in four different formats:**

   • **FDF or Form Data Format:** Exports data as an FDF file and allows you to include field data, comments, and incremental changes to the PDF. The incremental changes feature sends data such as a digital signature in a format that can be easily read and stored by the server application. (See "Importing/exporting form data," later in this chapter, for more on this file format.)

   • **HTML:** Form data is exported as an HTML file.

- **XML:** Exports as an XML file and allows you to also send field data and annotations.

- **Complete Document (PDF):** Sends the entire PDF form rather than just the field data. This option is useful for preserving written digital signatures in a PDF form.

6. **In the Field Selection area, you can select which fields to export. Click the All Fields radio button to export data in every form field. If you choose the All Except or Only These radio buttons, click the Attached Select Fields button to open the Field Selection dialog box. Choose which fields to include or exclude by clicking the Add button to move a field to the Include Fields list, or the Remove button to move a field to the Exclude Fields list. Click OK after making your selections. To export selected form fields even if they contain no data, click the Include Empty Fields check box.**

7. **If you want to export all the dates entered in your form regardless of how they are entered, click the Convert Dates to Standard Format check box in the Date Options area.**

8. **Click OK to accept your choices and close the Submit Form Selections dialog box.**

9. **Click Set Action to close the Edit an Action dialog box and finally click OK to close the Field Properties dialog box.**

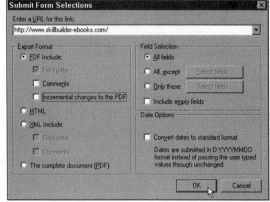

Figure 14-9:
Options that
appear on
the Submit
Form
Selections
dialog box.

To view and test your Submit button, click the Hand tool on the Basic Tools toolbar or press (H), then enter data in the fields of the form before you click the submit button.

Getting familiar with the Format tab

The commands on the Format tab are applicable only to Combo Box and Text field types. The same can be said of the Validate and Calculate tabs as well. These format options enable you to specify a particular numerical format for data entered in the form field. For example, you can create a text field for entering a Social Security number that must contain nine numbers and automatically place dashes after the third and fifth numbers.

The Format tab presents a list of format categories in the Category list on the left side of the tab. Clicking a category displays specific options for that category in the Options area on the right. Figure 14-10 shows the Number Options that appear when the Number category is selected. Choose formatting options and then click OK to apply that formatting to your form field. The following list describes the categories and options provided:

- ✔ **None:** The default setting that specifies that no formatting is applied to data entered in a field.

- ✔ **Number:** Type a number in the Decimal Places field or click the attached spinner buttons to set the number of decimal places for the number entered in the text field. Click the arrow on the Currency Symbol drop-down list to select from a wide variety of foreign currency symbols. Click the arrow on the Separator Style drop-down list to select a comma and decimal separators preference. Select how negative numbers appear in a field by choosing a style in the Negative Numbers Style list box.

- ✔ **Percentage:** Automatically displays the percent symbol with numbers entered in a Text or Combo Box type field. Type a number in the Decimal Places field or click the attached spinner buttons to set the number of decimal places. Click the arrow on the Separator to select a comma and decimal separators preference. The sample area provides a preview of your selected percentage options.

- ✔ **Date:** Choose from a wide variety of date-only or date and time formats (choose the Time category for time-only formats) in the Date Options list box. The formatting code for the selected format style appears in a text field below the Date Options list. For example, selecting 1/3/81 in the Date Options list displays its formatting code as m/d/yy. When you're familiar with these simple date and time codes, you can select any format in the Date Options list and alter its formatting code to create custom date and time formats.

- ✔ **Time:** Choose from four time formats provided in the Time Options list. Note that formatting codes are not provided for time-only formats.

- ✔ **Special:** Choose from the list of four options that appear in the Special Options list: Zip Code, Zip Code+4, Phone Number, or Social Security Number.

✔ **Custom:** Provides a means of using JavaScript to format text or apply keystroke validation to text entered in a field. (See the next section to find out about field validation.) Click the Edit button next to either the Custom Format Script or Custom Keystroke Script area to open the JavaScript Edit window. If you're familiar with JavaScript language, you can write your own or copy and paste a predefined JavaScript in the script editing window. Click OK to close the JavaScript Edit window. The keystroke or formatting script appears in its proper Custom Options area. Note that you can use the arrow keys to view the script, but you can't edit it.

Figure 14-10:
The Format tab on the Field Properties dialog box appears when you select Text or Combo box field types.

Viewing the Validate tab

Like the Format and Calculate tabs, options on the Validate tab apply only to Combo box and Text field types. You use these commands to restrict data entry in a field to a specific range, such as a dollar amount less than or equal to $1,000. Note that in order to specify a data range, the selected form field must be formatted with either the Number or Percentage category on the Formatting tab of the Field Properties dialog box.

You can accomplish more sophisticated validation, such as restricting data to specific values and characters, through the use of JavaScript. You might, for example, want to limit a date entry to only the years between 1950 and 2000 or allow a password that only contains three letters and four numbers separated by a dash.

To set a data range or attach a JavaScript to validate a field, click one of the three radio buttons on the Validate tab:

- ✔ **Value Is Not Validated:** The default state. This radio button is selected automatically if a field does not use number or percentage formats (selected on the Format tab). Otherwise, click this option if you don't want validation applied to data entered in a field.

- ✔ **Value Must Be:** Provides two fields in which to define upper- and lower-range parameters, as shown in Figure 14-11. Type a number in either the greater than or equal to field, the less than or equal to field, or both to specify limits on a data range.

- ✔ **Custom Validate Script:** Click the Edit button to open the JavaScript Edit window. If you're familiar with JavaScript language, you can write your own or copy and paste a predefined JavaScript in the script editing window. Click OK to close the JavaScript Edit window. The validation script appears in a preview box below the Custom Validate Script radio button. Note that you can use the arrow keys to view the script, but you can't edit it.

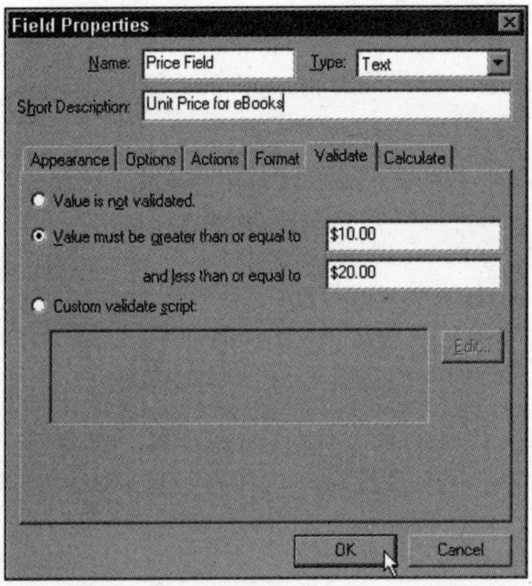

Figure 14-11:
Defining
data-range
parameters
for a field on
the Validate
tab of the
Field
Properties
dialog box.

Cruising the Calculate tab

Like its Format and Validate tab brethren, options on the Calculate tab apply only to Combo box and Text field types. You use these commands to perform mathematical calculations on data entered in two or more form fields and display the result in another field. This feature is often used in an interactive order form where the product of an item's quantity and price is automatically displayed in a total field. In addition, it is possible to perform more advanced calculations using JavaScript.

To define the fields in a form that will perform calculations, or attach a JavaScript calculation to a field, click one of the three radio buttons on the Calculate tab:

- ✔ **Value Is Not Calculated:** The default state. Click this option if you don't want to perform a calculation on data entered in a field.

- ✔ **Value Is the <Operation> of the Following Fields:** Provides a drop-down list of five operations: sum (+), product (×), average, minimum, and maximum. Select an operation option and then click the Pick button to open the Select a Field dialog box, which displays a list of fields in your form. Select a field and then click the Add button. You can only select fields one at a time. When you're finished selecting fields, click the Close button.

- ✔ **Custom Calculation Script:** Click the Edit button to open the JavaScript Edit window. If you're familiar with JavaScript language, you can write your own or copy and paste a predefined JavaScript in the script editing window. Click OK to close the JavaScript Edit window. The calculation script appears in a preview box below the Custom Calculation Script radio button. Note that you can use the arrow keys to view the script, but you can't edit it.

By default, field calculations are performed in the same order as the form field's tab order — that is, the order in which the fields are selected when the user presses the Tab key (see "Tabbing through a form," later in this chapter). This is not always a good idea, especially if your form contains multiple calculations where the result of one calculation depends on the result of another calculation. To override the default, set your own calculation order by choosing Tools⇨Forms⇨Set Field Calculation Order on the menu bar to open the Calculated Fields dialog box. Select fields in the window and use the Up and Down buttons to arrange their calculation order and then click OK to save your changes.

Sizing up the Selection Change tab

The Selection Change tab provides you the means to execute JavaScript actions when making a selection in the List Box field type.

To use this feature, click one of the two radio buttons on the Selection Change tab:

- ✔ **Nothing Happens When a Listbox Selection Changes:** Use this option if you don't want to run a JavaScript action when a user makes a list box selection.

✔ **This Script Executes When the Listbox Selection Changes:** Use this option to attach an action, click the Edit button to open the JavaScript Edit window. If you're familiar with JavaScript language, you can write your own or copy and paste a predefined JavaScript in the script editing window. Click OK to close the JavaScript Edit window. The JavaScript appears in a preview box on the Selection Change tab. Note that you can use the arrow keys to view the script, but you can't edit it.

Singling out the Signed tab

Options on the Signed tab apply only to the Signature field type. Its commands enable you to specify actions that occur in a form when data is entered into a blank signature field. You add signature fields to a form in the same manner as you do other form fields by using the Form tool. (See "Adding Fields to Forms," earlier in this chapter, if you need a refresher.) The Form tool creates a blank signature field that can be filled out as part of completing a form. (To find out all about digital signatures, see Chapter 11.)

To configure a blank signature field, click one of the three radio buttons on the Signed tab:

✔ **Nothing Happens When the Signature Field Is Signed:** Use this default option if you don't want any actions to occur to data entered in a field.

✔ **Mark as Read-Only:** Provides a means of locking portions of a form at the time it is signed off in the signature field, in essence "freezing" the form at that moment in time. Choose one of three items on the drop-down list: All Fields, Just These Fields, and All Fields Except These. If you click either of the latter two options, click the Pick button to open the Select a Field dialog box where you choose the fields you want to render as read-only. Select a field from the list and click the Add button. When you're finished adding fields, click the Close button.

✔ **This Script Executes When the Signature Field Is Signed:** Click this radio button to execute a specific JavaScript action when data is entered in a signature field. Click the Edit button to open the JavaScript Edit window. If you're familiar with JavaScript language, you can write your own or copy and paste a predefined JavaScript in the script editing window. Click OK to close the JavaScript Edit window. The action script appears in a preview box below the radio button. Note that you can use the arrow keys to view the script, but you can't edit it.

Looking at the Layout Grid

Acrobat 5 provides a wealth of tools that make the process of laying out and modifying form fields quick and easy. One of these tools is the Layout

Grid — a non-printing, customizable on-screen grid that provides guidelines for drawing field boxes with the Form tool. To show or hide the Layout Grid, choose View⇨Grid or press Ctrl+U (⌘+U on the Mac). The best part of the Layout Grid, however, is its Snap to Grid feature, which causes field boundaries to snap to gridlines when they're being drawn, as shown in Figure 14-12. To turn this feature on or off, choose View⇨Snap to Grid or press Ctrl+Shift+U (⌘+Shift+U on the Mac). Note that because these two features are discrete, the Snap to Grid feature will still work even if the Layout Grid is hidden and vice versa. A check mark next to either command's name on the menu bar lets you know the feature is turned on.

Setting Layout Grid preferences

Layout Grid preferences let you specify a grid's spacing, position on a page, subdividing lines, and color. Choose Edit⇨Preferences⇨General or press Ctrl+K (⌘+K on the Mac) to open the Preferences dialog box, shown in Figure 14-13. These are your options:

- ✔ To specify the space between major gridlines, click the spinner buttons or enter a measurement in the Width and Height between Lines text boxes.

- ✔ To offset the Layout Grid from the top-left corner of the page, click the spinner buttons or enter a measurement in the Grid Offset from the Left Edge or Grid Offset from the Top Edge text boxes.

- ✔ Click the spinner buttons or enter a number in the Subdivisions text box to display a specified number of subdividing lines between major gridlines.

- ✔ To specify the color of the gridlines, click the Grid Line Color button and select the desired color on the color palette (Windows) or the color picker dialog box (Mac) that appears.

When you're finished selecting Layout Grid preferences, click the OK button to apply your changes and close the Preferences dialog box.

You'll probably find that the Layout Grid isn't really very useful for adding fields to ready-made forms that you've scanned into Acrobat 5 because its gridlines will rarely match the cells that are already drawn in your paper form. In these cases, use the Align commands (see "Move those fields!") to keep your fields straight. Where it really makes sense to use the Layout Grid is in designing and building a form from scratch. Here's a quick and easy method of getting a blank page into Acrobat 5 so you can use the Layout Grid to custom build a form. Open a new blank document in Microsoft Word (Windows or Mac) and click the Convert to PDF button on the PDFMaker 5.0 toolbar. You can open the resulting blank PDF in Acrobat 5, configure and display the Layout Grid, and then start cranking out a form of your own design. For more on converting Microsoft Office documents to PDF, see Chapter 5.

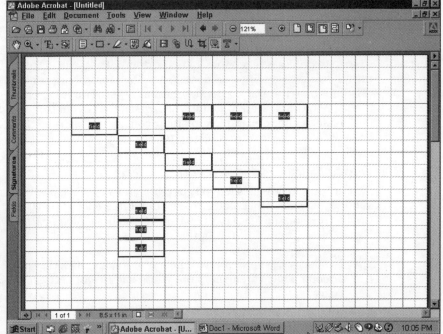

Figure 14-12:
Drawing
form fields
using the
Layout Grid
with its
Snap to Grid
feature
turned on.

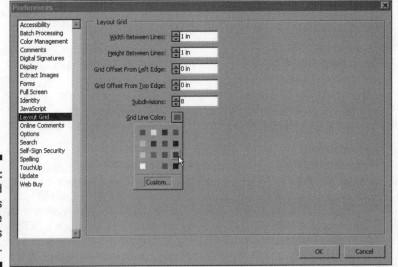

Figure 14-13:
Layout Grid
options
in the
Preferences
dialog box.

Creating form field tables

Building a table of form fields is a snap. The fields can be all the same type or different types, and the methods for creating a table vary slightly, depending on which case is true. To create a table made up of form fields that are all the same type, follow these steps:

1. **Press Ctrl+U and Ctrl+Shift+U (⌘+U and ⌘+Shift+U on the Mac) to display the Layout Grid and turn on the Snap to Grid feature, which is really helpful when building a form field table.**

2. **Add a form field to your PDF in the area you want to serve as the corner of your table.**

   See "Adding Fields to Forms," at the beginning of this chapter, for details.

3. **Hold down the Shift key (the ⌘ key on the Mac) and draw a marquee around the single field.**

   A blue line appears, overlapping the red border of the selected field, which is now a dotted red line.

4. **Hold down the Ctrl key (the ⌘ key on the Mac) and drag any of the corner sizing handles of the selected field in the direction you want your table to fill, using the rectangular marquee line as a guide.**

   When you let go of the mouse button, the rectangle you just drew is filled with blue outlined cells, as shown in Figure 14-14.

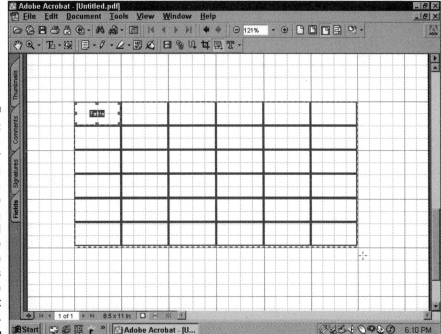

Figure 14-14: Dragging the corner sizing handle of a single cell to create a form field table. Note that the initial field is in the upper-left corner.

5. **Click inside the new table (Windows) or anywhere in the PDF (Mac) to change the blue cells to form fields.**

   Note that if you click outside the table in Windows, your table selection disappears, and you have to start over from Step 3. The fields are given sequential names based on the name of the initial field. You can double-click any cell to edit its properties in the Field Properties dialog box.

To create a table made up of different field types, you need to vary the preceding steps slightly. Instead of creating a single field (as in Step 2), you need to create an initial row or column of different field types that will serve as a basis not only for the number of rows or columns that appear in your table but also for how the different field types will occur in the table. After establishing that, you then drag the sizing handle that appears on the sides of the column or row of selected fields (rather than the corner sizing handles mentioned in Step 4) to draw your table.

Creating fields for tables in the manner just described is not the same as duplicating form fields (see "Duplicating form fields," earlier in this chapter). In this process, you give each field a unique name, which allows a higher degree of individual editing choices. Therefore, it's not the method to use if you want to create a group of related radio buttons that must have the same name. See "Understanding the Options tab," earlier in this chapter, for more on creating radio buttons.

When your form is in the development stage and you're beginning to accumulate a number of fields, it's a good idea to take advantage of the Fields palette in the Navigation pane. Click the Show/Hide Navigation Pane button on the File toolbar and then click the Fields tab. The Fields Palette provides a hierarchical, icon view of the fields in a PDF. It allows you to remotely select, rename, delete, edit the properties of, and more importantly, lock/unlock a field. Locked fields can't be moved or edited, which comes in handy when you've gotten a number of fields just where you want them but are still fiddling with others in the form. To access these commands, right-click (Control+click on the Mac) a field icon in the Fields palette and choose from the context menu that appears. (See Figure 14-15.)

What to do with all these fields?

As you go merrily along stacking up form fields and bringing your PDF form design to fruition, you'll want to know some of the handy features Acrobat 5 provides to ready your form for distribution over a company intranet or the World Wide Web. In the following sections, you find out all about the features that make an interactive form top-notch.

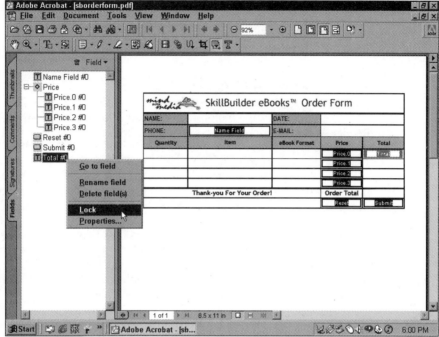

Figure 14-15:
Using the
context
menu
attached to
a field
displayed in
the Fields
palette.

Tabbing through a form

A form's tabbing order is the order in which the user selects fields when he or she presses the Tab key. This order is initiated when you add the first field and continues from there as you add fields to a form. Now if you know this ahead of time and are keeping track of the way you want the form filled out as you add fields, everything will work out fine. If you're like the rest of us, you'll probably have to set the tabbing order after you've finished adding fields to your form. Here's how:

1. **Choose Tools➪Forms➪Fields➪Set Tab Order.**

   The current tab order is displayed by numbers that appear in the upper-left corners of the fields in your form.

2. **Click individual fields in the order you want them numbered.**

3. **Click anywhere outside of a field to set your new tab order.**

If you find that some of your fields are in the correct tab order and you want to skip them in the reordering process and start your selection at a number other than 1, press the Ctrl key (the Option key on the Mac) and then click the form field that is numbered one less than the number you want to start with. The next field you click will be given your desired starting number. For example, say the tab order of the first four fields in your form is correct. You would hold down the Ctrl or Option key and click the field labeled (4). The next field you click will be labeled (5).

Importing/exporting form data

Acrobat 5's Import/Export feature allows you to move data in and out of a PDF form. That data can be imported into another PDF form or archived in a file format that is optimized to save space. When you export data from your form, Acrobat creates an FDF (Forms Data Format) file. This file contains only the data found in a form's fields, so it's much smaller in size than the original PDF form. After converted to FDF, any other PDF can import that data as long as its field names match those of the original form. Field names that don't match are ignored in the import process.

After you have your form up and running, you can export its data by choosing File⇨Export⇨Form Data. Type a file name for the FDF file in the Export Form Data As dialog box and click Save. To import data from an FDF file, choose File⇨Export⇨Form Data and then, in the Select File Containing Form Data dialog box, locate the file and click Select (Open on the Mac).

Keep in mind that importing and exporting field data is not the same as collecting and distributing form data through a browser on the World Wide Web. FDF files can reside on a network server, and users can access them on a company intranet, and you can even e-mail the FDF files to others to perform import/export functions right on their desktops. In order to collect your form data and distribute it over the Web, you need to use a CGI script written specifically for the form you want to use. If you're not familiar with coding CGI scripts, you'll have to leave it to the IT administrator of your company or Internet service provider's Web server. See the "Exporting CGI values" sidebar, earlier in this chapter.

Acrobat 5 also allows you to import data from a tab-delineated text file into a PDF form. This type of file is a text table that you create by placing a tab space between each entry to create table rows. The first row serves as columnar field headings for the table and is filled with names that correspond to the field names found in your PDF form. Subsequent rows correspond to the data to be entered in those form fields. You can create this text file in a word processor such as Microsoft Word, but I find it easier to create the data table in Microsoft Excel and then save it as a tab-delineated text file in that program.

Chapter 15

Building and Publishing eBooks

*I*f you've browsed any of your favorite online bookstores lately, you've probably noticed the burgeoning presence of eBooks for sale. Like it or not, eBooks are definitely the wave of the future, and while they'll never replace a nice cuddly printed book, they do have distinct advantages that ensure their future widespread use. Portability and ease of navigation are just two of the many advantages eBooks have over traditional books, and as I've mentioned throughout this book, these are areas where the Adobe PDF really shines.

In this chapter, you discover all the ways that Acrobat 5 allows you to build a better eBook. You see how easy it is to design and create a PDF file specifically for the eBook market. You also find out how to add interactivity to an eBook and create the kind of graphically rich page layouts that are only possible using Adobe PDF. More importantly, you discover how to create tagged PDF files that allow Acrobat eBooks to at last be viewed on handheld devices running Palm OS or Microsoft Pocket PC software. Finally, you find out how to package and distribute your eBooks and, in the process, ready yourself to catch the next big wave in digital publishing.

But First, a Little eBook History . . .

The origins of eBook technology are directly descended from SGML (Standard Generalized Markup Language), the grandmother of all markup languages. This venerable document structuring language (developed in 1986), along with its offspring HTML (Hypertext Markup Language) and the more recent and dynamic XML (Extensible Markup Language), are responsible for the billions of Web pages floating around the Internet today.

Markup languages like HTML use *tags* to define the structure and function of a document, in this case, a Web page that allows two remarkable features: The document content can be *reflowed,* meaning the reading order of the text is preserved no matter what screen size it is being viewed on, *and* it can contain hyperlinks.

To see an example of reflowed text, just crank up your favorite Web browser, visit your favorite Web site, and use the browser's text zoom feature to shrink or enlarge the text. Even though the text gets bigger or smaller, the reading structure of the Web page remains the same. This is accomplished through the use of tags that define the order of a document's headings, paragraphs, fonts, graphics, and other elements. The "link" tag, on the other hand, is what makes hyperlinks possible, and the ability to click a hyperlink to navigate from one document to the next is what makes the World Wide Web interactive.

Reflowing text and creating hyperlinks were the main reasons HTML was used early on in the development of eBooks. These features engendered two of the biggest advantages eBooks have over printed books. Because text could reflow, the entire content of a book could be viewed on a screen as small as a handheld computing device, allowing you to carry dozens of books in the palm of your hand. The use of hyperlinks in eBooks is just as compelling. You only need to imagine the difference between clicking a Table of Contents heading and having the beginning of a chapter appear instantly in an eBook reader, and using the traditional look-up-and-thumb-through-pages technique required for printed books. The only drawback to using HTML as a development tool for eBooks is that, like Web pages, they cannot be as graphically rich or as precisely laid out as printed books, which from a reading experience standpoint, is an innate expectation eBook users bring to the party.

Acrobat PDF files, on the other hand, rely on PostScript (see Chapter 1 for more on the origins of PDF), which is a page-layout language invented by Adobe specifically to create both electronic and printed documents that preserve the look and feel of their original counterparts. In versions prior to Acrobat 5, the problem with the standard PDF file as an eBook was that because it emphasized page layout, reflowing text was impossible. This fact relegated Acrobat eBook viewing to computer screens and laptops. Handheld devices as PDF viewers were never an option in the early stages of the Adobe Acrobat eBook development game. All that has changed with the release of Acrobat 5. Adobe has integrated the structure and navigational advantages of markup language with the "just like a printed book" reading experience of PDF. Acrobat 5's ability to create tagged PDF files offers the best of both worlds when it comes to designing and developing an eBook.

Designing eBooks for Different Devices

You design Adobe Acrobat eBooks in a word processor or page layout program and then convert their documents to PDF. You can then perform any last-minute tweaks, such as adjusting text flow or linking multimedia objects, in Acrobat and then view your final product either in the Adobe Acrobat eBook Reader on your computer or laptop or on a Palm OS or Microsoft Pocket PC handheld device. (See Chapter 2 to find out how to use Adobe's eBook Reader program.)

PDF files come in three document structure flavors — unstructured, structured, and tagged. Structured PDF files enable you to convert or *repurpose* a PDF for another format, such as RTF (Rich Text Format), while retaining much of the original page layout and reading structure. Tagged PDF files have the highest degree of success in retaining their original formatting when converting to RTF and are also able to reflow text, which is not the case with unstructured or structured PDF files. For the purpose of creating eBooks, then, you should always use tagged PDF files because they offer the most flexibility when it comes to viewing the final product on the greatest number of viewing devices.

To get more information about PDF file types, choose Help⇨Acrobat Help on the Acrobat 5 menu bar and see "Repurposing Adobe PDF Documents" on page 82 of the online Adobe Acrobat Help.

The following programs allow you to convert their documents to tagged PDF files in order to build an eBook:

- PageMaker 7.0 (Windows and Mac OS)
- InDesign 2.0 (Windows and Mac OS)
- Microsoft Office (Windows, versions 2000 and XP only)

The Adobe Acrobat eBook Reader was developed to provide a means of viewing PDF eBooks on a computer screen or laptop. Because of their size, computer screens are well suited to display graphically rich page layouts that re-create the reading experience of a printed book. For designing these types of eBooks, page layout programs (PageMaker, InDesign, or FrameMaker) are the best tools to use. In addition to allowing complex page layouts, their ability to create tagged PDF files adds a higher degree of accessibility for visually challenged users viewing PDF files in Acrobat eBook Reader.

Graphic size and page layout are definitely restricted by the screen size of handheld devices so it's better to develop eBooks that you want to view on those devices in Microsoft Word, which is text based and has Acrobat 5 features built in that enable you to create tagged PDF files with the click of a button. (See Chapter 5 for more on creating PDF files in Microsoft Office programs.)

Here are a few considerations to take into account in order to optimize eBooks designed for Palm OS or Microsoft Pocket PC handheld devices:

- ✔ **Graphics:** With handheld device screen resolutions running between 160 x 160 for Palm OS devices and 320 x 240 for Pocket PC devices, graphics must be optimized for the target screen size if used at all. Note that while the majority of Pocket PC devices in use have color screens, many more Palm devices are out there right now without color. You could consider preparing your graphics in grayscale (thus creating a smaller file) for this reason. For more on optimizing graphics for eBooks, see Chapter 4 as well as "Designing Library and Cover Graphics," later in this chapter.

- ✔ **Fonts:** Use the common Base 14 system fonts that are installed on your computer. These typefaces have been optimized for on-screen viewing and produce the best results when viewed on a handheld device.

- ✔ **Paragraphs:** Separate paragraphs with an additional hard carriage return for clearer visibility on the Palm handheld screen.

- ✔ **Conversion settings:** For grayscale Palm handheld devices, Adobe suggests some slight changes to the eBook job option in the Acrobat Distiller. You can get the specifics on creating a custom job option for these handheld devices at:

  `studio.adobe.com/learn/tips/acr5acropalm/main.html`

Adobe recently released two free products, Acrobat Reader for Palm OS and Acrobat Reader for Pocket PC. You can download these products at:

`www.adobe.com/products/acrobat/acrrmobiledevices.html`

The Acrobat readers are applications that are installed on their respective handheld devices and are designed to accommodate their specific screen characteristics. In addition to the reader software, each product includes a Windows desktop application for preparing and transferring a PDF to a user's handheld device. The Palm OS reader includes a HotSync conduit, and the Pocket PC version includes the ActiveSync filter, which has an added feature that attempts to create tags from untagged PDF files prior to uploading them to the Pocket PC handheld device.

Turning Out Tagged PDF Files

As I mention earlier in this chapter, a number of programs enable you to create a tagged PDF file. They do this either by exporting tags during the process of creating a PDF or, in the case of Microsoft Office programs, by converting them using the PDFMaker 5.0 plug-in. You can find out all about converting Office documents to tagged PDF files in Chapter 5. Keep in mind that if you're designing an eBook with little or no graphics for display on a handheld device, Microsoft Word is the tool of choice. On the other hand, if your goal is to create a beautifully stylized eBook for viewing in Acrobat eBook Reader, then PageMaker, InDesign, or FrameMaker is the best bet.

Perfecting your eBook in PageMaker

Authoring programs that export their tags to PDF perform a vital function when developing Acrobat eBooks. They allow you to complete nearly all of the mechanical and structural work on your eBook before you send it upstream to Acrobat 5. After your eBook is converted to PDF, you'll find that Acrobat's functional but limited editing toolset is best suited for fine-tuning the graphic and interactive elements of your PDF file. Take an eBook table of contents for example. Creating a table of contents (TOC) with more than a handful of headings in Acrobat is a tedious proposition (to put it mildly), especially compared to automatically generating an exportable, tagged, table of contents in PageMaker. The following sections take you through the process of preparing your eBook content so that 99 percent of your work is finished by the time you export it, tags and all, to Acrobat 5.

Setting up your eBook document

The following list provides a number of important tips to utilize that will ensure high-quality output when you convert your eBook to tagged PDF. Some of the items deal with conversion settings that you specify in Acrobat Distiller prior to exporting your eBook document to PDF. (See Chapter 4 to find out about selecting Distiller options.)

- When creating eBook content in PageMaker or any other layout program, make sure to set up a smaller page size so that your text won't be distorted when rendered in the smaller screen area provided by Acrobat eBook Reader. A 6-x-9-inch page dimension with ½- or ¾-inch margins all around translates well to the Acrobat eBook Reader's 4:3 screen ratio.

- Target output resolution should be 300 dpi or better to ensure clear, crisp text when the file is downsampled and compressed during the PDF conversion process.

- Try to use your system's Base 14 fonts in your eBook document. Otherwise, choose fonts that have strong serifs and strokes. If these font properties are too delicate, they'll distort and cause reading difficulty when displayed in the eBook Reader. In addition, be sure to embed those fonts you decide to use in the converted PDF. You can experiment with the readability of a chosen font by converting a test document to PDF and viewing it in Acrobat eBook Reader using a variety of magnifications and CoolType settings. You might also check for differences when viewing the eBook on a CRT or LCD computer screen.

✔ The minimum font size for body text should be 12 points. Use at least 2 points of leading. If you want to spread out your text, select a wider tracking value for your chosen font rather than using character kerning. Tracking can be applied globally and produces more significant visual enhancement than kerning, which also bulks up the size of your file.

✔ When creating paragraph heading styles in PageMaker, make sure you specify their inclusion in your table of contents by clicking the Include in Table of Contents check box in the Paragraph Specifications dialog box. You can open this dialog box by selecting the heading text in your document and choosing Type⇨Paragraph or Ctrl+M (⌘+M on the Mac). You can also access this dialog box while editing styles. Choose Type⇨ Define Styles, select a heading style in the Style list box, click the Edit button to open the Style Options dialog box, and finally, click the Para button.

Figure 15-1 shows the first page of my eBook example using the document setup parameters I just described. I used ½-inch margins all around with the exception of the ¾-inch margin on the bottom of the page to accommodate page numbers. The font is 12 point Georgia, using 2.4 points of leading for body text and up to 3 points for bulleted and numbered lists.

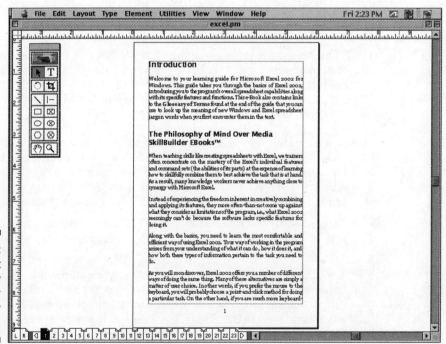

Figure 15-1:
The first page of my SkillBuilder eBook body section.

Generating a TOC

You can create a table of contents from those heading styles that are marked for inclusion in your PageMaker publication. The TOC can reside in the same document as your eBook body or in a separate publication for use with PageMaker's Book utility. I cover both methods in the following steps for creating a table of contents with hyperlink tags that can be exported to Acrobat 5.

To create a table of contents in the same publication as your eBook body, follow these steps:

1. **Select the first page in your publication and choose Utilities⇨Create TOC.**

   The Table of Contents dialog box, shown in Figure 15-2, appears.

2. **Type a new title or accept the default "Table of Contents" title in the text field provided and select one of the radio buttons in the Format area to specify the appearance and position of page numbers in the TOC. You can also specify a special character to appear between the entry and the page number (a tab space is the default) here.**

3. **Click OK to generate your table of contents *story*. A story in PageMaker terms is an independent text object with unique formatting that can be positioned anywhere in a page layout.**

   The mouse pointer changes to the story flow cursor. Now you need to create empty pages in which to flow your TOC story.

4. **Choose Layout⇨Insert Pages and enter the desired number of empty pages you want inserted, select Before the Current Page from the drop-down list, and click the Insert button.**

5. **Go to the first of your newly inserted pages and click to flow your TOC story onto the empty pages from there.**

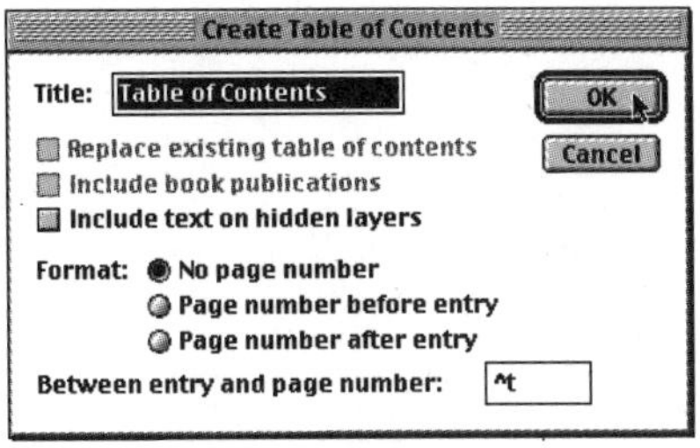

Figure 15-2:
The Create Table of Contents dialog box.

Create Table of Contents

Title: [Table of Contents]   OK

☐ Replace existing table of contents   Cancel
☐ Include book publications
☐ Include text on hidden layers

Format: ● No page number
○ Page number before entry
○ Page number after entry

Between entry and page number: [^t]

To create a table of contents in a separate publication from your eBook body, follow these steps:

1. **Create a new document from your eBook template containing the desired number of pages for your TOC and then save and name the publication.**

2. **Choose Utilities⇨Book.**

   The Book Publication List dialog box opens, as shown in Figure 15-3. This dialog box is used to specify the order of the publications you want to include in your book. Your current TOC document appears in the Book List on the right side of the dialog box.

3. **In the list on the left, locate the documents you want to include and add them to the Book List using the Insert button located between the two lists. Click OK to save your changes.**

   You can remove files and change the order of files in the list using the appropriate buttons. In Figure 15-3, I've added the body publication to the Book List after the TOC publication.

4. **Choose Utilities⇨Create TOC.**

   The Table of Contents dialog box opens.

5. **Type a new title or accept the default "Table of Contents" title in the text field provided and select one of the radio buttons in the Format area to specify the appearance and position of page numbers in the TOC. You can also specify a special character to appear between the entry and the page number (a tab space is the default) here.**

   Note that when you're creating a TOC from a document listed in a book publication, the Include Book Publications check box is automatically selected as opposed to being grayed out as in Figure 15-2.

6. **Click OK to generate your table of contents story and then go to the first page of your TOC publication and flow your TOC story from there.**

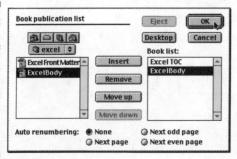

Figure 15-3: Define the order of your eBook sections in the Book Publication List dialog box.

Your brand-new table of contents contains tagged hyperlink entries that will produce accurate bookmarks and page references in your eBook when converted to PDF and viewed in Acrobat 5. You can check your links in PageMaker by selecting the Hand tool on the floating toolbox. The links appear in blue outline in Layout view, as shown in Figure 15-4, and you can click the hyperlinks in order to test their accuracy.

PageMaker inserts a text marker in front of every entry in the placed table of contents story in order to create hyperlink tags that will function when exported to tagged PDF. These text markers are visible only in story editor, (PageMaker's text editing window) and if they are removed, the links will not operate. For this reason, if you are editing a TOC entry, be very careful not to press the Delete key when the insertion point is directly in front of a TOC entry or page-number reference because this will remove the text marker from the publication. Your only recourse in such an event is to either close and reopen the document without saving (if you haven't saved the changes already) or regenerate the TOC.

You can make text edits to your TOC entries (heeding the warning in the preceding paragraph), but if you decide to add any new entries in either the TOC or the body of your eBook, you will have to regenerate a new TOC to create links for those entries that will export to tagged PDF.

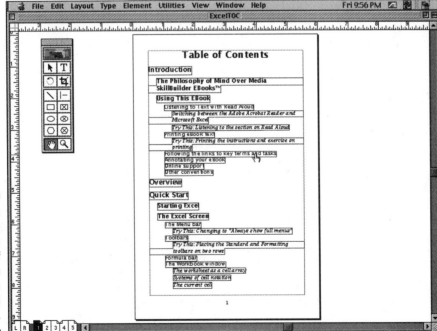

Figure 15-4: Displaying and testing table of contents links with the Hand tool.

Using mixed page-numbering schemes

The main reason for using PageMaker's Book utility to combine separate sections of your eBook is that doing so enables you to create different numbering schemes for those parts. A typical example is the way printed books use Roman numerals for their front matter (copyright, title, acknowledgment, and table of contents pages) and Arabic numerals for the body. Some books will also use different number formats for their appendixes and index. PageMaker allows you to renumber pages in a single publication but not change their format, which works well for many types of publications. As an eBook publisher though, it's nice to know you can add these little details to re-create the look and feel of printed books.

To apply a different number format to one of your eBook publications, follow these steps:

1. **Open the publication you want to reformat.**

2. **Choose File⇨Document Setup, and in the Document Setup dialog box, click the Numbers button.**

   The Page Numbering dialog box opens, as shown in Figure 15-5.

3. **Click one of the five radio buttons to select a numbering format and then click OK.**

4. **Click OK to close the Document Setup dialog box and view your newly formatted page numbers in the document.**

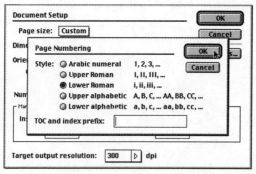

Figure 15-5: Choose a page-numbering format for your PageMaker publication.

You can apply these steps to any other eBook sections as desired. The beauty of the PageMaker Book utility is that it compiles your eBook sections in the order in which they appear in the Book List and, at the same time, preserves all your links when you export the eBook to PDF.

Creating a tagged PDF file

When you're satisfied with the look and feel of your eBook, your final step is to export the publication and its tags to PDF. The following steps show you how to export your PageMaker publication to PDF, which can then be opened up in Acrobat 5 for final adjustments prior to distributing your eBook:

1. **Open the publication you want to export to PDF.**

   Note that if you've compiled your PageMaker publications into a book, you need to open the first publication in your Book List. This should be some element of the front matter such as the table of contents. The Book utility takes care of sending the parts of your book in their correct order to Acrobat 5.

2. **Choose File⇨Export⇨Adobe PDF.**

   Acrobat takes a few moments to configure itself for this task and then opens the PDF Options dialog box, shown in Figure 15-6.

3. **Select options in the PDF Options dialog box. See the next section for details on specifying options that pertain to eBooks when exporting them to tagged PDF in PageMaker.**

4. **Click Export to send your publication to Acrobat 5.**

Figure 15-6:
Specifying options for your eBook export in the PDF Options dialog box. Note that the Embed Tags in PDF check box is checked.

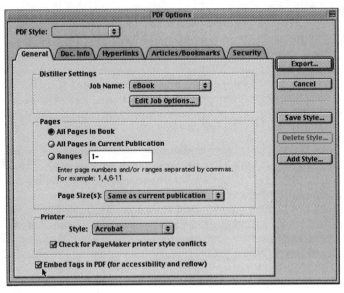

Specifying PDF options for eBooks

The PDF Options dialog box in PageMaker contains five tabs of options for configuring the way your eBook publication is exported to Adobe tagged PDF. Many of the options add functionalities that are specific to electronic publishing, such as setting up document information metadata that can be used as search criteria. The printing options don't really apply to eBooks because they will most likely stay in their electronic form. The following list describes these tabs and their options:

- **General:** Make sure to place a check mark in the Embed Tags in PDF (for Accessibility and Reflow) check box. This is the only way to specify that your eBook be converted to tagged PDF. To use a preconfigured Distiller job option, select from the Job Name drop-down list. Click the Edit Job Options button to make changes to the selected job. To find out more about Distiller job options, see Chapter 4.

  Choose one of the appropriate radio buttons in the Pages area to either export all the pages in a Book publication, all the pages in the current single publication, or a range or ranges of pages in the current publication. Select Same as Current Publication in the Paper Size(s) drop-down list to send the optimized PageMaker document settings you specified for your eBook to PDF. If you created separate document settings, choose Apply Settings of Each Publication. Leave the Style as Acrobat and the Check for PageMaker Printer Style Conflicts check box selected, which are the default settings; these options don't affect your eBook.

- **Doc. Info:** Information entered in the Doc. Info tab appears as metadata in the document properties of the tagged PDF file. For this reason, it can also be used as search criteria. You can specify the author, title, subject, and keywords of a document and create a note that appears on the first page of your PDF document that might contain an introduction or instructions for your PDF file. For more info on searching and cataloging a PDF file, see Chapter 13.

- **Hyperlinks:** These commands let you specify the links you want to activate in your eBook and their appearance and magnification after conversion to PDF. Select all applicable link types in the Export Links area. If you haven't defined these types of links in the PageMaker publication, the check box will be grayed out. Choose the Type, Highlight, Width, Color, and Style of your hyperlinks in the Default Appearance area. Note that most of these settings are more appropriate for PDF documents other than eBooks. Choose Fit Page in the Magnification drop-down list to have your linked destination page fit in the Acrobat eBook Reader window. Note that you can add, delete, and edit hyperlinks in Acrobat 5 after you've converted your eBook. See "Looking into eBook Links," later in this chapter.

- **Articles/Bookmarks:** PageMaker allows you to export text stories as PDF articles. It automatically finds these when you use the export command, and you can also define your own within the PageMaker story by clicking the Define button in the Articles area. (For details on PDF articles, see Chapter 10.) If you've created index or table of contents links in your publication, you can convert these to PDF bookmarks by selecting the appropriate check box in the Bookmarks area. Use the Fit Page setting in the Magnification drop-down list to have your bookmarked destination page fit in the Acrobat eBook Reader window.

✔ **Security:** You can select security settings for a PDF document such as limiting access by assigning passwords and restricting printing and editing. (For more on using security options with PDF files, see Chapter 11.) Use these settings if you don't plan to distribute your eBook commercially through an online retailer or distributor. Note that if you do plan to market your eBook, you must leave these settings blank because security for commercial eBooks is determined as part of the distribution process. See "Distributing Your eBooks," later in this chapter.

When the export job is finished, your new tagged PDF opens automatically in Acrobat 5 for viewing, as shown in Figure 15-7. The first page of the document is displayed (in this case, the inside cover page of my Excel SkillBuilder eBook), and the Bookmarks palette shows the table of contents headings that were converted to PDF bookmarks. You can now test your links and use Acrobat's PDF editing features to make final adjustments to your eBook.

Figure 15-7:
Your tagged
PDF is
opened in
Acrobat 5
after being
exported
from
PageMaker.

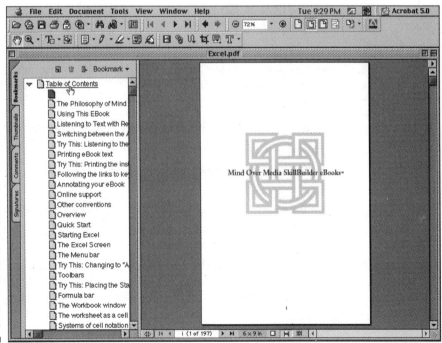

What about other layout programs?

As mentioned earlier, InDesign 2.0 is capable of converting its documents to tagged PDF, and the process is similar to the export function in PageMaker 7.0. The following sections provide an overview of this program as well as FrameMaker 6.0 and Quark 4.1, should you prefer using those authoring programs to create your eBook, rather than PageMaker.

Acrobat Distiller 5.0 does not provide the ability to specify the exporting of tags to PDF as part of configuring its job options. All layout programs, whether they are Windows or Mac OS versions, perform the conversion of documents to PDF by using either a Save as PDF, Export to PDF, or Print to Distiller type of command. The Save As and Export to PDF commands allow you to choose or edit Distiller job options right inside the program, and Adobe has only recently integrated the export tags feature within those programs listed at the beginning of this chapter. Older versions of these programs do not have this capability, and this is also the case with programs such as QuarkXPress 4.1 and FrameMaker 6.0 that use the Print to Distiller command for converting their documents to PDF.

Using InDesign 2.0 to create tagged PDF files

The latest version of InDesign is a feature-rich hybrid of layout and graphics editing programs. To date, it has the most advanced integration of Distiller properties of any Adobe program and allows complete configuration within the program. It also has the advantage of directly opening Quark 3.3-4.1 and PageMaker 6.5-7.0 documents. InDesign 2.0 is a great tool for designing and developing eBooks because of its extensive PDF conversion tools, but for this overview, here are the simple steps for exporting a document to tagged PDF:

1. **Open the document you want to export and choose File⇨Export.**

   The Export dialog box opens.

2. **In the Save as Type (Windows) or Formats (Mac OS) drop-down list, choose Adobe PDF.**

3. **Type a name for the converted PDF file, select a location on your hard drive, and click Save.**

   The Export PDF dialog box opens.

4. **In the Export PDF dialog box, shown in Figure 15-8, select an export style from the Style drop-down list. To edit a selected style choose the panel names on the left side of the dialog box and go to town.**

5. **Click Export.**

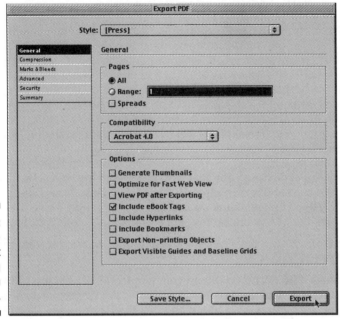

Figure 15-8:
The options-
laden Export
PDF dialog
box in
InDesign 2.0.

Converting QuarkXPress 4.1 documents to PDF

QuarkXPress 4.1 does not provide the export to tagged PDF feature for its documents that are converted to PDF. This may change with the release of Quark 5.0, which was in its pre-release stage at the time of this book's writing. To check out the program's new features, go online to:

```
www.quark.com/products/xpress/
```

You can also get information about the PDF Filter XTension utility that integrates Distiller options into Quark. Otherwise, to convert a Quark 4.1 file to Adobe PDF, follow these steps:

1. **Open the document you want to export and choose File⇨Page Setup or File⇨Print.**

   The Print dialog box appears.

2. **Choose Acrobat Distiller (Windows) or Create Adobe PDF (Mac) on the Printer drop-down list.**

3. **Select the eBook job option on the PDF options drop-down list.**

4. **Click Print.**

Converting FrameMaker 6.0 documents to PDF

FrameMaker is much like PageMaker in that you can create linked tables of content and indexes as well as compile book publications from separate documents. It's designed to create long, content-rich documents and also comes in a version (FrameMaker+SGML) that lets you publish complex documents in Standard Generalized Markup Language, which is a required format in some industries. Although FrameMaker 6.0 provides a Save as PDF command, this results in a "structured" but not tagged PDF document. Adobe recommends that you print your FrameMaker file to the Acrobat Distiller for the most reliable results. Here's how:

1. **Prior to exporting your FrameMaker document, open Distiller, choose Settings⇨Security, deselect all security settings if necessary, and click OK. Then choose eBook on the Job Options drop-down list. To reconfigure the eBook job option, choose Settings⇨Job Options.**

2. **In FrameMaker 6.0, open the document or book you want to convert to PDF.**

3. **Choose File⇨Print, and then (for Windows) click Setup in the Print dialog box, choose Acrobat Distiller on the Printer drop-down list in the Page Setup dialog box, and click the Print button. For the Mac, select Create Adobe PDF from the Printer drop-down list and then click the Print button.**

It's not the end of the world if your program doesn't export its documents to tagged PDF files. You can still add internal and external interactive links to your document in Acrobat 5, as you find out later in this chapter, and Windows users have the added ability to use Acrobat's Make Accessible plug-in to scan their PDF files and create tags that allow the document text to reflow. The plug-in is designed to create tagged files out of older PDF files so that they can be used in screen-reading programs for the visually challenged. Users of Acrobat 5 for Windows can download the plug-in at:

`www.adobe.com/support/downloads/detail.jsp?ftpID=1161`

There is not, as yet, a Make Accessible plug-in for Acrobat 5 for Macintosh (somebody write Adobe a letter!). After you've downloaded and installed the plug-in, open your PDF file in Acrobat and choose Document⇨Make Accessible. The utility scans your document's formatting structure, and if enough structure is available, it converts that information to reflowable tags.

Designing Library and Cover Graphics

You can definitely integrate graphics and digital photos into the design of your Adobe eBooks, especially those you create solely for viewing in Acrobat eBook Reader. Because there is no added expense for color use as there is with printed books, you can feel free to embellish your eBook with colored text, borders, and fills. In addition to the graphics you might use to illustrate your eBook, you also need to consider the use of library and cover graphics. There are three different kinds of library and cover graphics: your actual eBook cover and two thumbnail versions of the eBook cover. Although none of these graphics are required to create a functioning eBook, they add to the overall look and feel of your eBook and are required if you plan to market your eBook commercially.

When specifying color conversion settings in either the Distiller or the export settings of your eBook authoring program, always choose the sRGB model. Because computer screens use the RGB model, this device-independent color setting ensures that the graphics and colors in your eBook appear accurately in a wide variety of displays.

The Cover thumbnail is used for marketing purposes when you distribute your eBook online. (See "Distributing Your eBooks," later in this chapter.) eBook sellers use it on their Web sites to identify and advertise your eBook. The Library thumbnail is displayed in the Acrobat eBook Reader Library and used as a navigation button for selecting and opening an eBook. (See Chapter 2 for details about the Acrobat eBook Reader Library.) The actual eBook cover graphic is set as the first page in your eBook in Acrobat 5 and appears full screen (momentarily) in Acrobat eBook Reader when a user double-clicks the library thumbnail graphic to open the eBook. You can create these graphics in any editing program, though recent versions of Photoshop (5.0–6.0) have the advantage of using the sRGB color model as a default.

Here are the basic specifications for these three graphics:

- ✔ **Cover thumbnail:** Create a thumbnail of your cover graphic in GIF format. The image should be 100 pixels wide. A 3:2 aspect ratio works well, so at that width, your image would be 150 pixels tall by 100 pixels wide. Make sure to adjust the image resolution to 96 dpi so that the thumbnail display is sharper with fewer artifacts or pixel distortions when viewed online in a Web browser.

- ✔ **Library thumbnail:** The image that appears in the Acrobat eBook Reader Library is slightly different than the Cover thumbnail. For this graphic, create a thumbnail of your cover graphic in JPEG format. The image should be 100 pixels wide with the same 3:2 aspect ratio as the Cover thumbnail. Make sure to use the sRGB color model if possible (RGB otherwise) and adjust the image resolution to 96 dpi.

- ✔ **eBook Cover:** You should also create your eBook Cover in JPEG format. To fill the Acrobat eBook Reader window, it should be 600 pixels tall and 400 pixels wide using sRGB color and 96 dpi image resolution.

The graphics and illustrations you create for the body of your eBook can be developed in any graphic or photo editing program such as Illustrator or Photoshop. When you export your eBook to PDF, these graphics are optimized for viewing via the Distiller job option you choose during the export process. (To find out how Distiller optimizes graphics to reduce file size for Web distribution, see Chapter 4.) Because the Library and cover graphics are added to your eBook in Acrobat 5 after it has been exported or converted to PDF, make sure to create GIF and JPEG format graphics and use the sRGB color model so that they are fully optimized for the Web when you upload the cover thumbnail to a bookseller's server or insert the cover and Library thumbnail in your eBook.

Adding a cover graphic to your PDF eBook

Because an eBook cover graphic is designed to fill the Acrobat eBook Reader window, it's nearly impossible to add this graphic to your eBook in a layout program, let alone a word processor, and achieve satisfactory results. Imagine placing a 300 dpi graphic that covers the entire page (beyond the margins) into a document created in your favorite layout program and then hoping that Distiller will compress it nicely for full-screen display in the eBook Reader. It's best to create the graphic separately and use Acrobat 5 to insert it into your eBook after it has been exported PDF. Here's how:

1. **Open the tagged PDF eBook file you exported from your layout program.**

2. **Choose File➪Open as Adobe PDF.**

3. **Locate and select your JPEG cover image in the Open dialog box and click the Open button.**

   The Open as Adobe PDF dialog box appears.

4. **Click the Append to Current Document radio button and then click OK.**

   The cover image is imported into the PDF file as the last page in the document. (Unfortunately, you want this to be the first page.)

5. **Click the Thumbnails palette tab and scroll down to the last page in the document, select the cover image, and drag it up the Thumbnails palette and drop it at the beginning of the thumbnail list.**

6. **Note that because the cover graphic was appended to the end of the document, it was automatically given the last page number in the PDF. You can resolve this issue by choosing Document➪Number Pages.**

   Acrobat lets you renumber pages as well as change numbering formats one section at a time, so you can make sure the numbers you created for your eBook pages correspond to page numbers that appear in the page navigator bar in Acrobat eBook Reader. See Chapter 10 for details on using this feature.

Whenever you convert a document to PDF that is either a multisection book with different numbering schemes or a single document that starts with a page number other than the number one, you must use the Number Pages command in Acrobat 5 to renumber the PDF so its page numbers mirror your original document's numbering scheme.

When you add a front cover graphic to your Adobe eBook, it's important to insert an inside front cover page, such as the page shown in Figure 15-7, though this page could be blank as well. Also, make sure that you end up with an even number of front-matter pages, using a blank page at the end of the front matter if needed. This ensures that your Adobe PDF eBook displays properly in Two-Page View in Acrobat eBook Reader, with odd-numbered pages on the right. It's best to create these pages in your eBook authoring program rather than inserting them into the eBook in Acrobat 5.

Adding a library thumbnail graphic to your PDF eBook

After you've created your Library cover thumbnail, you need to attach it to your eBook in order for it to appear in the Acrobat eBook Reader Library. Here's how:

1. **Open the eBook file and select the cover page graphic in the Thumbnails palette (it should be the first page in the document) and then reduce the magnification so that the work area surrounding the page is visible.**

   100% usually works well for this.

2. **Select the File Attachment tool located on the Note Tool pop-up menu.**

   You can also hold down the Shift key while pressing the S key to cycle through the tools found on this menu. The cursor changes to a pushpin icon.

3. **Click in the workspace surrounding your cover page (not on the cover page itself), and, in the Select File to Attach dialog box (Windows) or the Open dialog box (Mac) that appears, locate and select your Library thumbnail graphic and then click the Select button.**

   The File Attachment Properties dialog box appears.

4. **Accept the default settings for your attachment and click OK.**

   A pushpin icon appears in the workspace next to the cover page, as shown in Figure 15-9. Make sure that the pushpin is in the workspace and not on the cover graphic page.

After you've attached your Library thumbnail graphic, you can open your eBook in Acrobat eBook Reader to view the thumbnail in the Library, as shown in Figure 15-10.

Pushpin icon

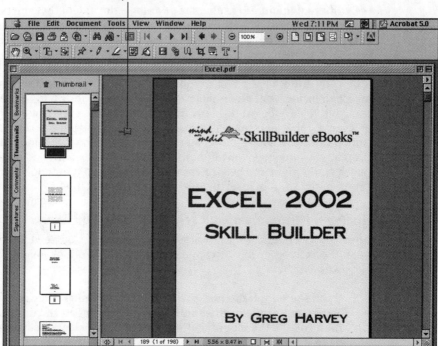

Figure 15-9:
The pushpin
icon in the
Acrobat
workspace
indicates an
attached
Library
thumbnail
graphic.

Figure 15-10:
The
attached
Library
thumbnail
appears in
the Acrobat
eBook
Reader
Library.

Looking into eBook Links

Hyperlinks add interactivity to an eBook by providing a means of navigating to desired information quickly and easily. Using links, an eBook reader can jump to a different place in the current page, call up other pages in the eBook, and even retrieve other documents on a network or download pages from the World Wide Web. When you create a link in Acrobat 5, you define an area in the document for the link, choose whether it appears visible or invisible to the user, and specify what occurs when the user clicks the link. Acrobat 5 lets you create internal links that navigate to destinations in the current document — a table of contents link, for example — as well as external links that retrieve other documents on a network or Web pages from the Internet.

One of the main goals in using an eBook authoring program that can export its documents to PDF is that the majority of links you might need in your eBook can be set up in the authoring program and automatically converted to PDF during the export process. There are times, however, when you'll want to edit those export-generated links or add new links to your eBook. The following sections take you through the process.

Adding an internal link

You create all links with the Link tool found on the Editing toolbar. To select the tool, click its button on the toolbar or press the L key. To add an internal link to your eBook, follow these steps:

1. **Open the eBook file and navigate to the page in which you want to add a link.**

2. **Select the Link tool and use its cross-hair pointer to draw a rectangle in the area of the page you want users to click to activate the link.**

   The Link Properties dialog box opens, as shown in Figure 15-11. See the next section for details on the options provided in this dialog box.

3. **Select Go to View in the Action Type drop-down list and then navigate to the page that you want to appear when the link is clicked.**

   You may have to move the Link Properties dialog box out of the way (but don't close it) to do this.

4. **When you arrive at your destination page, specify how you want the page to appear to the user by choosing a zoom level and page magnification setting in Acrobat 5.**

5. **Click the Set Link button on the Link Properties dialog box to return to the location in your PDF where the link was created.**

6. **To test your new link, right-click (Control+click on the Mac) the link with the Link tool and choose Follow Link on the pop-up menu. To return to the original link, click the Go to Previous View button on the Navigation toolbar.**

   You can also use the Hand tool to test the link. Note that when you hover the Hand tool pointer over a link, it changes to a pointing finger.

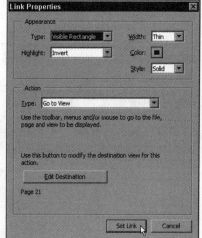

Figure 15-11:
The options provided in the Link Properties dialog box.

Using Link Properties options

The Link Properties dialog box lets you specify the appearance of a link and what action occurs when you click the link. The following list details these options:

✓ **Appearance:** Specify whether or not your link is visible or invisible to users by making an appropriate selection in the Type drop-down list. If you choose Visible Rectangle, the Width, Color, and Style options appear so that you can specify how a link is displayed:

  • Click the Width drop-down list and choose a Thin, Medium, or Thick outline border for the link.

  • Click the Color button to choose a color for the link border on the palette that appears.

  • Click the Style drop-down list to select either a Solid or Dashed border style.

The Highlight drop-down list lets you specify a momentary change in appearance for a link when the user clicks it. The effect is displayed until the user releases the mouse button. These options are available for both visible and invisible links. Choose None to have no change in appearance, Invert to invert the colors of the link, Outline to highlight the border on a visible link or to display a thin line around an invisible link, or Inset to create a 3-D button effect.

✔ **Action:** Choose from 12 options in the Type drop-down list that define an action that occurs when the user clicks a link. Go to View is the default and is used for internal links. The other choices on this list are used to perform a variety of actions when a link is activated, such as opening a file, playing a sound or movie, or running a JavaScript. These actions are explained in detail in Chapter 14, and the majority of them are either impractical or not appropriate for eBook use. An exception is the World Wide Web Link action, which is detailed in the next section.

✔ **Edit Destination:** Click this button if you decide that you want to change the view of the destination page you specified when you created a link. The destination page is displayed, and you can then use the Acrobat 5 zoom and magnification controls to create the desired view.

Adding an external link

You can allow eBook users to jump back and forth between the World Wide Web and Acrobat eBook Reader by adding external Web links in your eBooks. Keep in mind that users must have Internet access at the time they are reading the eBook for this to be possible. To create an external link in an eBook, follow these steps:

1. **Open the eBook file and navigate to the page in which you want to add a link.**

2. **Select the Link tool and use its cross-hair pointer to draw a rectangle in the area of the page you want users to click to activate the link.**

   The Link Properties dialog box opens (refer to Figure 15-11).

3. **Select World Wide Web Link in the Action Type drop-down list and then click the Edit URL button.**

   The Edit URL dialog box opens.

4. **Type the URL in the Enter a URL for This Link text field. When you're finished entering a Web link, click OK.**

   You can also copy a URL from your browser's address bar and paste it in this field.

5. **Click the Set Link button on the Link Properties dialog box to return to the location in your PDF where the link was created.**

6. **To test your new link, right-click (Control+click on the Mac) the link with the Link tool and choose Follow Link on the pop-up menu. To return to the original link, click the Go to Previous View button on the Navigation toolbar.**

To delete, edit, or test (follow) a link you've created in Acrobat 5, right-click (Control+click on the Mac) the link and choose the appropriate command on the pop-up menu that appears. You can also open the Link Properties dialog box to edit a link by double-clicking it with the Link tool.

Controlling the Way Text Flows

After you've converted your eBook to tagged PDF, you may discover that the page elements don't flow properly, especially when the page is viewed on a smaller screen. For example, a text caption for a graphic might appear above the image rather than below it. In other cases, you might have an image that has a text wrap around it, but you want to have the image appear after the text when it is reflowed. In such cases, you can use the TouchUp Order tool in Acrobat 5 to edit the reflow order of tagged items in the document. The TouchUp Order tool is located on the TouchUp Text Tool pop-up menu. You can select the tool by either choosing it from this pop-up menu or tapping the T key, while holding down the Shift key, to cycle through the TouchUp tools until the TouchUp Order tool appears.

To change the reflow order of elements on a tagged PDF page, follow these steps:

1. **Open the eBook file and navigate to the page containing the elements for which you want to change the reflow order.**

2. **Select the TouchUp Order tool.**

   Selecting this tool displays the separate elements on the page outlined in blue, as shown in Figure 15-12. Numbered boxes also appear in the upper-left corner of the outlined borders that indicate the current reflow order of each element. When you hover over an element, its blue outline turns red. This is helpful when you view a page that's chock full of such elements.

3. **Click the number boxes in the order in which you want them to appear when the page is reflowed.**

   If you want to start the process over, you have to deselect the TouchUp Order tool by selecting any other tool and then reselecting the TouchUp Order tool.

4. **Point to an element and right-click (Control+click on the Mac) to display that element's context menu, which contains commands for making specific order and position changes.**

5. **Click the Hand tool or press the H key to deselect the TouchUp Order tool.**

6. **To view your reflow order changes first, click the Reflow button on the Viewing toolbar and then use the Zoom In and Zoom Out buttons to observe how the elements reflow under different page magnifications. (See Figure 15-13.)**

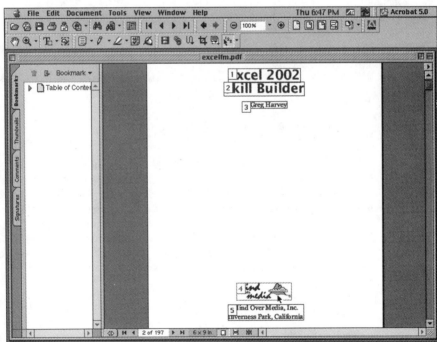

Figure 15-12:
The current order of page elements is displayed when you select the TouchUp Order tool.

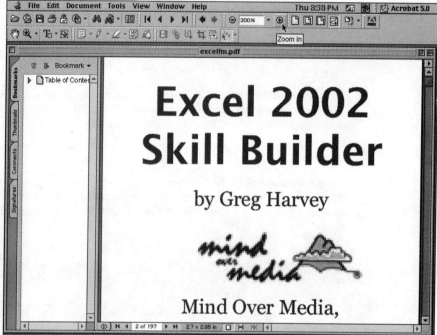

Figure 15-13:
Change
magnifi-
cation
settings to
view
reflowed
text.

Distributing Your eBooks

When you're satisfied with the look and feel of your eBook, including the way
its text reflows, and have checked that all links are working properly, your
next step is to decide how you want to distribute your eBook. Adobe sells a
server software package called Adobe Content Server that online eBook dis-
tributors use to encrypt, store, and distribute eBooks for sale. The latest version is 2.1.1, and at $5,000.00 for the Standard Edition (which allows you to
store 250 titles on a single Web site), it's definitely for only those serious
eBook publishers among you. To find out more about Adobe Content Server
software, go to:

www.adobe.com/products/contentserver/main.html

If you're not quite ready to make the plunge into the world of eBook self-
distributorship, a number of companies online have made the plunge and don't
mind helping you distribute your Adobe eBooks for a percentage of your
gross sales. Adobe provides a list of links to these digital fulfillment company
Web sites for your convenience. Go to Adobe's eBooks Central page here:

www.adobe.com/epaper/ebooks/main.html

Whether you use your own server or sign an agreement with an online distributor, the actual process of uploading an eBook is fairly simple. The Content Server software provides an interface that takes you step by step through the process of filling out the necessary information about your book (including ISBN numbers, which you'll have to procure from the Library of Congress), specifying the level of encryption and printing privileges you'll allow for your eBook and, finally, uploading your Library and Cover thumbnails along with your PDF eBook to the server. After your eBook is uploaded to the Content Server, the distributor then makes it available to various online retailers, and you're in business!

Chapter 16

Making PDFs into Multimedia Presentations

In This Chapter

▶ Creating a PDF presentation

▶ Enhancing a presentation with movies and sound

▶ Adding interactivity to a presentation

▶ Viewing a presentation

*M*ore and more, paper easels and overhead transparencies are giving way to electronic presentations as a means of imparting information to groups of people. Whether in business or education, slide show–type presentations and their ability to incorporate multimedia components make everything from sales meetings and seminars to student academic reports more interesting and exciting.

In this chapter, you discover how Acrobat 5 lets you create interactive PDF presentations in graphics editing programs or from Web content. Plus, you find out how easy it is to convert existing slide shows created in Microsoft PowerPoint. On the way, you gain knowledge of how to add interactive elements such as navigation buttons and also add multimedia objects like movies and sounds to your PDF document. Finally, you find out how to design and display a project in Full Screen mode to give your Acrobat PDF presentation a more cinematic look and feel.

Converting a Presentation to PDF

Probably the easiest way to create a presentation in Acrobat 5 is simply to convert an already made Microsoft PowerPoint presentation to PDF. Users of Microsoft Office versions 2000 and XP are provided with the PDFMaker 5.0

macro utility when they install Acrobat 5. After the installation, when you open PowerPoint, Acrobat buttons appear on the PDFMaker 5.0 toolbar, and Acrobat commands appear on the menu bar that let you convert your Power Point presentations to tagged PDF. Just click the Convert to Adobe PDF button on the PDFMaker 5.0 toolbar or choose Acrobat⇨Convert to Adobe PDF on the PowerPoint menu bar, as shown in Figure 16-1. If you choose Acrobat⇨ View Result in Acrobat before you run the macro, your PDF presentation opens in Acrobat 5, as shown in Figure 16-2. (See Chapter 5 for more on converting Microsoft Office documents to Adobe PDF.)

PDFMaker 5.0 converts any hyperlinks you added in your PowerPoint presentation so that you don't have to re-create those interactive elements in your new PDF presentation. In addition, PDF portability makes it possible for you to easily distribute your PDF presentation over a company intranet or the World Wide Web and be assured that the greatest numbers of people are able to view it.

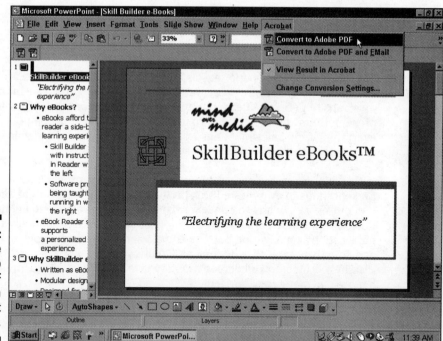

Figure 16-1:
Using the
Convert to
Adobe PDF
command in
Microsoft
PowerPoint.

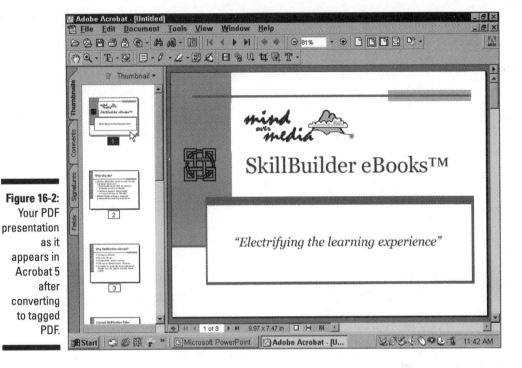

Figure 16-2:
Your PDF
presentation
as it
appears in
Acrobat 5
after
converting
to tagged
PDF.

Building Your Own PDF Presentation

You might find that PowerPoint's design-template approach to developing a slide show presentation has limitations. For example, the simple slide show I created for my eBook publishing company, shown in Figures 16-1 and 16-2, doesn't match the design of my Web site. And, although I love PowerPoint's ability to create an appealing slide show in a hurry, it would take far longer to re-create the look and feel of my site in that program.

Acrobat 5, on the other hand, lets you use graphics editing or page layout programs to design a presentation to your exact specifications and then convert it to a PDF presentation. You probably already have a great deal of your own "branded" content developed in such programs, which makes the job of incorporating your designs in a PDF presentation all the more easier. Check out Chapter 15 for details on page layout programs that convert their documents to Adobe PDF. On the graphics editing side, Illustrator or Photoshop are likely choices to use because of their close integration of Acrobat 5 features.

Having Fun with Photoshop

Photoshop 6.0 users can take advantage of the unparalleled design features of that program to create unique presentation pages. Figure 16-3 shows a page that more closely mirrors my Web site's design than the PowerPoint presentation shown earlier. When you've finished developing a design, you can convert a Photoshop document to PDF in two ways. The first is to use the Save As command in Photoshop 6.0, as described in the following steps:

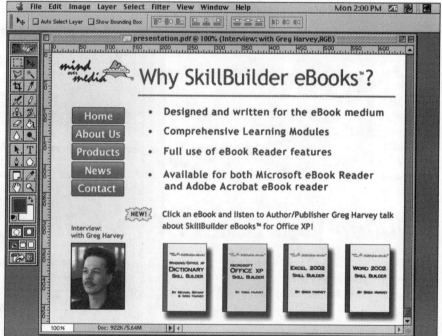

Figure 16-3:
Creating a
custom
design for a
presentation
in
Photoshop
6.0.

1. **Choose File⇨Save As.**

   The Save As dialog box opens, as shown in Figure 16-4.

2. **Specify a location for your saved PDF file and then type a title for your document in the Name text field.**

3. **Select Photoshop PDF in the Format drop-down list.**

4. **The Color area of the dialog box provides two options for selecting a color gamut conducive to either print or on-screen viewing. Click the Embed Color Profile: sRGB IEC61966-2.1 check box to ensure that the colors in your presentation will display accurately on the widest variety of monitors and then click Save.**

   The PDF Options dialog box opens, as shown in Figure 16-5.

5. **Select the JPEG radio button in the Encoding area. You have three ways in which to select the amount of compression when using JPEG encoding: Type a number between 0 and 12 in the Quality text field, or choose a fixed setting in the pop-up menu, or use the slider. Then click OK to convert the document to PDF.**

Note that applying more compression reduces a file's size with a corresponding reduction of image clarity.

The remaining options in this dialog box pertain to printed output and don't apply in this case. Note that Zip compression is also provided and can be used if your presentation has large areas of single colors using 4- or 8-bit color.

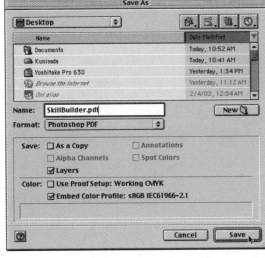

Figure 16-4:
Selecting
Save As
options
when
converting a
Photoshop
document to
PDF.

The converted PDF document is saved in the specified location. You can then open it in Acrobat 5, as shown in Figure 16-6. You can continue to build a PDF presentation by first converting your finished Photoshop image layouts to PDF and then consolidating them into a single PDF document using the Insert Pages command. For more on inserting pages into PDF documents, see Chapter 10.

You can also convert your Photoshop documents from inside Acrobat 5 by using the Open as Adobe PDF command. Keep in mind that you have to first save your Photoshop document in a format that can be converted to PDF in this manner. Acrobat 5 supports these graphic formats: BMP, GIF, JPEG, PCX, PICT (Mac OS only, unless you have QuickTime installed on your Windows computer), PNG, and TIFF. To convert your Photoshop presentation page to PDF in Acrobat 5, follow these steps:

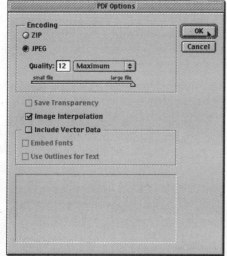

Figure 16-5:
Selecting
JPEG
encoding
options prior
to saving
your file.

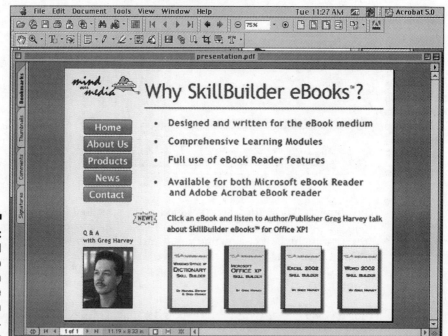

Figure 16-6:
A converted
Photoshop
presentation
page
viewed in
Acrobat 5.

1. **Choose File⇨Open as Adobe PDF.**

   The Open dialog box appears.

2. **On the Files of Type pop-up menu, choose the file format in which you saved your Photoshop document and then locate and select the file you want to convert to PDF.**

3. **Click the Settings button to choose a color and grayscale compression setting (JPEG or Zip) that Acrobat will use during the conversion process and then click OK.**

   Note that if you left the default option All Files selected in the Files of Type pop-up menu, this button will be grayed out.

4. **Click the Open button to convert the Photoshop document to PDF.**

5. **If you already have a document opened in Acrobat 5 when open a Photoshop document as PDF, you get an Alert box asking you what to do with your new PDF page. Select one of the following radio buttons and then click OK:**

   • **Create a New Document:** Select this radio button if you want to make a separate PDF file out of your Photoshop document.

   • **Append to Current Document:** Select this radio button if you want to add the Photoshop document as a new page in the currently opened PDF document.

You can invoke the Open as Adobe PDF command by dragging an image file onto the Acrobat application icon located on your desktop (Windows) or in the Acrobat 5 folder (Mac). Windows users can also drag an image to the open Acrobat 5 window to convert an image to Adobe PDF. In this case, if you already have a document opened in the Acrobat window when you drag a new image into it, a dialog box will appear to let you specify whether or not the new image should be placed before or after the currently opened PDF document.

Using Multimedia Objects in a Presentation

Acrobat 5 lets you enhance a PDF presentation with the addition of movies and sounds. Before you add these objects to your PDF page, consider the following points about using these objects in your presentation:

✔ **Formats:** Acrobat PDF documents play all video and sound files that are compatible with Apple QuickTime software. The most common (therefore, best to use) of these include MOV and MPG formats for movies and AIF and WAV for sounds. The user must have a minimum of Quick Time 2.5 for Windows or Mac (though versions 4.0–5.0 are recommended), or Windows Media Player for Windows only, to play these objects in your presentation.

✔ **Embedding:** Sound clips are embedded in the PDF document, meaning that the actual sound file is attached to the PDF. Because sound files can be quite large, you should take care when using them because they can increase the size of PDF files significantly. Movies, because of their greater size, are not embedded. They are linked to the PDF via a place-holder that points to the movie clip's location. For this reason, all linked movies must accompany a PDF document, so it's important to use the correct filenames and relative path locations for the actual movie clips when you distribute them to others. If your presentation is bound for network or World Wide Web distribution, playback quality will also depend on the user's network access speed.

Inserting a movie in a presentation

Follow these steps to insert a movie in a presentation:

1. **Open the PDF presentation to which you want to add a movie clip.**

2. **Select the Movie tool on the Editing toolbar or press M.**

3. **Click a spot on your presentation page where you want the movie to play.**

   This spot represents the center of the movie frame, and the movie playback area will be the same size as the actual movie frame. Clicking the Movie tool also opens the Movie Properties dialog box, shown in Figure 16-7.

4. **In the Movie File area, click the Use File on Local Volume radio button and then click the Choose button to locate the movie clip on your hard drive. Select the Use Remote URL radio button if your movie will be streamed from a remote location on a network or the Internet.**

5. **To allow the user to pause or stop a movie, select the Show Controller check box in the Player Options area. Select a playback option from the Mode pop-up menu: Play Once Then Stop, Play Once, Stay Open, Repeat Play, or Back and Forth. To have a movie float on top of a presentation window, click the Use Floating Window check box and select a playback window size on the pop-up menu.**

6. **Movie posters are image placeholders for the playback area in a PDF. They can be any image but are usually the first frame of the linked movie clip. In the Movie Poster area of the Movie Properties dialog**

box, select Don't Show Poster, Put Poster in Document, or Retrieve Poster from Movie on the pop-up menu. If you choose to display a movie poster, select its color display — either 256 Colors (8-bit) or Millions of Colors (32-bit) — on the provided pop-up menu.

7. **If you want a border to appear around the playback area, select a Width, Style, and Color option in the Border Appearance area.**

8. **When you're through selecting movie options, click OK.**

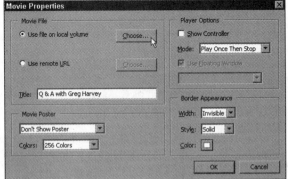

Figure 16-7:
Options provided in the Movie Properties dialog box.

A border highlighting the play area appears in the PDF document. This border is displayed only when using the Movie tool for editing purposes. You can right-click (Windows) or Control+click (Mac) this window and then Play, Delete, or Edit the movie's properties by selecting the appropriate command on the pop-up menu that appears.

When choosing a playback area with the Movie tool, it's best to just click the area as described in the preceding steps, even though it's possible to draw a marquee for a movie playback area. Clicking ensures that the playback area will be the exact size of the selected movie frame. If you try and draw this area or resize it after the movie link has been created, it's very likely your playback area won't match the movie clip's aspect ratio causing distorted playback. You should also set the magnification view of pages that have movies in them to 100% to avoid this type of scaling so that the user sees the best quality playback when viewing your presentation. If you find that a movie clip you want to use isn't the right size for your presentation, plan on using your movie editing software to make adjustments rather than Acrobat 5.

Inserting a sound in a presentation

The process of adding a sound clip to a presentation is nearly identical to that of adding a movie clip with the following exceptions:

- ✔ You drag the Movie tool to define a rectangular playing area for sounds rather than pointing and clicking as you do for movies.

- ✔ If you navigate to locate a sound in the Movie Properties dialog box, you have to select All Files rather than the default QuickTime Movies in the Type pop-up menu in order for sound clips to appear in the navigation window.

- ✔ If a desired sound clip is not QuickTime-compatible, you will be asked to convert it by following on-screen instructions.

You can test movie and sound clips added to a PDF presentation in this manner by selecting the Hand tool and then moving the mouse pointer over the playback area until it turns into a filmstrip pointer. Click the playback area to play the movie or sound clip. To stop playback, click again or press the Esc key. Note that you can also attach movie and sound playback to buttons, as described in the next section. To get details on attaching actions to these and other Acrobat interactive elements such as links, bookmarks, and so on, head to Chapter 14.

Making Your Presentation Interactive

You can add interactivity to a PDF presentation by adding links that navigate the user through the presentation and/or buttons that have actions assigned to them, such as playing movies or sound. (To get details on inserting links into a PDF document, see Chapter 15. To find out about adding buttons created in Acrobat 5 to a PDF document, see Chapter 14.) If you decide to develop a custom-designed presentation in an editing program such as Photoshop, it's better to create the graphics for your button in that program and add interactivity to it using Acrobat's Form tool. Here's how:

1. **Navigate to the presentation page in which you want to add an interactive button, and select the Form Tool button on the Editing toolbar or press (F).**

2. **Drag the Form tool pointer to draw a box in the desired field area of your PDF form and then release the mouse button.**

   The Field Properties dialog box opens. In Figure 16-8, I've created a button out of the Dictionary book cover that, when clicked, will play an interview movie in the area to the left.

3. **Type a name for the field in the Name text box, and select Button as the field type on the Type drop-down list.**

4. **On the Appearance tab, deselect all default appearance options.**

   Because the button graphic is already created in the document, you have no need for Acrobat's appearance embellishments.

5. **On the Options tab, select Invert on the Highlight drop-down list, which contains a variety of action effects that visually enhance button interactivity. Selecting Invert causes the colors to invert on the button area when the button is clicked. Leave the other options on this tab in their default state.**

6. **On the Actions tab, click Mouse Up in the When This Happens list box and then click the Add button.**

   The Add an Action dialog box appears.

7. **Select Movie on the Type drop-down list.**

   The Movie Action dialog box appears.

8. **Click the Select Movie button to choose a movie.**

   Note that prior to performing this step, you need to link movies to the page as described in the previous section in order to select them in this dialog box.

9. **Click the Set Action button and then click OK to close the Form Properties dialog box.**

The button field appears in the PDF outlined in red to indicate that it is selected for editing. To test your button, select the Hand tool and click the button, as shown in Figure 16-8.

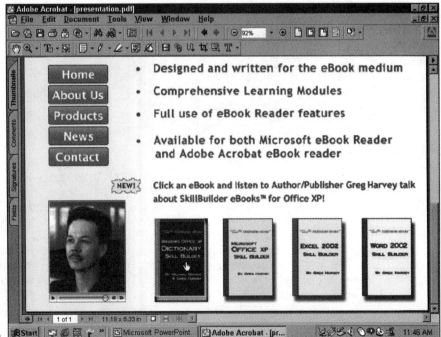

Figure 16-8:
Testing an interactive button that plays a movie in a PDF presentation.

Viewing a Presentation Full Screen

Acrobat's Full Screen mode allows users to view your presentation without the distraction of the menu bar, toolbars, or window controls. Document pages fill the entire screen, allowing viewers to focus completely on your presentation. Acrobat lets you set full-screen presentations to run automatically using timed page advancement and transition effects, and you can use the mouse pointer to activate on-screen controls in your presentation such as buttons or links. In addition, users can navigate and change views of a presentation by using standard keyboard shortcuts associated with Acrobat menu commands. To set up a PDF presentation so that it opens up automatically in Full Screen mode, follow these steps:

1. **Open the PDF presentation you want to display in Full Screen mode.**

2. **Choose File⇨Properties⇨Open Options.**

   The Document Open Options dialog box appears.

3. **Click to place a check mark in the Open in Full Screen Mode check box, as shown in Figure 16-9, and then click OK.**

4. **Save the presentation and then close and reopen it to view it in Full Screen mode.**

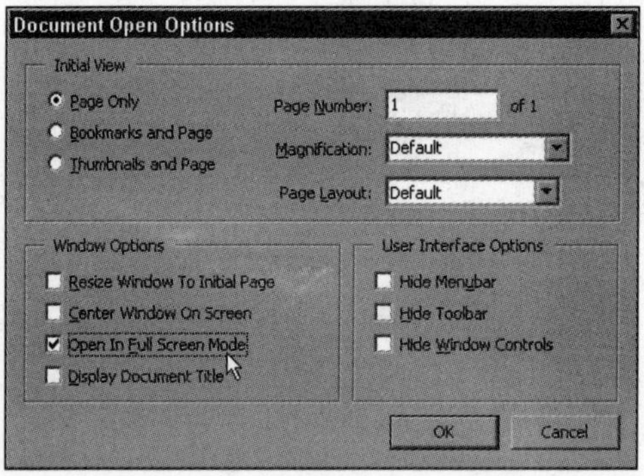

Figure 16-9: Specifying Full Screen mode in the Document Open Options dialog box.

Your full-screen presentation is displayed in Acrobat 5, as shown in Figure 16-10, and you can page back and forth through your slide show by using any of the following keys: Pg Up, Pg Dn, Enter, Return, or any of the arrow keys. Of course, you can also use any on-screen interactive navigational controls you've set up using Acrobat 5 or your presentation authoring program. To exit Full Screen mode, press Esc. To toggle Full Screen mode off or on at anytime, choose View⇨Full Screen on the menu bar or press Crtl+L (Windows) or ⌘+L (Mac).

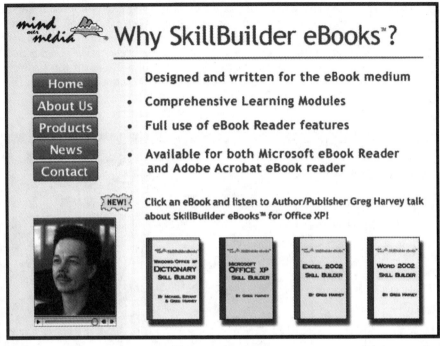

Figure 16-10:
A PDF
presentation
displayed in
Full Screen
mode.

Selecting Full Screen Mode Preferences

You can specify a number of navigation and appearance options that apply
to PDF Full Screen mode. Choose Edit⇨Preferences⇨General to open the
Preferences dialog box, shown in Figure 16-11. Choose Full Screen in the list
box on the left side of the dialog box and then select options in areas
described in the following list:

- ✔ **Full Screen Navigation:** To automatically page through the slides in your
  presentation at a specific rate of time, place a check mark in the Advance
  Every check box and type a number in the Seconds text field that is activated. To use the mouse to advance slides, choose Advance on Any Click.
  To have your presentation run continually from beginning to end, choose
  Loop After Last Page. You can deselect the default Escape Key Exits check
  box, but you'll have to remember that in order to exit Full Screen mode
  at that point, you have to press Ctrl+L (Windows) or ⌘+L (Mac) to toggle
  the Full Screen command.

- ✔ **Full Screen Appearance:** Click the Default Transition drop-down list to
  select from a variety of transition effects that will display when moving
  from page to page in your presentation. Note that the selected transition

will apply to all the pages in your document. To specify the appearance of the mouse pointer while a presentation is running, choose Always Visible, Always Hidden, or Hidden After Delay in the Mouse Cursor drop-down list. To change the color of the presentation background that appears as a thin border around your slide or during slide transitions, click the Background Color button and choose a color on the palette that appears. The default is black.

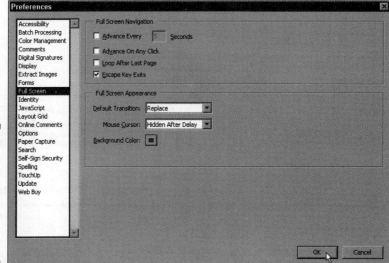

Figure 16-11:
Selecting
navigation
and
appearance
options for
Full Screen
mode.

Part V
The Part of Tens

The 5th Wave   By Rich Tennant

DENISE AND JERRY LEVIN — AUTHORS OF "LOST IN THE MALL PARKING LOT", "THE MISPLACED GALLERY INVITATION", AND, "THE BAD HAIRCUT — WHY ME?"

©RICHTENNANT

Truthfully? If it weren't for ePublishing, many of these stories would have remained untold.

In this part . . .

Possibly the most fun and certainly the most dynamic
section of the entire book, the Part of Tens brings
you a cursory view of top ten things that make PDF and
Acrobat so special. Chapter 17 gives you a list of the top
ten features in Acrobat 5, complete with references to
the chapters where you can delve into detailed how-to
information. Chapter 18 lists the Ten Commandments for
converting your Microsoft Office documents to PDF using
the built-in PDFMaker 5.0 utility. Chapter 19 shows you
how to extend the functionality of Acrobat 5 through the
use of what I consider currently to be the top ten third-
party plug-ins for this already most versatile program.
Finally, Chapter 20 rounds out the Part of Tens by giving
you the top ten online resources for extending your
knowledge of Acrobat and PDF files way beyond the basic
introduction I've offered you here in this book.

Chapter 17

The Top Ten Features of Acrobat 5

*I*f you're looking for a quick rundown of the best features in Acrobat 5, and perhaps a reason to upgrade, you need to look no further. Here is my list of the ten best things about Acrobat 5, along with references to the chapters in this book where you can get detailed information on how to use these nifty features.

Paper Capture Plug-in

Acrobat 5 not only lets you scan in paper documents for saving as PDF files, but also enables you to convert the text scanned as a graphic into fully searchable and editable text by installing the Paper Capture plug-in. For those of you using Acrobat 5 for Windows, you need to download this Adobe plug-in from the Adobe Web site (www.adobe.com). For those of you using Acrobat 5 for Macintosh, you need to use Adobe's Paper Capture Online service (available to you for free at createpdf.abobe.com). See Chapter 6 for details.

Web Capture Plug-in

The Web Capture feature in Acrobat 5 lets you download entire Web sites (or only as many pages of the sites as you want) and save them as PDF files. Web pages saved as PDF files for offline viewing with Acrobat or Acrobat Reader retain all of their Web links. See Chapter 7 for complete information on using this great feature.

Form Creation and Fill In

Acrobat 5 makes it easy to create your own electronic forms that users can fill in either with Acrobat or Acrobat 5. You can add a variety of different interactive fields and controls to the forms you create: text fields, combo boxes, check boxes, and radio buttons, along with buttons for submitting the form data by saving the information in a special form file that can be used with popular spreadsheet and database software. See Chapter 14 for details.

Review Comments

Acrobat 5 offers you a wide variety of commenting features that make it easy for a group of users to review copies of the same PDF document and give you their suggestions and corrections. The best thing about the Commenting features in Acrobat is how painless the program makes the process of collecting, collating, and summarizing all the comments made by individual members of the group into the original PDF document. See Chapter 9 for the ins and outs of using comments in reviewing PDF documents.

Tagged PDF Files

Acrobat 5 introduces tagged PDF files as the foundation of its new accessibility features designed to greatly enhance the online reading experience for users with visual disabilities. A tagged PDF file saves information about each structural element used in the PDF document as well as information about its reading order. Tagged PDF documents support the use of special screen-reading Windows software, the new Acrobat Reader for mobile devices (Palm OS and Pocket PC), and the new Reflow text feature in Acrobat 5 and Acrobat Reader 5 that reflows the document text to fit the left and right page margins no matter how much you increase the magnification. See Chapter 15 for details on creating and using tagged PDF files.

PDF Maker 5.0 for Microsoft Office (Windows Only)

This Microsoft Office macro for Office 2000 and Office XP for Windows lets you convert any Word, Excel, or PowerPoint document to PDF using either the PDFMaker toolbar or Acrobat pull-down menu that it adds to their applications. PDFMaker 5.0 not only makes PDF file conversion as easy as clicking the Convert to Adobe PDF button but also enables you to completely customize distilling settings, convert all Word document styles into PDF document bookmarks, retain all hyperlinks, and create tagged PDF files (as described in the preceding section, "Tagged PDF Files"). See Chapter 5 for details on using PDFMaker 5.0 for Windows.

Make Accessible Plug-in (Windows Only)

The Make Accessible plug-in enables you to automatically and effortlessly convert any of your unstructured, non-tagged PDF files into tagged PDF files as described in "Tagged PDF Files," earlier in this chapter.

Digital Signatures and Document Encryption

Acrobat 5 introduces Adobe Self-Sign Security, an encryption feature that enables you to protect your PDF files from being opened and edited by unauthorized users and enables you to digitally sign your PDF documents with a signature that other users can verify as yours. See Chapter 11 for all you'd ever need to know about digitally signing and encrypting PDF documents.

Extracting PDF Content

Acrobat 5 makes it easy to extract text and graphics saved in any PDF document so that you can reuse them in other application software. You can extract specific sections of text and specific graphics through the operating system's Clipboard feature or save the entire file in a simple text, Rich Text Format (RTF), or even an HTML text file format. See Chapter 12 for all the ways you can extract and repurpose the text and graphics in a PDF document.

Cataloging PDF Document Collection

Acrobat 5 makes it possible to do fast searching across a whole group of PDF files by organizing them into a PDF document collection, which you then index. By cataloging your PDF files, you ensure that you can retain access to valuable information in the files that you archive. See Chapter 13 for details on how to create, search, and distribute a PDF document collection.

Chapter 18

The Ten Commandments for Converting Office Documents into PDF Files

● ●

*P*DFMaker 5.0 for Windows makes it ridiculously easy to turn any Word, Excel, or PowerPoint document you create or edit with the Office 2000 or Office XP (2002) editions of these programs into the latest and greatest versions of PDF documents — all you have to do is click the Convert to Adobe PDF button on the PDFMaker 5.0 toolbar (automatically added when you install Acrobat 5.0 for Windows on your computer). But before you touch that button, you should have a gander at my ten commandments for making perfect PDF conversions.

Check for Consistent Use of Heading Styles in Your Word Document

Click the Document Map button on the Standard toolbar to display the headings and their hierarchical relationship in the Document Map pane in Word. Because PDFMaker can automatically convert all Word document headings into bookmarks in the resulting PDF document (see "Confirm That All Your Word Document Headings and Styles Will Be Converted into Bookmarks," later in this chapter), you should make sure that all the headings in your document use the appropriate Heading style. Word 2002 users can display the Styles and Formatting task pane (choose View⇨Task Pane and then click Styles and Formatting on the Task Pane pop-up menu) to check and, if necessary, reapply the Heading styles.

Check the Paging of Your Excel Worksheets

Choose View⇨Page Break Preview on the Excel menus. Because PDFMaker uses the current paging of the Excel worksheet in constructing the pages in the resulting PDF document, you will want to verify the page breaks before doing the conversion. Remedy bad page breaks that separate columns and rows of data that should appear together on a page by dragging the page break markers in the Page Break Preview mode.

Verify Which Type of PDF Document (eBook, Press, Print, or Screen) You're Creating

You do this by checking the name that appears in the Conversion Settings combo box on the Settings tab of the Acrobat 5.0 PDFMaker 5.0 dialog box (Acrobat⇨Change Conversion Settings). When selecting among these presets, keep in mind the major use of the final PDF document: Select eBook for online viewing, Press for professional printing, Print for in-house printing, and Screen for fast downloading and viewing on the Web. Also, keep in mind that you can customize any of these presets by selecting it in the Conversion Settings combo box and then clicking the Edit Conversion Settings button.

Confirm That the Document Info and Links Should Be Converted

Verify that the Convert Document Info, Convert Cross Document Links, and Convert Internet Links check box options on the Office tab of the Acrobat 5.0 PDFMaker 5.0 dialog box (Acrobat⇨Change Conversion Settings) all have check marks in them. When the Convert Document Info check box is selected, PDFMaker converts the data entered in the Title, Subject, Author, and Keywords fields on the Summary tab of the document's Properties dialog box (File⇨Properties) into the PDF document metadata that you can use in searching (see Chapter 14 for details). When you select the Convert Cross Document Links and the Convert Internet Links check boxes, PDFMaker retains the hyperlinks in the resulting PDF file (see "Verify How the Office Document Links Will Appear in the PDF Document," later in this chapter, for information on controlling how these links appear in the PDF file).

Confirm That All Your Word Document Headings and Styles Will Be Converted into Bookmarks

Verify which settings are selected on the Bookmarks tab of the Acrobat 5.0 PDFMaker 5.0 dialog box (Acrobat⇨Change Conversion Settings) in Word. Click the Convert Word Headings to Bookmarks check box to convert all Heading paragraph styles used in the document into bookmarks in the resulting PDF file. Click the Convert Word Styles to Bookmarks check box to convert all the other paragraph styles used in the document to bookmarks as well. To omit certain levels of headings or particular styles from bookmark conversion, click their individual check boxes that appear in the list box below.

Confirm Whether You're Converting All Worksheets in Your Excel File or Just the Current Worksheet

Check whether the Entire Workbook or the Active Worksheet Only radio button is selected on the Office tab of the Acrobat 5.0 PDFMaker 5.0 dialog box (Acrobat⇨Change Conversion Settings) in Excel.

Verify Which Word Features Are Marked for Conversion in the PDF Document

Verify which Word Features settings are selected on the Office tab of the Acrobat 5.0 PDFMaker 5.0 dialog box (Acrobat⇨Change Conversion Settings) in Word. To convert document comments to hidden notes in the PDF document, select the Comments⇨Notes check box. To add text boxes to the adjoining text using the PDF Articles feature, select the Text Boxes⇨Article Threads check box. To retain the page numbers used in the Word document, select the Page Numbers (e.g., iii, A-1) check box. To convert all cross-references and any table of contents generated in the Word document into links in the PDF document, select the Cross References & TOC Links check box. To convert all footnotes and endnotes added to the Word document into links in the resulting PDF file, select the Footnote & Endnote Links check box.

Make Sure That You're Creating a Tagged PDF File

Verify that the Embed Tags in PDF (Accessibility, Reflow) check box option on the Office tab of the Acrobat 5.0 PDFMaker 5.0 dialog box (Acrobat⇨Change Conversion Settings) has a check mark in it.

Confirm How the Converted PDF Document Is Set to Open in Acrobat

Verify the Document Open options on the Display Options tab of the Acrobat 5.0 PDFMaker 5.0 dialog box (Acrobat⇨Change Conversion Settings). To open the PDF document without displaying the Bookmarks palette in the Navigation pane, click the Page Only radio button. To display a page other than the first page upon opening, enter the page number in the Page Number field. To open the page at a set magnification, click the percentage (200, 400, 800, or 1600) or preset view (Fit in Window, Fit Width, or Fit Visible) in the Open Magnification pop-up menu.

Verify How the Office Document Links Will Appear in the PDF Document

Verify the Link Appearance options on the Display Options tab of the Acrobat 5.0 PDFMaker 5.0 dialog box (Acrobat⇨Change Conversion Settings). To enclose the links in a thin rectangle, click the Thin Visible Rectangle radio button and then select their line style (Solid or Dashed), highlighting upon clicking (None, Outline, Invert, or Inset), and color (Black, Blue, Cyan, Green, Magenta, Red, Yellow, or White) in the Line Style, Highlight, and Color sections of the Link Appearance area. To enclose the links in a thicker rectangle, click the Thick Visible Rectangle radio button and then select their line style, highlighting, and color in the appropriate sections of the Link Appearance area.

Chapter 19

The Top Ten Third-Party Acrobat Plug-Ins

• •

*A*s versatile as Acrobat 5 is right out of the box with the addition of the free Adobe plug-ins, you can make the program even more multitalented and yourself more productive by investing in third-party plug-ins for Acrobat. The following list presents you with a smorgasbord of plug-ins that enhance various aspects of Acrobat. For more information on these plug-ins, including information on pricing and how to order them, as well as a listing of other third-party plug-ins currently available, visit `www.adobe.com/store/plugins/acrobat` on the Adobe Web site.

Quite a Box of Tricks from Quite Software

This plug-in enables you to recompress the graphic images in a PDF document without having to re-distill the file. In addition, it can convert any RGB (Red, Green, Blue) PDF document to CMYK (Cyan, Magenta, Yellow, Black), transform, and get detailed information about any of the text and graphics in the file (including font and image dimensions).

Quite Imposing from Quite Software

The Quite Imposing plug-in enables you to compose PDF document pages on larger pages for printing and binding as books and booklets. This plug-in also enables you to reorder document pages and split or merge the even- or odd-numbered pages. It also enables you to compose foldable booklets from the pages of your PDF document.

WebPerfect PDF from Enfocus

The WebPerfect PDF plug-in enables you to convert large, high-resolution PDF files into small and faster pages optimized for viewing and downloading on the World Wide Web. This plug-in makes it possible for you to downsample images to 72 dpi (dots per inch), convert color images to RGB (Red, Green, Blue), delete any objects outside of the visible document, eliminate redundant fonts, as well as remove comments, article threads, and thumbnail images in the PDF document.

Jade (Windows only) by BCL Computers

This plug-in enables you to accurately extract normal text, tables, and graphics for editing in Windows applications, such as Microsoft Word and Excel, simply by selecting the text, table, or image and then copying it (using copy-and-paste or drag-and-drop methods).

Redax by Appligent

This plug-in enables you to black out sensitive and private text and scanned images in a PDF document before distributing the file to others. You also have the ability to customize the palettes of exemption codes and generate reports on what text and graphics were censored.

Pagelet by CreoScitext

The Pagelet plug-in enables you to quickly and easily assemble different PDF files into a single PDF document. It includes orientation tools, its own set of customizable grids, rulers, and guidelines, to help you accurately position, resize, and rotate the pages of the composite PDF document.

Magellan by BCL Computers

This plug-in enables you to accurately convert PDF files into Web pages. It converts the text, graphics, and structure of your PDF file to the appropriate HTML tags to ensure that all the elements on the PDF page are correctly positioned in the resulting Web page.

Certify PDF by Enfocus

This plug-in enables you to preflight your prepress PDF files by storing both the preflight profile (identifying potential printing problems) and the preflight results in the same PDF file. It also tracks all editing sessions on the file and supports rollback to previous edited versions.

DateD by Appligent

The DateD plug-in enables you to date and time stamp any PDF document as required for ISO (International Organization for Standardization) compliance. After you use this plug-in to date/time stamp your PDF document, this information always appears when you view the document online in Acrobat or Acrobat Reader or in printed copies you make.

Sonar Bookends Activate by Virginia Systems

This plug-in enables you to automatically generate an interactive table of contents or index for your PDF document in a matter of seconds. You can also use this plug-in to link cross-references as well as e-mail and URL addresses found in the text.

Chapter 20

The Top Ten Online Resources

● ●

*L*ast, but never least, I present you with a list of ten of the top online resources for extending your knowledge of Acrobat and for getting service for PDF conversion jobs you're just not prepared to handle in-house. As you would expect, many of these top online resources are Web sites that are run and maintained by Adobe Systems.

Adobe Web Site

www.adobe.com

Check out the Adobe Web site for online support and to download all the free Adobe plug-ins for Acrobat 5, including the Make Accessible and Paper Capture plug-ins for Windows and the Save as XML plug-in for both Windows and Macintosh.

Acrobat Expert Center

studio.adobe.com/expertcenter/acrobat

This site offers white papers full of tips and tutorials on using Acrobat and integrating PDF into your workflow, access to the user forums and certified trainers, and the latest information on program updates and third-party plug-ins.

Adobe Access

access.adobe.com

Check out this site for general information on the accessibility features in Adobe Acrobat 5 and Adobe GoLive 5.

Adobe eBooks Central

www.adobe.com/epaper/ebooks

This site provides detailed information on creating, managing, and delivering PDF documents as Acrobat eBooks.

Create PDF Online

www.createpdf.com

Head for this site to have Adobe convert your documents into PDF files for you. You can test out this online conversion service by signing up for a free trial when you visit this Web page.

PDF Zone.com

www.pdfzone.com

This site provides all kinds of articles and tidbits on the Acrobat and PDF industry and professionals who inhabit it.

Planet PDF

www.planetpdf.com

Planet PDF offers all kinds of news and information on using PDF, including tips on how to get the most out of the file format, along with plenty of listings of PDF tools, consultants, and trainers that can help you get the job done.

Extensis Preflight Online

www.extensis.com

This site provides a complete online preflight service for checking prepress PDF files against the parameters that you specify.

Texterity

www.texterity.com

Texterity is a complete online service for converting documents saved in a wide variety of file formats (including Word, WordPerfect, QuarkXPress, PageMaker, and InDesign) into ready-to-publish Adobe eBook PDF files.

Adobe eBook Site

ebookstore.adobe.com/store

At the Adobe eBook site, you can download some free Acrobat eBooks for your reading pleasure with the Acrobat eBook Reader.

Index